MW00634133

The Cycles of Constitutional Time

The Cycles of Constitutional Time

Jack M. Balkin

Oxford University Press is a department of the University of Oxford. It furthers the University's objective of excellence in research, scholarship, and education by publishing worldwide. Oxford is a registered trade mark of Oxford University Press in the UK and certain other countries.

Published in the United States of America by Oxford University Press
198 Madison Avenue, New York, NY 10016, United States of America.

Library of Congress Cataloging-in-Publication Data
Names: Balkin, Jack. M., author.
Title: The cycles of constitutional time / Jack M. Balkin.
Description: New York : Jack Balkin, 2020. | Includes index.
Identifiers: LCCN 2020004528 (print) | LCCN 2020004529 (ebook) |
ISBN 9780197530993 (hardback) | ISBN 9780197531020 (oso) |
ISBN 9780197531006 (updf) | ISBN 9780197531013 (epub)
Subjects: LCSH: Constitutional law—Political aspects—United States. |
United States—Politics and government—2017–
Classification: LCC KF4552 .B345 2020 (print) | LCC KF4552 (ebook) |
DDC 342.73—dc23
LC record available at https://lccn.loc.gov/2020004528
LC ebook record available at https://lccn.loc.gov/2020004529

3 5 7 9 8 6 4 2

Printed by Integrated Books International, United States of America

For Bruce Ackerman

Contents

I. UNDERSTANDING THE CYCLES OF CONSTITUTIONAL TIME

1. The Recent Unpleasantness **3**
- A. Thinking in Terms of Cycles 3
- B. The Framework of the Argument 7

2. The Cycle of Regimes **12**
- A. Where Are We in Political Time? 19
- B. The Waning of Political Time 22
- C. Trump as the Great Reviver? 27

3. The Cycle of Polarization **30**
- A. The Long Cycle of Polarization 30
- B. Polarization in the Reagan Regime 31
- C. Is Polarization Permanent? 33

4. Constitutional Crisis **38**

5. The Cycle of Constitutional Rot and Renewal **44**
- A. Republican Insurance 47
- B. The Four Horsemen of Constitutional Rot 49
- C. The Political Economy of Republican Government 50
- D. Constitutional Rot Produces Demagogues 53
- E. A Demagogue for Our Times 55
- F. The Acceleration of Constitutional Rot 58
- G. The Bad News—and the Good News 62

II. THE CYCLES OF JUDICIAL REVIEW

6. Judicial Review in the Cycles of Constitutional Time **69**
- A. Judicial Time 71
- B. The Political Supports for Judicial Review 74
- C. Partisan Entrenchment: Judicial Review and the Party System 77

7. How the Rise and Fall of Regimes Affects Judicial Review **81**
- A. Three Questions About Judicial Review 84
- B. Judicial Review in the Life-Cycle of a Political Regime 85
- C. The Causes of Change 91
- D. Judicial Review on the Cusp of a New Regime 95

8. The Role of Constitutional Theory in the Cycle of Regimes **97**
A. The Cycle of Regimes and Living Constitutionalism 99
B. The Cycle of Regimes and Originalism 102
C. The Return of Liberal Skepticism About Judicial Review 108
D. Looking Ahead 110

9. How Cycles of Polarization and Depolarization Shape the Exercise of Judicial Review **112**
A. The Judiciary in a Depolarized World 113
B. The Changing Audience for Judges 118
C. The End of Elite Consensus 121
D. The Breakdown of the *Carolene Products* Model 123
E. The Collapse of the Distinction Between High and Low Politics 125
F. Disciplining Outliers Makes Less Sense 126
G. The Federal Judiciary as Policy Vanguard 127
H. The Stakes of Judicial Appointments in a Polarized World 130

10. Law in the Time of Constitutional Rot **135**
A. Courts and Party Politics in an Age of Constitutional Rot 136
B. Polarization Limits Judges' Abilities to Recognize and Halt Constitutional Rot 137
C. Judicial Decisions Can Exacerbate Constitutional Rot by Increasing Economic Inequality 138
D. Rot Increases as Courts Become the Policy Vanguard 139
E. Rot Generates Constitutional Hardball, Which Further Undermines Trust in the Courts 140
F. Courts Cannot Protect Democracy Because They Do Not Agree About What It Is 141
G. Constitutional Rot Generates a Reverse-*Carolene Products* Effect 142

11. Judicial Politics and Judicial Reform **148**
A. Judicial Politics in the Next Regime 148
B. Reforming the Supreme Court 151

III. CONCLUSION

12. The Turn of the Cycles **159**
A. How Polarization Leads to Disjunction 162
B. A New Regime Without a Social Movement Party 164
C. The New Party Configuration 165
D. The Limits of a Cosmopolitan Party 168
E. How Constitutional Rot Ends 170

Acknowledgments *175*
Notes *177*
Index *229*

PART I

UNDERSTANDING THE CYCLES OF CONSTITUTIONAL TIME

1
The Recent Unpleasantness

"The Recent Unpleasantness" is one of several Southern euphemisms for the American Civil War.[1] It is also a fitting description of our current political predicament. Of course, I am not suggesting that the United States is currently in the middle of a civil war, or that we will soon be in a civil war. Rather, the expression conveys a widespread feeling that something has gone seriously wrong with constitutional democracy in the United States. The stark political and cultural polarization of American life, the raucous 2016 election, and the tabloid meanderings of the Trump presidency have only seemed to confirm a growing despair about the future of democracy in the United States.

This book takes a longer view. It argues that the malaise is only temporary. I will use tools from constitutional theory and from political science to try to explain what is happening to American politics: how we got where we are, and where we are likely to be headed in the next few decades. But first, let me offer a little astronomical diversion.

A. Thinking in Terms of Cycles

On August 21, 2017, an amazing event occurred over large parts of the United States: a total eclipse of the sun.[2] These are very rare occurrences, especially this one, which moved across almost the entire breadth of the country.[3] In early times, eclipses were frightening events. They came suddenly; people feared that magical powers were at work and that the sun would never return. We don't fear eclipses today, of course, because we know that they are natural phenomena caused by the concatenation of different cycles. The sun and moon, when viewed from the earth, are just about the same size, depending on the earth's orbit around the sun, and the moon's orbit around the earth. And so, when the earth is at a particular position in its cycle around the sun, and the moon is in a particular position in its cycle around the earth, and the three line up in just the right way, the disc of the moon covers the disc of the sun for a brief period of time.[4] It is an amazing spectacle, and some people have called it a life-altering event. Stunning as these events are, we know that they will soon be over.

The Cycles of Constitutional Time. Jack M. Balkin, Oxford University Press (2020). © Jack Balkin 2020.
DOI: 10.1093/oso/9780197530993.001.0001

Our present condition is a little like an eclipse, although much less enjoyable. To understand what is going on today in the United States, we have to think in terms of political cycles that interact with each other and create remarkable—and dark—times.

In American constitutional law, however, people tend not to think in terms of cycles. Rather, they think about time in linear terms. The two most well-known approaches to constitutional interpretation in the United States involve linear visions of time. One is originalism, and the other is living constitutionalism.

Originalism is linear because it rests on an implicit story—about how we have moved further and further away from the moment in time that grounds the authority of the Constitution and the correct meaning of the Constitution. To interpret the Constitution correctly, we must restore the meaning at a moment that has long since passed.[5] We must return to that moment, metaphorically speaking. We must restore the correct interpretation and not stray from it again. The problem of interpretation arises precisely from the fact that time is linear: that we move ever further away from the moment that grants authority.

Originalism can also be a story of decay—a concern with what we have lost and about the need for restoration and renewal. As we move further and further away in time from the source of constitutional meaning and authority, we make mistake after mistake in our interpretations of the Constitution. Judges in particular are tempted to stray from the original meaning and impose their personal predilections. So we must find a way to retrace our steps and return to the original meaning that is the source of constitutional authority. That is the only way to restore and ground our constitutional system.

The other standard theory of constitutional interpretation is called living constitutionalism. This is the idea that as history progresses, so too should our Constitution.[6] In every day, in every way, our Constitution is becoming a better constitution—or at least, we should interpret the Constitution to make it so. Living constitutionalism also has a linear theory of time, because it rests on an implicit story of progress. We no longer live in the time of the Founders. We have left them behind. We honor the Founders' achievements in their time, but they are long dead. Their views may have been good enough for their day (or maybe not—after all, they owned slaves!). But their opinions may well be inadequate for our very different times and circumstances. Most living constitutionalists assume that if we adapt the Constitution to changing circumstances, this will represent improvement rather than decline, and gradual progress rather than gradual unraveling.[7] In other words, the theory implicitly rejects the idea that moving away from the past and forward in time signifies decay or loss. The arc of history is long, but it bends toward justice.

If we keep the Constitution in touch with the times, it will not only function better, but it will approach justice as well.

These views are obviously opposed to each other, and yet it's worth noting what they have in common. They are linear conceptions of time. We move away from the past, for good or for ill.

But that is not the only way to think about historical change. If you asked the Ancient Greeks or the Ancient Chinese, they would have disagreed. They would have argued that history moves in cycles, not in straight lines away from the past.[8] The Greek historian Polybius offered a famous account of cycles in politics: he argued that regimes cycled among monarchy, aristocracy, and democracy, with each form deteriorating and leading to the next.[9] Polybius's idea that politics moved in cycles and that forms of government inevitably decayed influenced Italian Renaissance thinkers such as Machiavelli and eventually, through multiple transformations, the Founding generation in the United States (I'll return to this idea in chapter 5).[10]

Modern American historians have also been fond of cycles. Henry Adams argued that American history moved like a pendulum between concentrations of power to diffusions of power.[11] Arthur Schlesinger Sr. argued that history spirals between episodes of liberal reform and conservative reaction,[12] an idea further developed by his son, Arthur Schlesinger Jr., in his book *The Cycles of American History*.[13]

In order to have a cyclic view of history, you don't have to believe that things occur exactly in the same way they occurred before. Rather, you can take the view, often attributed to Mark Twain, that history doesn't repeat itself, but it does rhyme.[14] That is the general approach I will develop in this book. I invite you to think of the events that we are going through like the strains of a ballad that repeatedly returns to its refrain, although with many changes and variations along the way.

But of course, things are not quite as simple as that. What is especially interesting about our current situation is that there is more than one cycle at work. In fact, there are three. And when these three cycles converge, when they all line up in a certain way, the result is a sort of political eclipse of the sun, a very dark and disturbing time. What one gets, in other words, is the recent unpleasantness.

Of course, the cycles that I will discuss here are quite different from the cycles that cause the eclipse of the sun. They arise through the interaction of political will with institutional structures. People cause these cycles through mobilization, organization, and the exercise of political will in a particular institutional environment. The institutions shape the actions, while the effects of the actions slowly remake the institutions.

In this book, I will talk about what I expect is going to happen in the next few decades. Unlike eclipses, however, one can't be entirely sure of the future. Politics is not astronomy, and human affairs do not operate like clockwork. Moreover, we can't assume that everything is already foreordained: that if people simply sit on their hands and do nothing, the cycles I describe in this book will take care of themselves. Quite the contrary. I am telling a story about what happens in the long run, but it is not a deterministic story. The actions of many individuals over time, pursuing their values and interests, but constrained by institutional arrangements, will tend to cycle in intelligible ways. But people have to actually pursue those interests. They have to be motivated to respond to the problems they face. Above all, they can't allow themselves to be overcome by despair and paralyzed into inaction.

Of course some people do despair today. They fear that we are headed inexorably toward fascism, authoritarianism, and the end of democracy. That is not what I think is going to happen. Nor do I expect that the American public will sit on its hands. I believe that Americans will respond to the misfortunes of our present age, just as they have many times before. And for that reason, although I will mention President Donald Trump at various points in my discussion, I will not be delving into great detail about the crazy and often disturbing things that have happened since his election. Instead, I will view him, and the party he leads, as exhibiting the effects of the cycles of constitutional time on political life in the United States.

My purpose, then, is not to tell people that their democracy will take care of itself without any effort on their part. Rather, it is to offer a bit of hope for people who read the news every day and fear that things are only going to get worse. Hope does not guarantee action, but it makes beneficial action more likely. If people misunderstand our situation, and conclude that American decline is inevitable, they may unwittingly help to make that fate a reality; but if they understand the cycles of constitutional time, they may come to believe that their democracy can be redeemed, and do their part to realize that worthy goal.

What are the three cycles at work in American politics? The first is the cycle of the rise and fall of political regimes in American history. The second is the cycle of polarization and depolarization. And the third is the decay and renewal of republican government, which I call the cycle of constitutional rot and constitutional renewal. (I explain the idea of constitutional rot in chapter 5.) Each of these cycles operates on a different time scale. I will introduce each of them in turn, and explain how they interact. Together, the interaction of these three cycles—of the rise and fall of regimes, of polarization and depolarization, and of rot and renewal—generate *constitutional time.*[15] Think of the analysis that follows like a chronometer that tells you where we are in constitutional time.

B. The Framework of the Argument

Before I describe these cycles in detail, however, it might be helpful to offer seven central points that will frame my argument. First, we are not in a constitutional crisis. Second, we are suffering from a severe case of constitutional rot. Third, we are at (what one can only hope is) peak polarization, and this polarization is connected to constitutional rot. Fourth, the federal judiciary, which is a lagging indicator of events, is not likely to be very helpful in getting us out of our current difficulties; it is part of the problem, not part of the solution. Fifth, the path out of constitutional rot will be political mobilization and reform movements, like those in the first decades of the twentieth century. We are in our Second Gilded Age, and on the cusp of a Second Progressive Era. Sixth, it is already possible to see how the reorganization of our major party coalitions will lead to depolarization, which, in turn, will make bipartisan solutions possible once again. Seventh, and perhaps most important, our recent unpleasantness is only a temporary condition. We are in transition—a very difficult, agonizing, and humbling transition—but a transition nevertheless.

When I say that it is a temporary condition, however, I do not mean that things will go back to the way they were before the 2016 election. They will not; they cannot. We are moving into a new constitutional order, with a new party structure, and with many new and unfamiliar elements.[16] The recent unpleasantness is the awkward, uncomfortable, and occasionally frightening transition to that new political order.

The majority of this book was written in 2018 and 2019 during the Trump administration, but before the 2020 election. As the book went to press, a dizzying sequence of events shook the country. In the fall of 2019, a scandal rocked Washington, as the press and congressional investigators discovered that Trump had tried to coerce Ukraine into smearing Trump's likely Democratic opponent in the upcoming presidential election. Congressional Democrats impeached the President in December 2019, but the Republican-controlled Senate held a perfunctory trial and acquitted Trump in early February 2020 without hearing any witnesses.

No sooner had Trump's impeachment trial concluded when the country was thrown into upheaval by a world-wide pandemic. Businesses shuttered, the stock market crashed, unemployment skyrocketed, and the United States seemed headed for a deep recession. The pandemic threw into uncertainty how and whether the public would vote in the 2020 election, how overtaxed and unprepared states would be able to count their ballots, and whether the results would be challenged in the courts, as in the 2000 election.

This quick succession of twists and turns makes short-term predictions foolhardy. Instead, the analysis in this book aims at the medium to long-term. It predicts that the Reagan regime that has dominated US politics since the 1980s is slowly grinding to its conclusion. The United States is on the cusp of a new political regime, probably one led by the Democratic Party. A new cycle of political time is about to commence. It will take about five to ten years before we can be confident that such a new era has begun.

In Chapter 2 I argue that Trump represents the end of the road for the Reagan regime. And if he is like other presidents presiding over exhausted regimes, he will probably not win a second term. The opposition party—the Democrats—will begin a new political regime and a new cycle of political time.

But given the confusion of the past year, it remains entirely possible that Trump will win a second term, especially if he squeezes out another Electoral College victory. In the modern era, incumbent presidents usually win second terms. If that happens, our current political regime will continue for a while longer. Our recent unpleasantness will be extended—especially if Trump loses the popular vote and forms a minority government for a second consecutive time. Like all things good and bad, the Reagan regime will eventually come to an end, and a new cycle eventually will begin. But if Trump wins in 2020, the transition will be even more fraught than it is today, if such a thing can be imagined. Throughout the book I will try to suggest the different paths that might occur if Trump does win a second term.

Finally, this is a book about the United States, its constitutional structures, and the cycles of American constitutional history. But events in this country do not happen in splendid isolation from events elsewhere. One of the reasons why people are so alarmed today about the fate of American democracy is that they see democracy decaying around the world—in Turkey, in Hungary, in Poland, and Brazil, to name just a few examples. Britain's proud democracy has been thrown into a tailspin by the debate over Brexit. Elsewhere in Europe democracy is threatened by the rise of new forms of anti-immigrant populism.

The aftershocks of the global financial crisis of 2008 and the Eurozone crisis that followed it continue to shape the political future of countries around the world. In much of the developed world, politics is consumed by anger over elite failures to protect the working class from the consequences of globalization. Democracy, which seemed to be on an unstoppable march only three decades ago, has been forced into an ignominious retreat. Russian manipulation of social media has stoked polarization, anger, and outrage in multiple countries. The European Union seems more precarious now than it has for years.

Perhaps a book about cycles of *American* constitutional development seems superficial, if not wholly irrelevant in light of these larger global trends. Indeed, many people—including many of my friends and colleagues—have taken precisely this approach. They warn us that tyranny, authoritarianism, and the end of democracy are just around the corner. People fear that what happened elsewhere will soon happen here.

History helps us understand how to think about these questions. This is not the first time political upheavals have shaken the world. When these upheavals occur—especially in Europe—similar upheavals also tend to happen in the United States. Yet American institutions tend to absorb these upheavals and process them differently than European states and most other countries do. Why this happens is probably overdetermined—a combination of institutional differences, geographical separation, and different historical starting points.

As we move from the eighteenth century to the twenty-first, we discover a remarkable pattern: the causes may be the same, but the effects are often different. In the 1770s and 1780s, the Americans and the French both have revolutions, but the American Revolution turns out differently than the French. Another set of convulsions hits Europe in the late 1840s, leading to a series of failed revolutions. The parallel unrest in the United States leads to a devastating civil war and political reconstruction. Europe responds to a period of economic globalization in the 1890s with a world war in the 1910s, while Americans engage in an imperialist war at the turn of the century and then fight over progressive reforms until entering—and helping conclude—that same world war.

Fascism rears its ugly head in Europe in the 1920s and 1930s, and a worldwide depression shakes democracy to its core, leading to Mussolini and Hitler, and a small fascist movement in Great Britain. Yet fascism doesn't prove as successful in the United States, and the country winds up not with Mussolini or Hitler, but with Franklin Delano Roosevelt and the New Deal. Social unrest in the 1960s throws France into unrest and confusion, while Americans, equally beset, manage to culminate a civil rights revolution.

Global economic turmoil upends the Labor Party in Britain in the 1970s, leading to Margaret Thatcher and providing an entry point for neoliberal governance, whose smiling visage in the United States is Ronald Reagan. But Thatcher and Reagan take somewhat different paths, in part because Reagan was able to dismantle far less of the New Deal and the Great Society, and in part because the United States never had as elaborate a system of nationalized industries to privatize.

Even when the United States and the rest of the world face the same set of causes, history repeatedly shows that the effects in the United States diverge in important respects. This is not because of "American exceptionalism" in the style of Louis Hartz.[17] Rather it is because different institutions with different histories are likely to absorb shocks and influences differently.

My task in this book is to consider how these global trends are affecting the institutions of American democracy, filtered through our party system, institutional history, and constitutional structures. Although analogous problems are roiling the wealthy democracies of the world, institutional and cultural structures in the United States affect the way that our politics processes them. These institutional and cultural features are the primary reason why my argument focuses on the cycles of American constitutional time. They are also among the reasons why I believe the fate of the United States is not going to be the same as that of Turkey, Brazil, Hungary, or Poland.

Part I of this book takes us through the three political cycles: of the rise and fall of constitutional regimes, of polarization and depolarization, and of constitutional rot and renewal. The message of Part I is ultimately optimistic. We have been through these cycles before and we will ultimately get out of our present troubles, not simply by waiting for things to get better, but by actively working to renew our democracy.

Part II asks how these cycles of constitutional time affect the work of the Supreme Court and the federal judiciary, which interpret and apply our Constitution. Here my answer is darker and more pessimistic. Although courts have played an important role in promoting and protecting democracy in other periods of American history, we cannot and should not expect courts to extricate us from our current difficulties. In a period of high polarization and advanced constitutional rot, the courts are likely to be as compromised as the rest of the government, and because they are a lagging indicator of politics, they will remain polarized and compromised for some time to come. The Supreme Court and the federal judiciary are unlikely to be the source of constitutional renewal. Only democratic mobilization that calls upon the best parts of our constitutional tradition can bring the country out of its current problems, and this effort will take some time.

Part II is not an argument for abandoning judicial review; rather it is a sober assessment of where the appropriate cure to our constitutional difficulties lies. We should not expect too much from the courts at this point in history. They may be ineffectual, or they may actually make things worse. Although judicial review remains a valuable feature of constitutional design, we should not treat courts as saviors during this difficult period, or look to an institution that cannot do much to help.

Part III of the book briefly considers what the new constitutional regime will look like, and how to understand the emerging structures of American party competition. The big takeaway is that our Second Gilded Age is likely to give way to a Second Progressive Era, which, like the first, will come with its own blindnesses, faults, and foibles. Even in our bitterly polarized world, we can already see signs of how American politics will eventually depolarize, creating new opportunities for cross-party collaboration.

Although the long-term view is optimistic, it will not be a smooth ride. The First Progressive Era was a turbulent time, and today we see all too clearly its flaws and moral failings. Our current case of constitutional rot is not and need not be a fatal condition. But the future of our democracy is not guaranteed, and we still have a long way to go to restore it.

2

The Cycle of Regimes

Our current political problems stem from the fact that we are in the final days of a crumbling, decadent political regime, and no new regime has yet appeared to take its place. This is a difficult and agonizing transition, a very sad time in American life. Its difficulty is enhanced by the fact that this transition between political regimes occurs at a time of peak polarization[1]—the crest of the cycle of polarization and depolarization—and at the low point of a cycle of constitutional rot. For that reason, the transition to a new political regime is going to be very difficult. But we will get through it. And when we get through it—about five to ten years from now—the present will seem like a distant, unhappy nightmare, or an illness from which one has recovered. Our politics will be quite different.

Many people my age or older have lived through another transition between political regimes, although they may not remember it as such. The last transition was not half as wrenching as this one. It occurred in the last years of the 1970s though the first years of the 1980s.[2] In a lecture I gave several years ago, I referred to it as "The Last Days of Disco."[3] This was the transition from the final years of the New Deal/Civil Rights regime, when Jimmy Carter was president, to the current regime we are living in now, the regime begun by Ronald Reagan, which I will call the Reagan regime.[4]

The transition from the New Deal/Civil Rights regime to the Reagan regime did not occur in circumstances as fraught as ours. First, it was not a time of strong polarization.[5] Polarization had been growing slowly since the 1960s, but it really took off during the Reagan regime, for reasons I will describe. In fact, one of the characteristic features of the Reagan regime is the development of political parties with strong polarization and conflict extension.[6] Polarization means that people in the two parties disagree strongly on particular issues. But they might still agree on some things, or there might be policy disagreements that cross party lines. Conflict extension means that Democrats and Republicans have simultaneously become polarized on multiple policy dimensions and multiple policy issues, even issues that ostensibly have little to do with each other, so that all of the disagreements line up.[7]

Just as the change of regimes in the late 1970s did not occur during a period of strong polarization and conflict extension, it also did not occur during

The Cycles of Constitutional Time. Jack M. Balkin, Oxford University Press (2020). © Jack Balkin 2020.
DOI: 10.1093/oso/9780197530993.001.0001

a period of advanced constitutional rot. The rot mostly came later. As I will also describe, a characteristic feature of the Reagan regime is a series of policy decisions that significantly increased economic inequality, and this, together with increasing party polarization, made the political system especially susceptible to constitutional rot.

To explain these ideas in more detail, I will begin with the central idea of constitutional regimes and explain the life cycle of these regimes. To do this, I will draw on the work of a distinguished political scientist and scholar of the presidency, Stephen Skowronek, at Yale University. He developed a theory of presidential leadership within political regimes that has been very influential, and deservedly so.[8]

Here is the big idea: American political history has featured a series of successive governing regimes in which political parties compete.[9] During each regime one of the parties tends to dominate politics practically and ideologically.[10] That doesn't mean that the party wins all of the elections. But it does win more of the elections than the other parties, and, more importantly, the dominant party's ideals and interests construct the basic agenda for politics during the regime. Put another way, the dominant party sets the baseline of what is considered possible and impossible politically. It structures the basic ideological assumptions of the politics of its time.

The easiest way to see this point is by contrasting the last two regimes. Our present governing regime, which began around 1980, is the Reagan regime, in which the Republican Party has been dominant. American conservatism and neoliberal ideology have set the basic agendas of politics, even if the conservative movement has not won every battle. This is an era of deregulation, privatization, tax cuts, weak labor unions, increasing economic inequality, and racial retrenchment.

The ideological assumptions of the Reagan regime differ from those of the previous regime—the New Deal/Civil Rights regime. It lasted from around 1932 to 1980, and the Democrats were the dominant party. This was an era of increasing government regulation, higher taxes, the creation of major social insurance programs, protection for organized labor, and the civil rights and civil liberties revolutions. American liberalism shaped the basic political assumptions of the period, even though liberals did not achieve everything they sought.

The idea of political regimes should not be confused with the theory of realigning elections—the theory that there are crucial elections in which large numbers of voters suddenly shift from one party to the other, inaugurating a new political era.[11] Political coalitions may change slowly rather than through quick transitions in the way that realignment theory proposes. Perhaps more important, political regimes feature dominant parties that manage to set the terms of political debate for long periods of time, even as electoral alignments shift beneath them. They manage to maintain dominant electoral coalitions even though the coalitions themselves constantly change. For example, although electoral patterns changed greatly between 1860 and 1932, the Republican Party remained the dominant political party in the United States during this period. For this reason, Andrew Polsky has defined a partisan regime as "a political coalition organized under a common party label that challenges core tenets of the [previous] established political order, secures effective national governing power, defines broadly the terms of political debate, and maintains sufficient power to thwart opposition efforts to undo its principal policy, institutional, and ideological achievements."[12]

Political regimes rise and fall. A dominant party depends on a political coalition to bring it into ascendance and keep it in power. In its early days, the regime may seem quite strong. It decisively rejects the politics that came before it. But as time goes on, and the regime normalizes, its coalition evolves and fractures. Circumstances change. The country faces new problems and threats. Demographic, social, economic, and technological changes test the coalition's dominance. Moreover, successful coalitions are often the victims of their own past successes.[13] As they achieve policy victories they change the political world around them, but in so doing, they often create new problems for themselves and produce new institutional impediments that make further change difficult.

Over time, opposition parties regroup and reorganize, appealing to new constituencies and finding new issues that threaten to split the coalition apart. The dominant party's positions, agendas, and standard policy solutions begin to seem stale, irrelevant, and out of touch with current problems. Elements of the dominant party divide into factions, and some become radicalized and demanding. Parts of the coalition become impatient and feel increasingly slighted or marginalized; they demand that the coalition take care of their needs. Compromise becomes more difficult. Existing voters leave the party, or new generations of voters reject it, so that the party cannot reproduce its majority over time. The coalition shrinks and fragments, becoming weaker and less resilient. This creates an opening—not always successfully taken—for a different party to begin a new regime. The new party is supported by a new political coalition, and it promotes a different set of commitments of ideology and interest. The cycle of political time begins again.

What I have just described is the life cycle of a political regime in American politics. A party that was once subordinate gradually grows in strength. It forms a rising coalition. It dominates politics. It promotes its distinctive agendas of ideology and interest. Its influence peaks. It becomes the victim of its own success. Its factions struggle with each other. It weakens, it withers, and it is eventually pushed aside by a new regime headed by another political party.

As Table 2.1 indicates, this cycle has happened about six times in American history.[14] The first regime is led by the revolutionary party, the Federalist Party, which loses power in 1800 and eventually falls apart. The next regime is the Jeffersonian regime, which begins with Thomas Jefferson's election in 1800. It is so dominant that for a brief time the United States effectively has one-party rule. This is sometimes known as the "era of good feelings." But that expression disguises a growing set of disagreements and factions. The good feelings don't last, and the Jeffersonian regime begins to fall apart in 1824, with a contested election that is thrown into the House of Representatives. The Jeffersonian regime is succeeded by the Jacksonian regime, beginning with Andrew Jackson's election in 1828. This regime is led by the Democratic Party, the first mass political party, the party of the white working man, and also the party of slavery. Eventually it becomes the vehicle and the mouthpiece for the Slave Power.

The Jacksonian regime falls apart because of increasing factionalism and radicalism among defenders of slavery, who try to preserve and extend their political power as the country develops into its western territories. This leads to the original "recent unpleasantness"—the American Civil War. Political struggles over the growth of slavery destroy the old Jacksonian coalition—as well as the coalition of the opposition party, the Whigs—and create an opening for a new regime, led by the ascendant Republican Party, created in 1854.

The Republican Party is the party of the Union, and following the Civil War, it dominates American politics for a very long time; for this reason it well

Table 2.1 The Cycle of Regimes in American Constitutional History

Name	Years	Dominant Party	Opposition Party
Federalist	1789–1800	Federalists	Jeffersonians
Jeffersonian	1800–1828	Democratic-Republicans	Federalists (until mid-1810s)
Jacksonian	1828–1860	Democrats	National Republicans; Whigs (after 1834); Republicans (after 1854)
Republican	1860–1932	Republicans	Democrats
New Deal/Civil Rights	1932–1980	Democrats	Republicans
Reagan (Second Republican)	1980–?	Republicans	Democrats

deserves its nickname of the Grand Old Party or GOP. The first Republican regime is the longest-lived regime in American history. It lasts from 1860 until 1932. The Republican regime weakens, however, with the increasing corruption of the Gilded Age. The Democrats—the party of the Old South, slavery, and secession—eventually grow stronger. They retake the House in 1874 and finally return to the presidency in 1884, almost twenty years after the conclusion of the Civil War. The Democrats have a chance to start a new regime in the 1896 election, allied with the insurgent populists. But for complicated reasons, the Democrats blow their chance, the Republicans regroup under William McKinley, and the Republican regime is revived and continues until the New Deal.

The Republican regime, however, is finally done in by the Great Depression. It is succeeded by the New Deal/Civil Rights regime, which begins with Franklin Roosevelt's election in 1932. The Democrats, with a new coalition that includes Catholic immigrants, city-dwellers, and labor unions, become the dominant party. In contrast to the Civil War era, national politics is quite depolarized, and most political achievements result from a series of bargains between three groups: Northern Democrats, Southern Democrats, and Republicans. This is the regime that creates the modern state and eventually passes the great civil rights acts.

The New Deal/Civil Rights regime is the victim of its own success. The Democratic Party begins to split apart during the 1960s—in part because of disputes over race and the Vietnam War—and members of its Southern wing start to leave the party. What we now call the culture wars begin. The 1970s witness the emergence of the New Right and a collection of conservative social movements; they will eventually remake the Republican Party in their own image.

The New Deal/Civil Rights regime is on its last legs in the 1970s, buffeted about by internal dissention and economic stagnation. The collapse of the New Deal/Civil Rights regime creates the opening for the emergence of the Reagan regime, which begins with Reagan's election in 1980. The conservative movement gradually takes over the Republican Party, revives it, and pushes it decidedly to the right. The Republican Party becomes the dominant national party, and it sets the agenda for national politics for decades. This is the regime of neoliberalism, deregulation, declining labor unions, and lower taxes—especially for the wealthy.

This is the regime we have been living under through most of my adult life. And this is the regime that is cracking up before our eyes. For the better part of a decade, the Republican Party has been radicalized and factionalized.[15] As Republicans moved sharply to the right, polarization and mutual distrust between the two major political parties made American politics increasingly poisonous and dysfunctional. The Republican party has been taken over by populist demagogues and con artists, of whom Donald Trump is only the most recent example. The party is momentarily united under Trump's brand of populist nativism. Even so, it looks ripe for an electoral reckoning, if not in 2020, then within the next few election cycles.

Of course, one could have said the same thing in 2008, but it didn't happen. Barack Obama and an emerging coalition of women, minorities, suburbanites, and professionals—the "coalition of the ascendant"[16]—were not able to inaugurate a new political regime. After two terms of Obama's presidency, the rising coalition was not yet strong enough to elect Hillary Clinton in 2016.[17] Even so, the Reagan regime is far weaker and internally conflicted than it was in 2008. The old regime is dying, but a new regime has yet to be born.

Why do I say that this regime is dying? For those who follow American politics, that statement might seem quite strange. In an important sense, the Republican Party is stronger now than it has been for almost a century.[18] Following Trump's 2016 victory, commentators pointed out that the Republicans haven't dominated national politics this much since 1928, when the party controlled all of the branches of government.[19] Nineteen twenty-eight . . . gee, I wonder what happened after that. . . .

After the election of Donald Trump in 2016, the Republican Party controlled the presidency and both houses of Congress. It had a Supreme Court majority, controlled more than half of the governorships, and had unified control of the legislature in thirty-three states.[20] (Republicans lost the House in the 2018 elections, but gained two Senate seats.) On paper, at least, the Republican Party appears to be a strong and robust political party, especially at the state and local level.

At the national level, however, the regime has many weaknesses, some overt and some hidden.

First, the Reagan regime, like many previous regimes, is a victim of its own success. At the outset its central commitments of ideology and interest were to lower taxes, make government smaller, reduce business regulation, build up national defense, and defeat communism. The Soviet Union was gone by 1991. The War on Terror offered a replacement for Cold War politics, but it led to the policy disaster of the Iraq War. As time goes on, calls for lowering taxes, reducing regulations, and building up defense seem increasingly irrelevant to problems the country faces—stagnant wages, decreasing social mobility, an opioid epidemic, crumbling infrastructure, a decaying educational system, crippling student debt, unaffordable health care, and so on. What sounded good in 1980 sounds increasingly stilted and out of touch by 2018.

Second, the regime's commitments of ideology and interest eventually drove a wedge between the party's ideological elites and the party's rank and file, which increasingly consists of white working-class voters.[21] These voters may support reducing government programs for the poor, especially if they believe that the benefits will be enjoyed primarily by racial minorities. But they may not support dismantling Social Security and Medicare and other features of the social safety net on which they depend. Globalization also drove a wedge between businesses' support for free trade and immigration reform and working-class opposition to both positions.

Third, the regime strongly supported campaign finance deregulation and First Amendment challenges to campaign finance laws. Deregulation changed how campaigns are financed and ultimately undermined the Republican Party. Deregulation allowed huge sums of money to enter politics and allowed wealthy individual donors to act increasingly independently of the party's organizational leadership. The result was the rise of financial "warlords" who act independent of the party apparatus and who increasingly call the tune in candidate selection and in primary challenges.[22] This encouraged increasingly radical positioning on the right, as candidates lined up to please donors.

Fourth, the Reagan regime also committed itself to the defense of traditional sexual norms, family values, conservative views about race and race relations, and opposition to multiculturalism—in short, to fighting the culture wars. Although this often helped mobilize voters, it eventually produced mixed results. Conservatives repeatedly lost key battles in the culture wars, forcing them perpetually to retreat from more conservative positions, for example, on gay rights. These battles over sexuality, as well as the use of racially charged issues to mobilize the base, may have worked well in the short run. But in the long run, they turned off increasing numbers of younger voters, college-educated voters, and women, who became independents or defected to the Democrats.[23]

Fifth, the regime's strategy of polarization, opposition, and obstruction, which helped Republicans gain control of Congress and stymie Barack Obama's administration, eventually encouraged internal factionalism, radicalism, and hostility to compromise.[24] This made it more difficult to govern effectively when Republicans were in power.

Sixth, the regime has been increasingly unable to win national presidential majorities since 1992. From that point on the Republican Party has won the national popular vote only once, in 2004. The other two times it gained the presidency it had to rely on Electoral College victories. The last time this happened, in 2016, it lost the popular vote by almost three million votes.[25] To maintain political control, the party has had to rely increasingly on partisan gerrymandering and multiple devices designed to depress the vote and restrict minorities' access to the ballot.

A. Where Are We in Political Time?

Seventh, and finally, the most recent Republican President, Donald Trump, is in an especially precarious position in the life cycle of the Reagan regime. To explain this point, I will need to describe in some detail Skowronek's analysis of the different political situations in which successive presidents find themselves during the life cycle of regimes. Skowronek calls the progress of these various situations *political time.*[26] (As we will see presently, a more accurate name might be *presidential time.*)

Skowronek classifies the political situation presidents face—and therefore the kind of presidents they are likely to become—according to whether they take office when a regime is robust or debilitated, and whether they are allied to the existing regime or opposed to it.[27]

Donald Trump is a Republican who becomes president during the Reagan regime. According to Skowronek, Trump may have inherited one of four possible political situations.

Reconstructive presidents successfully overturn a weakened regime and begin a new one.[28] They lead the opposition party to become the newly dominant party. Examples of reconstructive presidents are the first presidents in each new regime: Jefferson, Jackson, Lincoln, FDR, and Reagan. Presidents who achieve such a reconstruction are usually considered as among our most successful.[29] If Trump is a reconstructive president, then he would be trying to overturn Reaganism and the conservative movement and create a new Trumpist regime.

Affiliated presidents are allied with the regime and take office later in political time.[30] They try to keep faith with the regime's commitments under changing circumstances. Skowronek describes them as "orthodox-innovators."[31] Examples in the New Deal/Civil Rights regime would be Truman, Kennedy, and Johnson; examples in the Reagan regime would be George H. W. Bush and George W. Bush.[32] If Trump were an affiliated president, he would present himself as an orthodox Reaganite who is trying to keep the factions in his party united.

Pre-emptive presidents come from opposition parties; they swim against the tide of a still powerful regime, so they must compromise, triangulate, and find a "third way."[33] Examples in the New Deal/Civil Rights regime would be Eisenhower and Nixon; examples in the Reagan regime would be Clinton and

Obama.[34] If Trump were a pre-emptive President, he would be opposed to Reaganism and the conservative movement and seek to find a third way between the two political parties.

The final category, *disjunctive* presidents, are leaders who come from the dominant party but have the misfortune to take over when the regime is on its last legs.[35] Here the president tries to repair and reform a decrepit regime that has lost its coherence and legitimacy; the leader attempts this by selectively breaking with party orthodoxy in specific ways to shore up public support and reform the party's base. But because the coalition has become so debilitated and weakened, the leader is not up to the task, and therefore presides over the regime's dissolution.[36] Jimmy Carter, the last Democrat in the New Deal/Civil Rights regime, and Herbert Hoover, the last Republican in the long Republican regime, are key examples. Disjunctive presidencies are usually regarded as failures.

Table 2.2 sums up Skowronek's account of the different styles of presidential leadership.

Where are we in political time? To decide this question, we should ask which description of presidential leadership best fits Trump's situation.[37]

It is unlikely that Trump is a reconstructive president. He did not run against the philosophy of Reaganism or claim that he sought to displace it. Like other Republican primary candidates, he sought to compare himself to

Table 2.2 Presidential Leadership Styles in Skowronek's Theory of Political Time

President Takes Office	When the Current Regime Is Vulnerable	When the Current Regime Is Robust
Opposed to the current regime	*Reconstructive* Repudiates old politics and clears ground for a new regime. Examples: Jefferson, Jackson, Lincoln, F. D. Roosevelt, and Reagan.	*Pre-emptive* Offers a third way to shore up legitimacy. Examples: Tyler, Fillmore, Cleveland, Wilson, Eisenhower, Nixon, Clinton, and Obama.
Allied with the current regime	*Disjunctive* Coalition falls apart; president presides over the dissolution of the regime. Examples: J. Adams, J. Q. Adams, Buchanan, Hoover, and Carter.	*Affiliated* Must articulate regime's commitments and balance party orthodoxy against the need for innovation; tries to mollify multiple factions. Examples: Madison, Monroe, Polk, Grant, T. Roosevelt, Taft, Truman, Kennedy, Lyndon B. Johnson, and George H. W. Bush.

Source: Balkin, *The Last Days of Disco*, note 16.

Reagan, and his primary campaign slogan, Make America Great Again, originated with Reagan.[38] He has strongly supported the religious right and nominated conservative pro-life judges vetted by the Federalist Society.[39] With only a few important exceptions (to be discussed later), his policies and his judicial appointments have been very conservative and characteristic of a conservative Republican President.[40]

For the same reasons, Trump is not a pre-emptive president; he did not come into office from an opposition party, trying to swim against the tide of Reaganism and seeking to find a way to compromise with the dominant party or triangulate between the two parties' positions. He is the leader of the regime's dominant party, the Republicans. The members of his party have strongly supported him not because they like his personal behavior or his political principles (he doesn't seem to have many settled principles), but rather because his policies have been largely consistent with those of a very conservative Republican.[41] The president he most sought to repudiate was not Ronald Reagan but Barack Obama, and if Obama was a preemptive president in the Reagan regime, it's hard to see how Trump could be one too.[42]

Trump might well be an affiliated president like George W. Bush. As noted earlier, after his election, Trump and his appointees have acted like very conservative Republicans on a wide range of issues. On the other hand, Trump has departed from Republican orthodoxy in several ways: his rejection of free trade, his defense of middle-class entitlements such as Social Security and Medicare, and his repeated calls for huge public works and infrastructure projects. During the campaign Trump also criticized George W. Bush's hawkish foreign policy, distanced himself from the Iraq War, and even blamed Bush for failing to prevent the 9/11 attacks.[43]

Trump's opposition to free trade and his draconian rhetoric and policies on immigration suggest that although he is not abandoning the regime's commitments to deregulatory capitalism, low taxes, and the culture wars, he is trying to renovate and repair the regime. He is adapting it to a changing Republican base of white, working-class voters, especially those without college degrees.

Trump, in other words, seems to be trying to give the Reagan regime a new lease on life, or a new shot of legitimacy, by pushing it in a strongly populist and nativist direction.[44] And he is offering himself as a nonideological outsider who has the special talents to fix things. According to Skowronek's model, this style of leadership makes him most like a disjunctive president. As Skowronek puts it:

> One of the great ironies of the politics of disjunction is that the Presidents who come to office in these sorts of situations tend to have only the most tenuous relationship to the establishments they represent. Long-festering problems within the regime tend to throw up leaders only nominally affiliated with it, and in their efforts to address the issues of the day, these affiliates often press major departures of their own from the standard formulas and priorities set in the old agenda. The political effect of these departures is disjunctive: they sever the political moorings of the old regime and cast it adrift without anchor or orientation.[45]

This description seems to fit Trump quite well.

Trump fits the disjunctive pattern in a second way. As differences within the coalition become increasingly obvious and difficult to manage, disjunctive candidates argue that they are able to fix things because they have special technical abilities. For example, they might portray themselves as extremely skilled politicians (John Quincy Adams, James Buchanan), outstanding technocrats and problem-solvers (Herbert Hoover, Jimmy Carter); or, as in Trump's case, outstanding dealmakers.[46] They explain to the public that what is important is not ideological purity but the ability to get things done. As Skowronek puts it, in the last days of a regime, mastery of technique—in this case dealmaking and business acumen—"is a hallmark of the politics of disjunction."[47] Focusing on technique allows the new president to remain ambiguous about his or her positions, allowing everyone in the coalition to believe that it will get what it wants.

We won't really know if Trump is a disjunctive president for several years after he leaves office. But many of the signs are present. And when we combine Skowronek's account of presidential leadership with the other pieces of evidence identified in this chapter, there is a very good chance that Trump does not represent the beginning of a new politics in America but the end of an older one.[48]

B. The Waning of Political Time

That is not, however, the end of the analysis. In addition to the cycle of regimes, Skowronek argues that long-term secular trends in American politics make political reconstruction increasingly difficult with each new regime.

As time goes on, the political system contains more and more veto points, conflicting interests and obstacles. (Think only of the difference between the state in 1860 and the state in 2019.) As older political regimes crumble, each new attempt at political disruption and ground clearing is less successful at destroying older, entrenched elements.

The effect becomes especially pronounced as the state grows larger and more complex during the twentieth century. Franklin Delano Roosevelt was unable to engage in the same kind of creative destruction as a president like Andrew Jackson or Abraham Lincoln. Ronald Reagan could muster even less change than FDR: Reagan left most of the administrative and regulatory and welfare state in place, and simply altered its beneficiaries.[49] Compared with Andrew Jackson, who dismantled the federal banking system, Abraham Lincoln, who destroyed the slaveholders' Republic, or FDR, who created the modern state, Ronald Reagan was a far less successful revolutionary.[50]

Skowronek argues that the cumulative effects of institution and state-building make it increasingly difficult for presidents to shatter old ways of doing things and thoroughly reconstruct politics.[51] He calls this phenomenon the "waning of political time."[52]

At some point in the future, Skowronek argues, institutions and interest groups will be so powerful that a new reconstructive politics will be impossible. Instead, presidents will be locked into a politics of "perpetual preemption."[53] All presidents will resemble pre-emptive presidents, bobbing and weaving through a constellation of conflicting forces, accumulated institutions, and powerful interest groups. Presidents will try to maneuver through this thicket of political obstacles, but they will not be able to demolish them to build anew. Each new leader will rail against the system, and will be elected on a promise to break it apart, but will wind up being unable to do very much.[54]

Have we reached the waning of political time? And has the cycle of the rise and fall of political regimes ended? It's important to separate out three different issues.

First, it is likely that revolutionary reform becomes increasingly complicated as the state becomes more complex and interests proliferate. Second, future presidents may find transformative political reconstruction difficult—at least in the short run—unless one party manages to win overwhelming majorities, as FDR did in the 1930s. Ronald Reagan lacked the kinds of overwhelming majorities that FDR (and LBJ) enjoyed to reshape the foundations of the American state. The parties have been highly competitive in the early twenty-first century—as they were in the late nineteenth century—and we simply have no way of knowing when we will return to the era of electoral landslides.

But a third, and quite different question is whether the cycle of regimes has ended—that is, whether there will be no new dominant party that sets the agendas of politics for an extended period, developing a winning coalition that ascends into power and eventually falls apart.

For purposes of this book, this third question is the crucial one. Even if Skowronek's prediction about the increasing difficulty of revolutionary change is correct, there is no reason to think that political time—much less constitutional time—is over. Perhaps there are fewer opportunities for truly reconstructive leadership on the order of Jackson or Lincoln, but the rise and fall of regimes continues unabated, because it is not solely caused by presidents.

Recall that Skowronek's is a theory of *presidential leadership*. He is interested in the kind of authority that presidents have for political action, and the limits of that authority imposed by the political and historical circumstances in which presidents find themselves. My interest, by contrast, is in *constitutional regimes*.

A constitutional regime involves far more than the presidency. It also includes, among other things, Congress, the courts, the administrative agencies, the military, the foreign policy establishment, the party system, and civil society organizations and actors. In many cases new constitutional regimes have been spawned by a powerful social movement that takes over a party and energizes it to remake politics. For example, anti-slavery and free soil movements, the labor movement, and the modern conservative movement played crucial roles in paving the way for the Republican, New Deal, and Reagan regimes, respectively. Each of these features may be connected to presidential leadership, but they have independent importance.

Moreover, a constitutional regime features a dominant party, with a reigning set of commitments of ideology and interest; a particular structure of party competition; the development of judicial doctrines reflecting the regime's commitments; new forms of state-building; and interactions between social movements, civil society organizations, and the party system. Skowronek's central concern—styles of presidential leadership—focus on how presidents behave within this larger environment.

If we want to know whether there has been a change in constitutional regimes, we should look to the following factors: (1) a newly dominant party; (2) new demographics that generate new party coalitions and support that party's dominance; (3) new methods of party organization; (4) a significant reorientation of the goals and agendas of governance; and, after the dominant party has appointed enough judges, (5) important changes in the composition of the judiciary and in the values and doctrines enforced by the judiciary on behalf of the dominant party. The last factor—the role of the judiciary—is quite important, and generally takes some time to develop. Most of the big changes in constitutional doctrine that are characteristic of the Reagan regime did not occur until the late 1980s, and especially after 1991, when Justice Clarence Thomas joined the Court.

These five signs of a change in constitutional regimes do not depend primarily on the emergence of a reconstructive, ground-clearing presidency—although it's easy to see why a transformative presidency would contribute to and accompany these kinds of changes.

New regimes involve a new dominant party and changes in governing coalitions. But a party can become newly dominant for reasons of demographic and technological change without affording presidents the same possibilities for reconstructive leadership that they enjoyed in the first hundred years of the republic.

Skowronek's "waning of political time" thesis is really a claim about presidential leadership styles; he argues that they are gradually converging. But even if he is right about this, there are larger forces at work that produce the succession of constitutional regimes. That means that the two ideas—the cycle of leadership styles and the cycle of regimes—may be coming apart. Regimes will keep rising and falling, but presidents may play a less central role in reconstructing politics when a regime begins. To the extent this is so, it marks the waning of *presidential time*, not political or constitutional time.

Put another way, Skowronek focuses on the changing relationship of the presidency to the constitutional regime. He thinks that, as time goes on, presidents will have fewer and fewer truly revolutionary opportunities. But he is not claiming that significant political change ceases altogether. He is not saying that the structures of American politics are the same in 1932 and 2016. That is why his argument is more properly called the waning of presidential time. And we do not know if this loss of revolutionary opportunity is truly permanent, or whether it, too, will change at some point in the future.

In fact, if Skowronek's "waning of political time" thesis is correct, then it actually shows why the forces that cause regimes to rise and fall do not depend on the existence of reconstructive presidencies. Reconstructive presidents take advantage of those forces, but they are not the primary, much less the sole cause, of them.

Reagan's example is instructive. Skowronek argues that Reagan was unable to change as much as FDR, much less Lincoln or Jackson. Yet there is no doubt that the Reagan regime's governing coalition, governing assumptions, and commitments of ideology and interest are very different from those of the New Deal/Civil Rights regime that preceded it. Constitutional practices also changed. In my work on constitutional theory, I employ the idea of the "Constitution-in-practice": the set of doctrines, institutions, and practices that characterize the constitutional system at any point in time.[55] Even if the constitutional text doesn't change very much, the Constitution-in-practice can change a great deal. It is pretty clear that the Constitution-in-practice as it existed in 1980, when the Reagan regime began, is quite different from the Constitution-in-practice in 2020, late in the regime. (I discuss the Reagan-era conservative judicial revolution in more detail in Part II of this book.) And, if Justices Neil Gorsuch, Brett Kavanaugh, and the rest of the Trump appointees to the federal courts have anything to say about it, the Constitution-in-practice of the future will increasingly look different from the Constitution of the New Deal/Civil Rights regime.

How can the Reagan era be so different, and its political assumptions so different, if Reagan wasn't as transformative a president as Jackson or Lincoln? The answer is that changes in constitutional regimes do not rest wholly on presidential leadership. The changing structure of the political parties, the organization of Congress, and the work of courts are also quite important. It is no accident that two of the most important features of the Reagan regime are (1) party polarization in Congress and the states and (2) a judicial revolution. Both are clearly related to the presidency, but neither is wholly subsumed by it.

If we take a broader perspective, this point should be obvious. After all, society continues to change, technology changes, demographics change, and new generations succeed older ones with different values, concerns, and aspirations. The party system changes too. Today's parties have been transformed by technology and systems of campaign finance. I call this transformation the "party as database."[56] Today's politicians rely heavily on data collection, surveillance, and analysis to raise money, target likely supporters, organize the party faithful, and turn them out to vote. The people and organizations who have control over data effectively control the party—and usually also have fundraising advantages too. The rise of data analysis and political surveillance mean that new players compete with the traditional party bureaucracy for control of the party's agenda and over who runs for office under the party's banner. This is a very different party structure than the one that existed during the New Deal or even the early years of the Reagan regime.

And then there's the Constitution itself, or, rather the Constitution-in-practice. No one would confuse the Constitution of 1969, in the heyday of the Warren Court, with the Constitution of 2019, fifty years later. Because presidents pick judges and Justices, there is every reason to believe that the Constitution-in-practice is going to keep on changing. In addition, we must consider how civil society is changing, the new forms of activism and protest, the changing structure of the bureaucracy, and . . . well, you get the picture.

Because party coalitions rise and fall, grow and fragment, there will be new constitutional regimes, whether or not we have reconstructive presidencies in the mold of Jackson and Lincoln. Put another way, if the Democrats (for example), manage to create a new winning coalition in the 2020s or 2030s and dominate politics for a long time, we may retrospectively bestow the mantle of transformative leadership on the first president in the new regime. But that leadership may be of a different order than previous reconstructive presidencies.

C. Trump as the Great Reviver?

In politics, as in life, however, nothing is certain. There is one possible pathway for the survival of the Reagan regime, and it would be folly not to consider it. Trump seems to have accelerated the movement of the Republican Party toward a coalition that depends heavily on white working-class voters, especially in rural areas and in the South. To please this coalition, Trump has adopted a new set of issues: he has moved the Republican party away from free trade and taken strongly anti-immigration stances. If this makeover succeeds, the Reagan regime might continue onward led by a nativist/populist Republican party. Working-class whites and conservative evangelicals would form the most significant block of the party. But the party would continue to be funded by business elites, wealthy individuals, and corporations with very different agendas.

Something like this happened once before. In the 1890s it looked as if the Democratic Party, allied with a populist insurgency, might form a new regime. But Democrats had the misfortune to control the White House during the panic of 1893.[57] William McKinley defeated William Jennings Bryan in the 1896 election, reorganizing the Republican Party and American politics around a new set of issues.[58] The 1896 election also produced a new coalition that kept the first Republican regime going until the Great Depression. So too, Trump might represent the second wave of the Reagan regime—a reorganized party, with a new coalition and a new set of issues that keep it dominant for decades to come.

A revived Trumpist Republican Party would be organized around a combination of American nationalism, conservative Christianity, and bare-knuckled capitalism. Following Trump's example, the party might become increasingly corrupt and kleptocratic. It would make ritualized feints in the direction of improving the lot of working-class families and protecting rural Americans. But because of the party's powerful business wing and donor base, its economic policies would remain largely deregulatory. It would continue the Reagan regime's upward redistribution of income and the downward redistribution of risk, and would actually do relatively little to improve the lives of its working-class constituents. Instead, a Trumpist party would please its working-class and evangelical base through cultural issues, immigration restrictions, and conservative versions of identity politics.

As I'll explain in the last chapter of this book, the Republican Party has indeed been undergoing a transformation like this. It is becoming a party with a large nativist and populist wing, in an increasingly awkward relationship to its neoliberal wing, which wants deregulation, ever lower taxes, and upward redistribution.

It is certainly possible that Trump will win re-election in 2020. He has a real shot at winning a second Electoral College victory without winning the popular vote. In addition, the Republicans retain a strong position in the United States Senate and in many state legislatures. Because of gerrymandering and because their political base is rural, Republicans also have a natural advantage in the House of Representatives. A Republican revival under Trump is not out of the question.

Even so, I don't think this is the most likely scenario. The percentage of white voters in the United States continues to shrink with each passing year. The party's brand is increasingly toxic among the millennial generation and younger voters. A party that continues to emphasize white identity politics combined with upward income redistribution does not seem well-calculated to maintain a durable national majority.

William McKinley's example is instructive. McKinley forged a new coalition that included not only businessmen and professionals, but also industrial workers and people living in cities. His opponent, the Democrat William Jennings Bryan, tried to put together a populist coalition centered around rural areas that were not growing as fast. Trump's electoral strategy seems closer to Bryan's than McKinley's, and indeed, as I will explain in the book's final chapter, the Republican electoral map in the last several presidential elections looks very much like that of 1896, but with the parties reversed. It is not clear that one can cobble a durable majority out of the segments of the American public that are growing older and losing population.

To be sure, the Electoral College, partisan gerrymandering, voting restrictions, and a friendly judiciary may keep Republicans in power for a bit longer. President Trump may squeeze out a victory in 2020. And certainly Republicans will continue to be a powerful force in the South and in the rural United States for years to come. But now matter how good a salesman President Trump may be, a long-term Republican revival faces long odds. The most likely candidate for a new political regime will feature the Democrats as the dominant party. Its winning coalition will be the natural evolution of the coalition that Barack Obama formed in 2008—of minorities, millennials, college-educated professionals, suburbanites, and women. In the last chapter of the book, I describe what this new party configuration is likely to look like.

3
The Cycle of Polarization

President Trump, as I have just argued, is a symptom of the decadence of the Reagan regime. But Trump is also a symptom of another political phenomenon, which brings me to the second of the three cycles of constitutional time that I'm interested in: the cycle of polarization and depolarization.

A. The Long Cycle of Polarization

American politics has featured a very long cycle of polarization and depolarization between the political parties.[1] As you might expect, political polarization grows markedly in the years leading up to the Civil War. Things stay pretty polarized for a long time. Until late in the nineteenth century, for example, Republicans ran political campaigns by "waving the bloody shirt"—reminding voters that the Democrats were the party of secession and slavery and therefore could not be trusted to govern.[2] Polarization continues through the Gilded Age, as waves of immigration and increasing income inequality keep politics strongly polarized.

In the first decade of the twentieth century, polarization begins to recede, and it continues to decline rapidly into the New Deal era.[3] The New Deal/Civil Rights regime features a largely depolarized politics. In fact, during this period there are effectively three different parties: Northern Democrats, Southern Democrats, and Republicans.[4] These three large coalitions have cross-cutting interests that make a wide array of legislative solutions possible. This is the political configuration that produces Social Security and the Fair Labor Standards Act during the New Deal, but it also produces the great civil rights acts of the 1960s, which are bipartisan projects of Northern Democrats and moderate to liberal Republicans.[5]

The civil rights reforms coincided with a transformation of Southern politics. Following World War II, and especially after the Voting Rights Act of 1965, the South gradually evolved from an apartheid region with one-party politics into a region more like the rest of the country, with two competitive political parties.[6] But the civil rights reforms had an unfortunate side effect. They precipitated realignment between the two parties, as white Southerners

The Cycles of Constitutional Time. Jack M. Balkin, Oxford University Press (2020). © Jack Balkin 2020.
DOI: 10.1093/oso/9780197530993.001.0001

flocked to the Republican Party and the two parties began to repolarize, especially around race and cultural issues.[7]

B. Polarization in the Reagan Regime

Polarization became a project of the Republican Party during the 1990s. Newt Gingrich saw it as the best way for Republicans to become a majority party that could not only win presidential elections (as Nixon and Reagan had) but could also control Congress and state governments. Gingrich perfected a new slash-and-burn style of rhetoric that portrayed his political enemies as sexually deviant, dangerous, and unpatriotic.[8] The conservative movement created counterinstitutions to promote conservative ideas, and conservative media—talk radio and Fox News being the most obvious examples—helped make political polarization a viable political strategy.[9] The result was *asymmetric polarization*. Democrats moved a little to the left, in part because conservative Southern Democrats gradually left the party, while the Republican base moved far to the right.[10]

Increasing polarization destroyed the system of compromise politics that characterized the New Deal/Civil Rights era. Conservative Democrats and liberal Republicans became increasingly rare to virtually nonexistent.[11] Unsurprisingly, because there was little overlap between the positions of members of the two parties, political compromise became increasingly difficult. Obstruction is a predictable result when there is no middle ground. Today there is a de facto rule that it takes sixty votes in the Senate to pass any important legislation because the party opposite the president will filibuster if they don't already control the majority. This phenomenon is relatively recent. It is a product of the 1990s, developed as a strategy of obstruction.[12]

One might have hoped that the disputed election of 2000 would have led the George W. Bush administration to attempt to mend political fences and work to tamp down the forces of polarization. Bush, who had cooperated with Democrats as governor of Texas, had sought to portray himself as "a uniter, not a divider."[13] A further opportunity for unity came after the September 11, 2001 terrorist attacks. But the forces of polarization were far too strong and, more to the point, far too tempting for politicians seeking short-term electoral gains. The Bush administration's chief political strategist, Karl Rove, recognized that Republicans were more likely to win national elections if they appealed to their base of loyal voters and got them out to vote in large numbers.[14] Such a base strategy encourages deliberately polarizing the electorate so that the base will be energized to turn out—because they come to believe that the other party can't be trusted to govern.

The problem with the rhetoric and strategy of polarization is that it is good for getting elected but not particularly good for governing—unless, of course, one can gain a sixty-vote majority in the Senate, a working majority in the House, and control of the presidency. The strategy of polarization helped Republicans become the dominant party during the Reagan regime,[15] but it had unfortunate effects—another example of how the path of victory for a dominant party in a political regime may contribute to its undoing later on.

Polarization and obstruction make it more difficult for Congress to reach compromises. For a time this meshed well with Republicans' ideological message that government is incompetent and therefore we should have smaller government and less regulation. But it made governing difficult when Republicans were in power. Polarization also helped encourage the rise of increasingly radical factions within the party who valued ideological purity over compromise and obstruction over legislative success.[16]

A gridlocked Congress also encourages presidents to assert ever-greater authority in governing, both in foreign policy and through creative uses of the administrative state.[17] An expansive conception of executive power and unilateral presidential action might have been fine when Republicans controlled the White House, but it created an opening for Democrats like Barack Obama to use similar strategies to push for immigration and environmental reforms. As a result, conservative Republicans have become increasingly critical of the executive's control of the administrative state.[18] This is a reverse of the conservative stance at the beginning of the Reagan era, when conservatives wanted the president to take greater control of the bureaucracy; in those years they developed the constitutional theory of the unitary executive and promoted the *Chevron* doctrine of judicial deference to administrative agencies.[19]

The final irony of the strategy of polarization and obstructionism was that when Republicans finally gained control of all three branches of government in 2017, they were unable to repeal Obamacare. Because Democrats could filibuster legislation when Republicans had less than sixty votes in the Senate, Republicans had to use complex reconciliation rules to repeal Obamacare by a simple majority. This greatly limited the kinds of reforms they could adopt. These limitations and the budgetary constraints of the reconciliation rules created divisions within their own coalition, ultimately dooming the repeal.

Polarization and obstruction have also led to an unwieldy form of governance. Congress no longer uses its ordinary appropriations process. Instead of a series of bills passed through the committee system, party leaders negotiate with each other for grand omnibus appropriations bills that are packed with multiple policy riders, conditions, tax breaks, and subsidies.[20] These bills keep the government running until the next deadline, at which point party leaders negotiate under time pressure to produce a new grand appropriations measure, which leaders then present to Congress without much deliberation, essentially on a take-it-or-leave-it basis. This policy of legislative brinksmanship—lurching from big appropriations bill to big appropriations bill—is the only way that congressional leaders can transcend the bitter polarization and political dysfunction characteristic of the late Reagan regime.[21] It keeps the government running, but it precludes serious policy deliberation, much less any sustained attempt to deal with serious public problems.

C. Is Polarization Permanent?

This book argues that polarization moves in cycles, and that our politics will eventually depolarize. But the cycle of polarization doesn't really commence until the party system stabilizes after the Civil War. To be sure, one could argue that polarization begins in earnest in the 1840s, when the country is increasingly divided by slavery, but this is also a period in which several parties come in and out of existence. The division of American politics between two major parties—Republican and Democratic—is the product of the Civil War era.

If Americans changed our system of representation—for example by moving to proportional representation or using ranked-choice voting systems—we could have more than two viable national political parties, and that would change how polarization operates.[22] These reforms merit serious consideration, and I happen to think that some of them are great ideas, but they haven't happened yet.

From the Civil War to the present day American politics has traveled through one great cycle of polarization, beginning with a period of high polarization in the nineteenth century, declining through the middle of the twentieth century, and then ramping up once again in the 1970s.[23]

In that same period of time, however, we have been through the rise and fall of three different regimes—assuming, as I believe, that the Reagan era is nearing its close. Given this history, what reason do we have to think that political polarization really does cycle—that it is not just a permanent condition of our politics, with the exception of parts of the early republic and one other period in the middle of the twentieth century? And if polarization actually does cycle, what causes it to cycle and why does that cycle move so slowly? Or to put it another way, why should we think that American politics will ever depolarize again?

To understand why polarization cycles, we need to know a bit about its causes. In fact, polarization has multiple causes, as I will describe.[24] But one of the most important is increasing income inequality.[25] In fact, polarization and income inequality tend to egg each other on. It is easier for politicians and political activists to polarize politics as income inequality gets worse. Conversely, when politics is polarized, it is easier for the wealthy to block reforms that might redistribute income downward, and easier to obtain deregulation and tax breaks that redistribute income upward. In this way, polarization and income inequality can create a vicious cycle—income inequality tends to makes polarization worse, while polarization blocks reforms that would ameliorate income inequality. That is one reason—although not the only one—why the cycle of polarization in American history is so long.

We can see the interaction of polarization and income inequality in the story I told at the beginning of this chapter. Income inequality rose markedly from the beginning of the republic to 1860, especially in the South.[26] The antebellum period—particularly after 1840—is also one of increasing polarization over the question of slavery; and, as I will argue in chapter 5, one of increasing constitutional rot.

The Civil War destroyed massive amounts of wealth, and this lowered economic inequality. But the political bitterness caused by the war continued for many years, so the political polarization between Democrats and Republicans did not decline. In fact, for many years afterward, politicians used the memory of the Civil War to whip up partisan resentments. In the meantime, rapid economic growth in the Gilded Age caused income inequality to rise sharply once again.

Once income inequality began to increase during the Gilded Age, other factors kept it going. One factor was the increasing influence of money in politics, as vast new fortunes were created. By today's standards, there were few effective limits on political corruption in the Gilded Age. So as economic inequality rose, politicians were likely to be far more responsive to the demands of the very wealthy than to the needs of the average citizen. As in our own time, this made inequality worse. That is why this is also a period of constitutional rot, as I describe in chapter 5.

A second factor that kept income inequality growing was immigration. During the Gilded Age the percentage of people not born in the United States increased considerably, reaching around 14.8 percent in 1890 and 14.7 percent in 1910.[27]

Immigration rates have interesting effects on the politics of redistribution. You might think that high immigration would cause voters to demand more income redistribution to compensate for economic competition from immigrants. But in fact the effect is the opposite.

Immigrants cannot vote until they are naturalized. (The story is actually a bit more complicated. During the nineteenth century, some immigrants, such as Chinese laborers, could not become citizens; conversely, some states allowed aliens to vote in local elections to encourage settlement.) Immigrants are also likely to be poor. Even after immigrants do become citizens, because they are poor, they are less likely to vote than the average citizen.[28]

In their study of income equality and polarization, Nolan McCarty, Keith Poole, and Howard Rosenthal point out that these facts have an important consequence. As large numbers of immigrants enter the country, they alter the ratio between the median income of *voters* and the average income of *all families* (which includes people who do not vote and those who cannot vote).[29] That is, an influx of poorer immigrants makes the people who do vote—who tend to be richer than nonvoters in the first place—comparatively better off, because they will compare their income with increasing numbers of people who are poorer and who cannot or do not vote.

Why does this matter? Electoral pressures for redistribution—through taxation and social programs—increase as the median income of the people who do vote sinks lower and lower relative to the average income of families.[30] In other words, what creates electoral pressure for redistribution is not whether median income increases in absolute terms, but whether the ratio between the median income of voters and the average income of all families is getting lower over time. As that ratio decreases, voters worry that they are losing ground. So they start replacing politicians who won't redistribute income through taxes and social programs with other politicians who will.

It is true that government capture by the wealthy can hold off redistribution for a time. It is also true that politicians can try to dilute redistributive pressures by disenfranchising more and more poor people, so that the people who actually get to vote are relatively better off as a class. But at some point, if income inequality gets too great, the median income of voters relative to the average income of families will fall too much, and voters will demand reform.

High rates of immigration counteract this effect. They bolster the median income of voters relative to the average income of all households. And this reduces the electoral pressure for redistribution that increasing income inequality would ordinarily produce.[31] In addition, the number of immigrants in the country affects how the benefits from government redistribution are shared. If voters think that noncitizens are relatively poorer than they are, they will also think that noncitizens stand to benefit more from redistributive programs than they will. So voters will be more likely to resist redistribution,[32] and politicians defending the interests of the wealthy will likely play on these fears.

During the Gilded Age political polarization stayed high because of increasing income inequality. But American democracy was unable to effectively counteract this inequality—because of Civil War politics, government capture by the wealthy, and high rates of immigration. Nevertheless, sometime in the 1910s there was a breakthrough, and polarization began to decline. Once again, there are multiple reasons.

First, the generation that fought the Civil War eventually died off, and new generations of voters had different priorities than continuing to fight the Civil War over and over again in politics.

Second, the party coalitions changed, making each party's coalition less ideologically coherent. The regime's dominant party, the Republican Party, reconfigured itself in the 1896 election, bringing skilled factory workers in large cities into the Republican coalition. Republicans also had many supporters in Western and midwestern states, whose interests differed from those in the East.

Something similar happened to the Democrats. Many European immigrants and urban workers joined the Democratic Party, making its coalition increasingly complicated. The more incoherent the party coalitions became, the easier it was for politicians from different parties to join forces on particular legislation. Increasing opportunities for cross-cutting alliances reduced polarization.

Third, income inequality became so pronounced that public opposition eventually overwhelmed the political blockages to redistribution and reform. Gilded Age corruption led to the creation of reform wings in both political parties, heralding the Progressive Era. And when the Supreme Court overreached and struck down the federal income tax in 1895,[33] it spurred a bipartisan movement for a federal income tax amendment—the Sixteenth Amendment—to overrule the Court. The passage of a new federal income tax in 1913 helped reverse income inequality. Although income inequality started to rise during the Roaring Twenties, it decreased once again during the Great Depression.

Fourth, the rate of immigration greatly slowed as a result of World War I. Pent-up hostility to immigration in both parties led to restrictions on new immigration in the 1920s that lasted until the 1960s. As the previous waves of immigrants were gradually absorbed into the country, they became voters in both parties. This further scrambled party coalitions.

The experience of the early twentieth century suggests why polarization eventually cycles into depolarization. At some point, rates of immigration slow, and political coalitions reform. Old issues replace new ones. Corruption becomes intolerable and economic inequality unacceptable. Demands for change overwhelm blockages and transform existing party configurations. Moreover, once reforms begin, they reshape political incentives and coalitions, making further reforms possible.

We can already see signs of how depolarization might occur in the next few decades. Income inequality, already at Gilded Age levels in the early twenty-first century, surged further as a result of the 2017 tax bill.[34] Although this will make wealthy donors happy in the short run, it will also increase hydraulic pressures for income redistribution in the future. In addition, although you would not know it from listening to President Donald Trump, the rate of new immigrants into the United States has already begun to drop.[35] The 2020 pandemic—and government responses to it—may slow immigration even further. Finally, as I describe more fully in chapter 12, the Republican and Democratic coalitions have slowly been shifting, creating populist wings in both parties. As the next regime develops, the growing incoherence and tensions within each party's electoral coalition will create new possibilities for cross-party alliances.

Of course, things will not happen exactly as they did a century ago. And the changes that do occur will not happen overnight. But all of these factors, taken together, give us reasons for hope that the cycle of polarization will slowly turn once again.

4
Constitutional Crisis

So far I have talked about the cycle of regimes and the cycle of polarization. The third cycle of constitutional time is the cycle of rot and renewal. But in order to explain this cycle, I need to introduce another key idea. This is the idea of constitutional crisis.[1]

One of the most common claims by journalists and commentators during the Trump administration has been that the United States is in the middle of a constitutional crisis, or that if a certain thing happened—for example, if Trump had fired Special Prosecutor Robert Mueller to undermine the latter's investigations—the country would be hurled into a constitutional crisis. People said this after the first travel ban was announced;[2] they said it again when President Trump fired FBI Director James Comey;[3] they have announced the imminent arrival of a constitutional crisis on any number of occasions since then.[4]

But at least as of this writing—the beginning of 2020—the United States is not in a constitutional crisis. Let me explain what a constitutional crisis is, and why we are not (currently) in the middle of one.

Constitutions do many things—they protect rights, and they distribute powers and duties. But above all, a constitution is a device for making politics possible—politics, that is, as opposed to violence, insurrection, and civil war. The central point of a constitution is to channel people's disagreements and struggles for power into a system of law and political procedures so that these disagreements and struggles for power do not break down or break out into violence, civil war, or insurrection.[5] We can therefore say that a constitution is achieving its central function when it can cabin the desire for power—and the desire for dominance, which is always present in human affairs—into political struggles within the constitutional system.

A constitution fails when it is unable to perform that central task. And this can happen in one of three ways.

First, at some point, political officials, most importantly the president, can simply announce that they will no longer abide by the rules of the Constitution.[6] Political leaders—or military leaders—might argue that things have gotten so bad and the country has strayed so far off course that they can no longer possibly stay within the boundaries of the Constitution. We have

The Cycles of Constitutional Time. Jack M. Balkin, Oxford University Press (2020). © Jack Balkin 2020.
DOI: 10.1093/oso/9780197530993.001.0001

to save the country, they will exclaim; we must deal with internal or external enemies and threats, and therefore we must—perhaps temporarily—stop following the Constitution. A constitutional crisis of the first type might also occur if political leaders refuse to obey a judicial order directed to them. That would undermine a central feature of constitutional government. For officials to say that they won't abide by the Constitution or direct judicial orders precipitates a constitutional crisis, because officials refuse to abide by the very device that keeps struggles for power and authority inside politics and within the basic law of the Constitution.

The second kind of crisis occurs when everybody thinks that they are following the Constitution, and the result is disaster.[7] For example, the Constitution might demand that leaders do something—or not do something—in a way that leads directly to disaster. Or people may believe that the Constitution does not provide for a certain event so that everyone is paralyzed and disaster strikes. In this second type of crisis, everyone goes off the cliff together, like a bunch of lemmings. If the first type of crisis is a crisis of constitutional disobedience, we might think of the second type as a crisis of excessive constitutional fidelity—or, more correctly, a crisis of fidelity produced by a total lack of constitutional imagination and innovation. This last point explains why this second sort of crisis almost never happens. When people find themselves in a predicament—for example, they don't know what the Constitution requires—they will usually be able to reinterpret the Constitution to get out of the predicament.[8] That doesn't mean that everyone will agree on the interpretive solution. But it does mean that the difficulty turns into a dispute about constitutional interpretation that can be resolved within the constitutional system.

The third type of crisis is closest to what people usually think of when they talk about a constitutional crisis. This crisis occurs when people disagree about what the Constitution means, and they disagree so strongly that they do not simply confine themselves to legislative votes and litigation, or to op-eds, tweets, press conferences, and protests.[9] Instead, they take to the streets and riot. They engage in violence. They engage in secession. Or they engage in civil war.[10] Now *that's* a constitutional crisis. The Constitution has failed to keep political struggle within its proper boundaries—that is to say, within the boundaries of political competition set by the Constitution.[11]

Constitutional crisis, in other words, means reaching a point in which the Constitution is about to fail, or has already failed, at its central task—of making politics possible. The US Constitution has been remarkably durable. There have been countless times during our history in which political officials have disobeyed the law—just think about the many times each year that local governments, states, and the federal government get sued—but these legal violations are not by themselves constitutional crises. There have been a small number of genuine crises in which the Constitution was on the verge of failure. But the Constitution has only broken down as a system of politics once in our history. That failure occurred during the Civil War. The Constitution failed because Americans were unable to keep the disputes that led to the Civil War within politics, and instead, the situation degenerated into violence and rebellion.

Political crises abound in American history—the Watergate scandal and the Clinton impeachment are good examples—but they usually are resolved within the constitutional order. And, as noted previously, government officials often violate the law—that's why we have a system of courts. Real constitutional crises, on the other hand, are very rare. Even political crises that veer on the edge of a genuine constitutional crisis are rare.[12]

Generally speaking, we almost never face the first kind of crisis—in which the president or other leaders announce that they will not abide by the Constitution or obey direct judicial orders. One reason for that is that lawyers are usually able to come up with creative interpretations so that politicians can assert that they are being faithful to the Constitution; at that point the dispute becomes a conflict over interpretation that is settled either in the courts or through the give and take of ordinary politics.[13]

The second kind of crisis is also very rare, and for much the same reason. Americans are very clever at interpreting the Constitution, so if lawyers and politicians come across a problem that they initially think can't be solved, or for which the Constitution appears to provide no solution, they will simply work at reinterpreting the Constitution until they think they have solved the problem.

The third kind of crisis is also very rare. The Civil War is the central example. People often disagree heatedly about what the Constitution means. But they usually turn to the courts to settle the question, or else the issue is resolved through politics. The point of a constitution is not to prevent disagreement and dispute; it is to channel disagreement and dispute into peaceful solutions within law and politics. That does not mean that disputes are always resolved correctly or justly. It merely means that disputes are settled within the constitutional system. Avoiding constitutional crisis is not the same thing as securing justice. One can have a great deal of injustice in a constitutional system without precipitating a constitutional crisis. In fact, one might note ruefully that injustice has often been the price of political stability in the United States. The US Constitution has been read to allow a great deal of injustice during its 230 or so years of existence. But it has faced few constitutional breakdowns.

Armed with this analysis of constitutional crisis, we can see that none of the things that people have complained about during the Trump Administration are genuine constitutional crises. When President Trump issued the first version of the travel ban and there was chaos at American airports, people said it was a constitutional crisis.[14] It wasn't. Rather, what happened is that the administration litigated the constitutionality of the travel ban (and its successors) in the federal courts.[15] That is how we are supposed to resolve constitutional disputes. Again, some people worried that firing FBI Director James Comey constituted a constitutional crisis, and other people worried that if President Trump dismissed Special Prosecutor Robert Mueller, that would be a constitutional crisis.[16] Neither of these things is the case. The president has the legal power to fire the FBI director,[17] and he also has the power to order officials in the Justice Department to dismiss the special prosecutor with cause.[18] To be sure, firing Mueller would have precipitated a *political* crisis—just as President Nixon's firing of Archibald Cox precipitated a political crisis that ultimately led to Nixon's resignation a year later. But a political crisis resolved through the courts and through constitutional processes of impeachment and removal is not a constitutional crisis.[19]

After the Democrats won the House in 2019, they began a series of Congressional investigations requesting documents and testimony from current and former executive branch officials. Trump's general strategy was to obstruct and delay, and, when pressed, to claim executive privilege. He sought to use every possible tactic to frustrate House Democrats who wanted to investigate him and engage in oversight. He has refused to release his tax returns to a House committee even though release is required by statute, arguing that the House has no legitimate interest in his tax returns. He has even tried to get the courts to prevent private third parties from handing over documents about his business practices to Congress. Some of Trump's legal positions—no matter how obnoxious they may seem—were taken by previous administrations of both parties. A few, however, are unprecedented.

Trump's stonewalling on document production, his claims of executive privilege, and his use of the courts are no doubt frustrating to his political adversaries. To the extent that his actions undermine norms of cooperation necessary for representative government to function properly, they probably also constitute examples of constitutional rot, as I discuss in the next chapter.

But these tactics do not, by themselves, create a constitutional crisis. Generally speaking, when Congress and the president disagree about documents and testimony for Congressional investigations, they work things out through negotiations. If negotiations break down, Congress can go to the courts to enforce its orders. This usually takes a very long time and allows the president to run out the clock, which is why these disputes are usually settled through negotiation instead. If all else fails, Congress can also threaten the president with impeachment to enforce its subpoenas.

If the president and Congress litigate these questions, or if Congress impeaches the president, there is no constitutional crisis. Impeachment (and removal from office) are part of the Constitution's processes of enforcement. If the Supreme Court issues a direct order to the president to hand over documents or provide testimony, and he refuses to obey, that would be a constitutional crisis.

This is what people feared would happen in the Watergate scandal: they feared that President Nixon would refuse to obey a subpoena ordering him to surrender the Watergate tapes.[20] But Nixon complied with the Supreme Court's order, and so there was no constitutional crisis. On the other hand, if Nixon had said, "I'm not going to give up the tapes, and I'm going to burn them on the White House lawn," that would have been a constitutional crisis.[21]

Here I will add an important qualification. Constitutional crisis doesn't have to refer only to the actual moment of constitutional failure. It might also refer to a period in which the possibility of constitutional failure is real and palpable.[22] The best analogy would be to a medical crisis, in which a patient's condition hovers between life and death. One might therefore argue that if there is a serious probability that the president will announce that he will discard constitutional limits or will refuse to obey a direct judicial order—that period of uncertainty is a constitutional crisis, even if the president ultimately backs away. Thus, if one believed that Nixon was planning to spurn the Supreme Court's order to surrender the Watergate tapes in 1974, one would be justified in saying that the country was on the brink of a constitutional crisis.

Therefore, if people reasonably believe that President Trump is about to jettison the Constitution or defy the courts, it is fair to say that we are in a period of constitutional crisis. (Imagine, for example, that the president loses the 2020 election, or had been impeached and removed from office, but refuses to leave and calls on the military to support him.) But such defiance has not yet occurred. The Trump administration has repeatedly fought out its disputes about the Constitution in the courts of law and the court of public opinion. In July 2019, after the administration lost its battle to include a citizenship question on the 2020 census, some observers speculated that Trump might defy the Supreme Court.[23] But nothing like this happened. Instead, the president engaged in rhetorical bluster, falsely claimed victory, and moved on to other controversies.

This means that we are not in a constitutional crisis at present in the United States, although we can expect many moments of political crisis in the next several years. I do not say that we will never be in a moment of constitutional crisis—merely that this is not our present situation. The pandemic that began in 2020 will test our electoral system, and it may lead to bitter contests over the outcome, as in 2000. But as long as people turn to the court system and the political system to resolve these disputes, as they did in 2000, there may be a profound political crisis, but no constitutional crisis.

Throughout Trump's presidency, many people have feared that we are on the brink of a constitutional crisis. They worry that any day now, the president is going to tweet: "That was a nice Constitution you had there, but it's over. Sad!" But no matter how outrageous some of Trump's public statements have been, he has not crossed that particular rubicon. Let us hope he never does.

Even so, people sense that there is something deeply wrong with American politics, and that is why they are using the language of constitutional crisis—incorrectly, in my view—to describe it. There is, however, a better, more accurate way to describe our current political situation. I turn to that question now. It lies at the heart of the third of the political cycles we are living through.

5
The Cycle of Constitutional Rot and Renewal

We are not living in a period of constitutional crisis. But we are—and have been for some time—living in a period of constitutional rot.[1] What is constitutional rot? It is the decay of those features of a constitutional system that maintain it both as a democracy and as a republic.[2] That basic idea has a number of entailments, which I will now try to elaborate.

The word "republic" comes from the Latin *res publica*, a public thing.[3] A republic is more than a representative form of government. It is a joint enterprise by citizens and their representatives to pursue and promote the public good.[4] As I will describe in a moment, republics are delicate institutions, often subject to decay, and both the public and the governing elites are often distracted from their public-spirited purpose. When a republic decays, it loses its connection to the joint pursuit of the public good. Government officials lose their connection to the public good. Then the country becomes an oligarchy or an autocracy.[5]

It is common to think of our current political problems in terms of gridlock. Government can't seem to respond to public problems, or, indeed, get anything of importance done. Congress can barely keep the government funded and running.[6] The diagnosis of gridlock made more sense when there was divided government. But during the first two years of the Trump presidency, the United States had unitary government with Republicans in charge. And yet we still had plenty of dysfunction. So although it is undoubtedly true that increasing polarization is part of the problem, something else much deeper is going on. That something else is constitutional rot.

In the past forty years or so, the United States has increasingly become both less democratic and less republican.[7] By less democratic, I mean that it is increasingly unresponsive to popular opinion and popular will. By less republican, I mean that representatives are increasingly less devoted to the public good, rather than to pleasing or paying off a relatively small set of powerful individuals and groups or using government to benefit themselves.[8]

The Cycles of Constitutional Time. Jack M. Balkin, Oxford University Press (2020).
DOI: 10.1093/oso/9780197530993.001.0001

Constitutional rot is the process through which a constitutional system becomes less democratic and less republican over time. When we talk of constitutional rot, therefore, we are interested both in failures of democracy—that is, responsiveness to public opinion and public will—and failures of republicanism—that is, public officials' devotion to the public good. When public servants are increasingly diverted into the pursuit of their own wealth, or when they are increasingly diverted into serving the interests of a relatively small number of very powerful individuals, democracy and republicanism decay, and we have constitutional rot. And when public officials are no longer responsive either to public will or to the public good, and instead serve the interests of a small group of powerful and wealthy people, the result is oligarchy—rule by the few.

Constitutional rot is a relative term, like being tall or short. It denotes a period of backsliding in democratic and republican norms and institutions, after a period of increasing democratization, or, at least, relative stability. This caveat is important because the United States has never been fully democratic or republican. In this book, I will point to three central episodes of constitutional rot: the 1850s, dominated by the Slave Power; the Gilded Age; and our own Second Gilded Age. But in each case, the periods of increasing democratization that preceded them were hardly perfect, and by modern standards, the country remained undemocratic in important respects. For example, the United States progressed toward universal white male suffrage in the antebellum era, but women were left behind, Native Americans were slaughtered or dispossessed, and blacks were held in slavery. Reconstruction's "new birth of freedom" still denied women basic civil rights and the right to vote, to say nothing of the treatment of Native Americans and Chinese laborers. And the twentieth century's long period of increasing democratization improved but hardly perfected American democracy. When I say that constitutional rot is the gradual loss of democracy and republicanism, therefore, I am speaking of a relative decline from an already imperfect system.

Constitutional rot has a second dimension: the gradual destruction of political norms of mutual forbearance and fair political competition that make it possible for people who disagree with each other to jointly pursue the public good.[9] Republics depend on more than mere obedience to the letter of the law. They depend on well-functioning institutions that balance and check power and ambition, and conventions that require government officials to behave in a public-spirited fashion.[10] Republics also depend on mutual toleration and forbearance that makes it possible for contending sides to view each other not as implacable enemies that must be eliminated but as fellow citizens who, despite their differences, all aim at the larger goal of serving the *res publica*.[11]

Some of these norms concern rule of law values. For example, political leaders must not misuse the executive power to punish their political enemies or attempt to imprison them. Others concern electoral integrity: politicians must respect the results of fair elections, and they must not try to rig the electoral system to entrench themselves in power. These and similar norms prevent ambitious politicians from overreaching, entrenching themselves and their ideological allies, and undermining public trust in democracy. When politicians abide by these norms, they help promote cooperation between different political parties and factions, even when opponents strongly disagree about the proper direction of politics. Finally, these norms prevent politicians from privileging short-term political gains over long-term injuries to the health of the constitutional system.

A third dimension of constitutional rot involves the gradual loss of the kinds of trust that are necessary for republics to function properly: trust between members of the public, trust between the public and government officials, and trust among government officials of different parties.[12] For republics to succeed, the public must not view their fellow citizens as incorrigible and implacable enemies. They must trust that government officials will usually exercise power in the public interest and not merely for their own personal benefit or for the benefit of private interests and cronies. Public officials need to trust that their political opponents will usually respect fair rules of political competition and will not overreach or manipulate the mechanisms of government to unfairly entrench themselves in power and seek to punish their political enemies.

Norms of mutual forbearance and fair competition ultimately depend on trust. When trust decays, these norms are weakened, producing a vicious cycle. If the public loses trust in public officials, they will become cynical and despairing, and they will turn to demagogues.[13] If public officials cannot trust each other to behave responsibly and fairly, they will refuse to cooperate. As their mutual suspicion grows, they will discard norms of fair competition; they will try to grab as much power as possible and punish their adversaries before their adversaries can lock them out of power and punish them instead.

When politicians become beholden to a small set of powerful interests and persons, discard norms of fair political competition, undermine public trust, and repeatedly overreach by using constitutional hardball to rig the system in their favor and keep themselves (or their allies) in power, they cause democracy and republicanism to decay.[14] All of these phenomena produce constitutional rot.

A. Republican Insurance

The Framers of the US Constitution understood that republics are especially susceptible to rot. Many people remember what Benjamin Franklin is supposed to have said when a woman asked him to describe the new Constitution—"A republic, Madam, if you can keep it."[15] But behind that famous quote is an important story. It sounds as if Franklin is joking when he says, "if you can keep it." But he wasn't joking. Near the very end of the Philadelphia convention, just as the Framers were about to ship the new Constitution off to the states for ratification, Franklin made an important speech, which appears in Madison's notes. Franklin told the delegates that the new American government "is likely to be well administered for a course of years, and can only end in Despotism, as other forms have done before it, when the people shall become so corrupted as to need despotic Government, being incapable of any other."[16]

When Franklin spoke, everyone in the room understood what he was saying. Many of the Framers had read the classics of ancient history, and they understood that republics are very difficult to keep going.[17] All republics are susceptible to constitutional rot. All republics eventually become corrupted. And up to that point in history, all republics had eventually fallen, turning into despotisms, tyrannies, or rule by the mob. The Framers had read Aristotle and Polybius, and they knew that ancient writers believed that this is how things usually ended up.[18]

Why are republics so difficult to maintain? Because of ambition, because of greed, because of the ever-present lust for power among human beings. The fragility of republics is a consequence of the fragility of human goodness. The people in republics may start out devoted to the public good, but over time they stray, for many reasons—including, ambition, wealth, power, and the urge to dominate others.[19]

The Framers knew that this had happened over and over again in human history. They believed it would eventually happen to the United States. And so they drafted their new constitution with various devices to try to limit the cycle of republican rot, to have things bottom out before the country turned to mob rule, oligarchy, or dictatorship.[20] Their goal, in other words, was to buy time for democracy so that the inevitable periods of constitutional rot would be followed by periods of constitutional renewal.

This way of understanding our constitutional system differs from our usual concern with constitutional doctrine, with principles of limited government, or even with the preservation of liberty. Focusing on constitutional rot is a structural consideration—but a consideration connected to the belief that history operates in cycles of rot and renewal. Many of the Constitution's structural features—federalism, separation of powers, checks and balances, an independent judiciary, staggered elections for the two Houses of Congress and the president, fixed terms for the executive—may be understood not only in terms of limits on government power, but also in terms of the dangers of constitutional rot. These structural features operate to dampen and limit the downside of inevitable decay in our republican institutions—to keep democracy afloat and republicanism running until the political system has a chance to renew and right itself. The goal is to ensure that although things may get bad at various points in time, the republic never completely falls apart, so that it can bottom out and renew itself eventually. Separation of powers, federalism, an independent judiciary, and staggered election cycles help guarantee that there is always a locus of opposition, a political space in which oppositional groups can safely form, in which pressures for reform can gain strength and are not completely snuffed out or shut out of power. So too, an independent judiciary helps ensure that federal judges aren't simply under the thumb of a charismatic leader.

If one looks at the Constitution this way, it is not merely a blueprint for liberty, it is also an insurance policy for republics.[21] Republics are at the mercy of time. They will get better and worse. They will get more public-spirited and less public-spirited. They will decay and they will renew themselves. Sometimes the people we elect will be very good people, sometimes they will be venal and incompetent. Sometimes they will be thoroughly corrupt. The country will cycle through decades of ebb and flow, renewal and decline. But the central point of a constitution like the United States' is to create a system that, even if ungainly in the best of times, can buffer itself against the worst of times.

There is a price to pay for these fail-safes, these forms of republican insurance. The most important price is that our constitutional system has many veto points that prevent it from being fully democratic. It is not very efficient in responding to popular will even in the best of times. That may lead to public frustration. But the ability of opponents to resist and derail change is the political price—the premium, if you will—that Americans pay for republican insurance. If you believe, as the Framers did, that rot and decay in republics are inevitable, that premium is probably well worth paying. Nothing is more certain than that American politics will go through periods of rot and decay, and that Americans will go through a cycle of corruption, cynicism, and despair. It has happened before. It is happening now.

Many factors have contributed to our present case of constitutional rot. They include the gradual breakdown in the party system; changes in how campaigns are financed; and the enormous power of dark money in deciding who gets elected, and in influencing what people do once they obtain office.[22]

Another important set of causes concern long-term changes in the structure of mass media, which have encouraged polarization and political distrust, and hastened the merger of politics with entertainment.[23] After all, we now have a reality TV star as president.

These changes in the structure of media have made the public more susceptible to propaganda, a term I use advisedly. Propaganda was an important tool for maintaining political power in the former Soviet Union. The United States is now flush with propaganda of the sort that would have done the Soviets proud. Some of this propaganda comes from outside the country,[24] but a lot of the propaganda comes from inside the country.[25] And whatever its source, it is having serious effects on American democracy.

Propaganda is more than false information. It is designed to confuse and divide people.[26] It sets people at each other's throats and makes it difficult for people to know what is true and what is false. As a result, people simply come to believe that no one and nothing can be trusted. This causes them to rely on their existing prejudices and to root ever more strongly for their political team. Propaganda discourages rational thought about policy and encourages emotional identification with one's tribe.[27] Thus, by blurring the line between the true and the false, and by making it difficult to know what is true and false, effective propaganda encourages polarization and exacerbates mutual distrust within society. It corrodes the public trust that is necessary to republican government, and it undermines the formation of public opinion that is necessary to democratic government.[28]

B. The Four Horsemen of Constitutional Rot

There are four basic causes of constitutional rot—I call them the Four Horsemen of Constitutional Rot.[29] The first is political polarization. A second is increasing economic inequality. A third cause is loss of trust. This includes loss of trust by citizens in their government; loss of trust between politicians of different parties who must cooperate to govern effectively; and loss of trust between fellow citizens who feel increasingly alienated from each other. Propaganda and strategies of political polarization can exacerbate this loss of trust. A fourth cause is "policy disasters"—a term coined by Stephen Griffin; it refers to major failures in policymaking by our representatives.[30] Recent examples of policy disasters in American history include the Vietnam War, the Iraq War, and the 2008 global financial crisis.[31]

These Four Horsemen of Constitutional Rot—polarization, economic inequality, loss of trust, and policy disaster—mutually reinforce each other.[32] Rising economic inequality exacerbates polarization, which encourages tribalism and diverts energies to symbolic conflicts.[33] This makes it easier for politicians supported by wealthy donors to sneak through policies that exacerbate economic inequality. Increasing inequality and polarization, in turn, generate loss of trust. People no longer trust government because they feel it does not protect their interests, and because of increasing polarization they lose trust in their fellow citizens, who they believe are stupid, biased, or out to destroy the country. Distrust of government and increasing tribalism make it easier for wealthy donors to manipulate politics and influence government officials behind the scenes, enhancing tendencies toward oligarchy. Polarization and oligarchy create a government that is unaccountable to more and more citizens, which creates even greater distrust and mutual recrimination. Polarization and unaccountable government also breed overconfidence; they insulate decision-makers from necessary criticism, which makes policy disasters more likely; policy disasters, in turn, further undermine trust in government, and so on.

One of the most important policy disasters in recent times has been America's inadequate response to the economic trends that produced the 2008 financial crisis. The 2008 financial crisis and its aftermath is a special case of the failure of our country's leaders to come to grips with the problem of globalization and how it affects republican government. In the face of globalization, American elites—including its wealthiest and best educated citizens—have taken pretty good care of themselves. But they have not taken good care of the country as a whole.[34]

C. The Political Economy of Republican Government

How does increasing globalization affect the stability of republics? Behind a successful republic is a republican political economy. How the economy operates—and how it distributes its benefits and opportunities—greatly affects how representative government operates. If the structure of the economy changes in certain ways, or changes too quickly, it can undermine the incentives of public officials to pursue the public good and lead to oligarchy or even autocracy. Put another way, although Americans often associate capitalism with democracy—and free markets with free institutions generally—not every version of capitalism can sustain a democratic system of government.

In particular, stable and effective democracies require a broad-based, stable, and economically secure middle class to create the right incentives for government officials to pursue the public good and represent the interests of the broad base of the citizenry.[35] That is because in republics, the people with the most economic power and the greatest wealth will usually attempt to leverage their superior economic power into political power that will allow them to keep their wealth and become even wealthier.[36] Therefore, the middle class is a necessary check on the ambitions of the wealthy. A big, stable middle class can check the wealthy more easily; a small and precarious middle class will find it harder to resist wealth's political power. This balance of power is by no means perfect, but it prevents a slide toward oligarchy and preserves republican government.[37]

If economic inequality in a democracy gets too pronounced, the wealthiest will tend, over time, to grab disproportionate political power. They will use that power to further entrench and enrich themselves, reshaping the content, interpretation and enforcement of the laws for this purpose. The wealthy can use their economic power to lobby for laws that benefit them and to promote political candidates who will be beholden to them and further their interests. They can leverage their influence over elected politicians to secure the appointment of executive officials who will enforce the laws and issue administrative regulations that favor their interests. They can use their wealth to push for the appointment of judges who will interpret the laws and the Constitution in a similar direction. They can also afford the very best legal counsel to represent their interests before courts and administrative agencies. Finally, they can use their wealth to influence think tanks, research institutions, and public opinion. They can leverage their economic power to influence media to push ideas and stories that promote their interests, insulate their business practices from scrutiny, and confuse, divide, and distract the public.

The result is a self-perpetuating cycle: the wealthier you are, the more political influence you have and the more political power you can exercise, the more you can enrich yourself, and the easier it is to use your increased political power and influence to build on previous gains. That is why middle-class entitlements like Social Security and Medicare, organizations like labor unions (which, in this country, have seriously declined), and progressive systems of taxation are important to maintain the republican political economy of modern democracies. They support the stability of the middle class and help it check the political power of capital.

We can trace these ideas about republican politics back to the founding, although the Framers lived in a very different economic world—one dominated by agriculture. Therefore, the mechanisms they would have seen as supporting what we now call the middle class would have been very different from those in a postindustrial economy like our own. At different points in American history, people have made the same basic argument about the effects of concentrated wealth on republican government, although the economic conditions have been very different.[38] In the early years of the republic, for example, Jeffersonian Republicans supported the idea of an agrarian republic premised on a broad base of self-supporting small farmers.[39] They pressed for the exclusion of primogeniture and slavery in the Northwest Territory.[40] Both slavery and the concentration of land ownership in first-born sons would concentrate wealth in a small number of people and give them economic leverage to gain ever more economic power. This would prevent ordinary Americans from supporting themselves in newly opening western lands. For similar reasons, Jeffersonians were deeply suspicious of Federalist support for the financial classes, which they believed would concentrate wealth, undermine the republic, and produce tendencies toward oligarchy and even monarchy.[41]

Half a century later, the anti-slavery Republican Party—named after Jefferson's early Republican Party—developed in opposition to an oligarchical system that Republicans called the "Slave Power."[42] These Republicans saw that a small group of plantation owners controlled vast amounts of property in land and slaves. Slave owners controlled both state governments and the national government; they had successfully leveraged their political power into ever greater economic power and had packed the Supreme Court with their supporters—the most prominent being Chief Justice Roger Taney.[43] Republicans feared that the Slave Power would succeed in spreading slavery—and slaveholders' economic dominance—throughout the rest of the country.[44]

We face the same issues of republican political economy today in the very different context of the globalized economy of the late twentieth and early twenty-first centuries. A globalized economy threatens republican political economy in three ways. First, it creates opportunities for rapid increases in income going to the very wealthiest individuals, enhancing their comparative political power. Second, it puts pressure on social insurance programs and on the economic stability and self-sufficiency of Americans, weakening their relative political power. Third, it empowers the wealthy to push for ever greater upward redistribution through tax reform, entitlement reform, and deregulation.

In the past several decades, American politicians have adopted policies that shifted income from the poor and middle class to the wealthiest

Americans, while simultaneously shifting the risks of capitalism from the wealthy onto the poor and the middle class.[45] One obvious example is the significant reduction of tax rates from where they stood at the end of the New Deal/Civil Rights regime.[46] A less well understood but equally important example is the shift from defined benefit retirement programs, such as employee pensions, to defined contribution programs, such as IRAs and 401(k)s.[47] The former place the risk of economic downturns and bad investment decisions on employers. The latter place the risk on workers saving for their retirement. On top of this are a vast number of changes in taxation and regulation largely invisible to the general public, but whose cumulative effect is an upward redistribution of wealth and power and a downward distribution of risk and danger.

The long-term result of these changes in political economy has been increasing tendencies toward oligarchy. That is true even though our political system remains formally democratic and there is intense competition between the two major political parties—just as there was, by the way, during the First Gilded Age. Despite the fact that we continue to have regular elections, and the two political parties are deeply polarized, a relatively small number of backers (small that is, in proportion to the mass of the general population) decides who stays in power and what kinds of laws and regulations get enacted.[48] In such a system, most politicians, regardless of their ideological priors, have strong incentives to divert resources to the small group of backers who help keep them in power. The result is predictable: most of the benefits of economic growth have gone to the wealthiest Americans; fiscal and regulatory decisions have diverted a great deal of money that might have been used for public services and public goods to wealthy groups and individuals.[49] Perhaps the most salient recent example of this tendency is the 2017 tax bill, which is likely to achieve a very significant upward redistribution of income from the poor and middle class to the wealthiest Americans.[50]

D. Constitutional Rot Produces Demagogues

Increasing constitutional rot has another troubling effect. It tends to encourage the worst kind of politicians: charlatans, snake oil salesmen, and demagogues. Constitutional rot causes the public to understand that their government is corrupt, and that their leaders can't be trusted. And so they turn to other leaders who tell them that they have been badly used, and who offer to wash away the corruption.

Traditionally, demagogues are people who affect a common, rough-hewn, folksy, even ill-mannered style, whether or not they are actually from humble origins.[51] Demagogues identify themselves with the common person. They flatter the public,[52] telling them that they have been misunderstood; that snobbish elites look down on them and are laughing at them; and that the demagogue understands how they have been mocked, neglected, and disparaged.

But demagogues usually do more than this. They also usually employ highly emotionally charged rhetoric. This rhetoric divides the public into the noble, wise, and honest common people—the real members of the country—and a group of immoral and deviant others—elites, foreigners, or minorities—who are not of the people and are the real source of the country's problems.[53] Demagogues appeal to prejudice and minister to fear.[54] Demagogues, in short, look for scapegoats; they look for opportunities to divide, frighten, and anger the public, and thereby forge a powerful emotional connection with their followers. They use their divisive rhetoric—and their emotional connection to their rapt followers—to gain power, and to justify violating political norms and the law.[55] They build on the elements of constitutional decay that always exist to some degree in a republic and nurture them for their own ends. Demagogues, in other words, exacerbate constitutional rot to gain political power and stay in power.

Demagogues praise the morality and decency of common people, whom they sharply distinguish from those hated others who lack the same morality, decency, and genuine connection to the country and its traditions. They denounce the country's cultural decline. They promise to restore the people to their lost greatness. They promise, to borrow a phrase, to make the country great again.[56]

Demagogues promise to make everything right, to sweep away the corruption, to restore order and decency. Demagogues tell us that they have special abilities, special skills that other leaders lack. They have the political will to succeed where others have failed. They alone can fix it.

Very often people are not hoodwinked by demagogues. They see them coming from a long way off. They know that these leaders are unscrupulous, that they exaggerate, even that they lie. Many people know, in short, that these leaders are demagogues. But because of years of constitutional rot, the public has become so frustrated—with government, with their current leaders, and even with their fellow citizens—that they are willing to take a chance on a demagogue. They are willing to roll the dice, to blow everything up, on the chance that the demagogue can clean up the mess of politics, on the chance that things can get better.[57]

E. A Demagogue for Our Times

All of which brings me to our current situation. Donald Trump is a symptom of advanced constitutional rot, and not its originating cause. He has not created our present misfortunes. But, like many unscrupulous politicians, he has taken advantage of them, and in many ways he is making them worse.

I won't mince words. Donald Trump is a demagogue. I don't know if our 45th president has ever read anything about the history of demagogues, but I do know that he likes to hire people who look the part—people who, as they say, come straight out of central casting. And I can say with some confidence that Donald Trump perfectly fits the role of a demagogue—he looks and acts as if he came straight out of central casting.

Trump, to be sure, is not a man of the common people, but he acts like one and he has shown repeatedly that he can connect emotionally with ordinary people. Trump is by turns uncouth, ill-mannered, boorish, corrupt, cunning, and entertaining. He offered himself as a sort of "people's billionaire," a persona he honed in his years as a reality television star. He affects a pose of bluntness, plain-spokenness, and honesty, even when he is obviously lying. He blames globalists and elites for demeaning and harming ordinary people. He warns against conspiratorial forces arrayed against him and the public. He engages in race baiting, he stokes fear of immigrants, he raises the specter of crime and loss of social order, and he finds ever new ways to divide and anger the public.[58]

Like many demagogues, Trump also is the master of projection and chutzpah. He says that he will "drain the swamp"[59] and eliminate corruption when he is probably the most corrupt person who has run for the presidency in my lifetime. He says that he will stick up for ordinary people who have been humiliated and laughed at by elites when he is doing everything he can to benefit the wealthiest and line his own pockets.[60] He is utterly without shame, a moral and political hypocrite who systematically attributes his own failings to others.

It is almost as if he read a book on how to be a demagogue—"Demagogues for Dummies"—and systematically went through each chapter, checking off each characteristic move and performing them flawlessly. I cannot say whether he studied up on the role or whether he simply has amazing instincts and natural talents for demagoguery. In any case, as the United States descended into ever greater depths of constitutional rot, Trump appeared, as if on cue: descending down the escalator of his gold-plated skyscraper to take advantage of the people of this country, just as he had taken advantage of so many other people before in his checkered business career.[61] It is as if someone called up

Domino's Pizza and said, "I'd like to order a large demagogue to go, with extra cheesiness and bile."

Trump's opponents misunderstand the basis of his appeal. They comfort themselves with the belief that he will not be able to keep his con game going forever. His administration is a mess, his executive branch is woefully understaffed, his backstabbing underlings leak like sieves, the country is perpetually in an uproar, and he lurches daily from scandal to scandal.[62] Surely, his opponents tell themselves, a president who has been exposed over and over again as a fraud, a liar, a cheat, and a scoundrel can't keep power for long. Surely his presidency is going to fall apart at the seams any day now.

Yet this is how demagogues operate. Demagogues gain and keep power by creating and sustaining negative emotions of fear, anxiety, upset, and suspense. They thrive on emotional upheaval and a sense of unresolved crisis; they maintain power by keeping people worried and uncertain. If you are perpetually upset and anxious about American politics, if you distrust and even hate the other half of this country, the demagogue's strategy is working. Polarization binds his followers more closely to him and frustrates and paralyzes his opponents. Emotional upheaval is the friend of the demagogue. Crisis is his brand.

Moreover, Trump is no ordinary demagogue. He is a twenty-first century innovator, a Michelangelo of political chutzpah. This particular demagogue has mastered the arts of the tabloid press and the narrative techniques of reality television. He understands that in the early twenty-first century politics can be represented and rearranged as a series of episodes in a reality television series, in which he is both the producer and the star—an addicting series of segments in which the various participants are shocked, outraged, and wondering whatever will happen next. Reality television deals in anger, emotional excess, and a compelling narrative of heroes and villains, scandals and blowups, delicious secrets, and surprise revelations. Trump has created a new form of political demagoguery that corresponds to the rhythms of reality television, one that keeps the media transfixed, entertains his supporters, and exhausts his opponents.

Like demagogues of the past, Trump has developed powerful strategies to weaken and undermine the political culture that undergirds representative democracy. Through skillful manipulation of both television and social media, Trump has changed how people understand their fellow citizens and the world around them.

Democracy and republican government cannot succeed without a commitment to a common, shared truth. That remains the case even though much of politics is about values and symbols, even though people often disagree about the facts, and even though people's understandings are often fallible and flawed. Without a common commitment to truth, you cannot persuade others that your policy is the best one rather than merely special pleading that benefits you or your group. Precisely because people in a democracy have different perspectives, interests, and values, a shared belief that there are facts and that those facts do matter is necessary for democratic debate, and thus for democracy itself. Belief in a shared reality has deep connections to the very idea of a republic—that the goal of politics is to pursue the common good. If there is no commonly held truth, there can be no common good to aim at.

Trump's political strategy has deliberately undermined these democratic and republican commitments in order to ensure an almost religious devotion among his followers and to confuse and disconcert his political opponents. Continuous lying signals to Trump's followers that what is actually true and false does not matter so much. What matters is loyalty to your team and to your political leader. Even if what the leader says is not literally true, you believe that he is trustworthy and standing up for you. Conversely, because your political opponents are bent on the country's destruction and cannot be trusted, you don't have to take their claims seriously.

Trump's attacks on the media were not new. They continued—and accelerated—a decades-long campaign by conservative politicians that sowed distrust in sources outside of conservative media. Meanwhile, conservative media—such as talk radio and Fox News—repeatedly emphasized that mainstream media could not be trusted. This campaign proved remarkably effective. Although pursued for ratings and short-term political advantage, it nevertheless hastened constitutional rot in the United States.

Trump recognized that media attention was crucial to his rise to power and to his ability to control the agenda of public discussion. But above all he wanted attention without accountability. To achieve this, he has combined continuous lying—even about easily disprovable matters—with repeated attacks on the mainstream press, which he labeled the "enemy of the people."[63]

Trump's strategy of lying and media attacks allowed him to have the best of both worlds—maximum attention with minimal accountability. He undermined belief in the trusted institutions that produce and disseminate knowledge and are necessary to representative government. This causes everything to be disputable and disputed, and therefore leads people to trust only members of their own group. His followers, cocooned in conservative media, no longer believed critical coverage from nonconservative media. Indeed, the fact that mainstream media were so relentlessly critical of Trump was evidence that they were biased. At the same time, media companies felt compelled to cover Trump's outrageous statements, thus ensuring that he continued to drive the agenda of public discussion. Finally, the fact that Trump could brazenly lie and get away with it showed that he was a powerful person who could discomfit his political opponents.

Of course, these demagogic strategies hardly began with Trump. To a lesser extent they have always existed in republics. Politicians often prevaricate and shade the truth. They often try to persuade their followers to distrust their critics. What Trump did was to take these problematic features of democratic politics and move them from the margin to the center, making them central engines of his rise to political power.

The fact that lies can be so effective is one reason why republics are always susceptible to corruption. It is best to think of demagogic strategies like an endemic disease that can be held at bay but never fully extinguished. When, however, under a demagogue like Trump, these strategies successfully take over public discourse, they eat away at representative democracy.

F. The Acceleration of Constitutional Rot

Trump's media strategy was not the only way he exacerbated constitutional rot in the United States. A central principle of republican government is that public officials should work for the public good rather than for their own personal benefit. Trump shredded these republican norms. He used his powers as president to funnel money to himself and his family, and he used his control over America's foreign policy to undermine his most likely political opponent in the 2020 election. He removed diplomats and other government officials who complained about his misconduct. He obstructed and undermined the nation's law enforcement agencies and intelligence services. He repeatedly stonewalled congressional investigations into his misconduct, making claims of executive privilege and testimonial immunity far broader than previous administrations had ever dared.[64]

Near the end of 2019, the House of Representatives—now controlled by the Democrats—impeached Trump for abusing his office and for stonewalling Congress's investigations into his misbehavior. But Trump's impeachment did not arrest constitutional rot. To the contrary, it showed how debilitated and decayed the political system had become.

The precipitating cause for Trump's impeachment was the Ukraine scandal. Trump had withheld military aid and a much-desired White House meeting from Ukraine unless the Ukrainian government publicly announced two investigations that would benefit Trump's 2020 presidential re-election campaign. First, Trump wanted an investigation into Trump's most likely

Democratic opponent, former Vice President Joe Biden, and Biden's son, Hunter, for corruption. There was no evidence that either Biden had violated the law. It was not even clear that Trump cared about an actual investigation—as opposed to a public statement by the Ukrainian government. The point was to make look Biden look like a criminal to distract from Trump's own corruption. This was the playbook he had employed so successfully in the 2016 election against former Secretary of State Hillary Clinton.

Trump's second request from Ukraine was an investigation into a bogus theory that operatives from Ukraine (as opposed to Russia) interfered in the 2016 election—and on behalf of Trump's opponent, Hillary Clinton. American intelligence services and diplomats had repeatedly debunked this far-fetched theory as Russian disinformation. They warned that Trump and his Republican political allies were doing the Russians' bidding by continuing to spread these falsehoods.[65]

Trump's desire to establish a conspiracy theory about Ukraine was the flip side of his concerns about his own legitimacy. Both US intelligence services and Special Counsel Robert Mueller's investigation confirmed that Russia had interfered with the 2016 election in order to harm Hillary Clinton and help Trump. Although Mueller did not find sufficient evidence that Trump or his campaign had directly conspired with the Russians, he found that the Trump campaign had welcomed the Russian involvement.[66] He also found that Trump had repeatedly tried to derail Mueller's investigation into Russian interference and its possible connections to the 2016 Trump campaign.[67] Trump worried that if people believed that the Russians had worked to put him in office, this would cast doubts on his legitimacy, so he sought to cast blame on Ukraine for trying to help Hillary Clinton; and he insisted, against all evidence to the contrary, that Russia had not interfered in the 2016 election on his behalf.[68]

Trump hoped that in the 2020 election, as in 2016, a foreign government would once again smear his opponent and clear a path to victory. The difference was that the second time, Trump used his powers as president to coerce the foreign government into doing his bidding.

Trump had shown that he was perfectly willing to undermine America's system of fair democratic elections to stay in power and that he would continue to do so unless someone stopped him. He simply did not care whether he undermined democratic accountability and republican government. Moreover, he demanded that his party unquestioningly support him while he did it. In this way, he accelerated constitutional rot.

The factual case against Trump was overwhelming.[69] His supporters simply ignored the evidence and engaged in distractions. Because Republicans controlled fifty-three votes in the Senate, there was little chance that twenty would defect and vote to remove Trump. Senate Majority Leader Mitch McConnell promised a speedy acquittal in the Senate and only one Republican, Senator Mitt Romney, ultimately voted to convict.[70] Upon acquittal, Trump became the first impeached president to run for re-election, supported by a supine party that dared not abandon him.

The Ukraine scandal, however, was only the tip of the iceberg. In addition to his abuse of his control over American foreign policy, Trump treated his presidency as a continuous opportunity to make money for himself and his family.[71] Trump's promises that he would distance himself from his businesses were quickly discarded, as Trump spent a large percentage of his presidency at his hotels, golf courses, and resorts, charging the US government millions for the privilege of protecting him.[72] Despite obvious conflicts of interest, Trump's sons continued to pursue foreign business ventures.[73] Both foreign and domestic government officials patronized his hotels and resorts in order to curry favor, and Trump wasted no opportunities to call attention to his properties and lavish praise on them.[74] As the most prominent member of the US government, Trump signaled, in other words, that brazenly profiting from control of government was perfectly normal and acceptable. The US Constitution contains two anti-corruption measures, which prohibit federal officials from receiving "emoluments"—that is, things of value—from domestic and foreign governments.[75] Consistent with his general insouciance about corruption, Trump treated the Emoluments Clauses as if they were not in the Constitution, at one point even referring to them as "phony."[76]

Trump's skill at media manipulation, combined with the enthusiastic cooperation of Fox News and other conservative media—which essentially became propaganda arms of his presidency—made it difficult for members of his own party to criticize him. They dared not cross Trump's loyal base of supporters—the Republicans most likely to vote in primary elections. Republican politicians lived in fear that Trump would attack them on social media, because they would be quickly ostracized by the party and find themselves unable to win re-election.[77] Politicians who had once warned the country about Trump's demagoguery, dishonesty, and unfitness to serve now became shameless lickspittles and sycophants.

The vast majority of Republican politicians followed Trump meekly, while others, eager for power and influence, became vocal cheerleaders, propagandists, and rationalizers. When they controlled the House of Representatives, Republicans declined to investigate him; and once Democrats took over the House, they tried to undermine and discredit any investigations.

Matters came to a head during the impeachment proceedings. Trump repeatedly refused to apologize and insisted that he had a perfect right to ask Ukraine to investigate his political opponent. He would allow no criticism from the members of his party. It was not enough for them to acknowledge that what Trump did was wrong but insufficient justification to remove him from office—what Democrats had argued during the 1998–1999 Clinton impeachment. Instead, Republicans had to say that what Trump did was perfectly proper and that it was the Democrats who were shredding constitutional norms by daring to impeach him.[78] Republicans slavishly followed Trump's lead, some even repeating Russian propaganda that blamed Ukraine for interfering in the 2016 elections.[79]

Trump demanded, in short, that Republican politicians accept that a president using political office for personal gain was appropriate behavior, and that they should tolerate and support a president who did this openly and shamelessly simply because he was from their own party. As Republican politicians capitulated to Trump's demands, some docilely, others enthusiastically, they too, accelerated America's constitutional rot.

What made this sorry state of affairs possible, however, is that the ground had long been prepared for it. Even before the Ukraine scandal, key Republican figures like Newt Gingrich and conservative media like talk radio and Fox News had slowly damaged the political culture of American democracy, capitalizing on polarization and propaganda to keep Republicans in power.[80] Trump himself had risen to political prominence by falsely asserting a conspiracy theory that President Obama was an illegitimate president because he was not born in the United States. During the 2016 campaign and afterward, Trump insisted that voter fraud was rampant in the United States and that Democrats had planned to rig the election against him.[81] Republican politicians who knew better accommodated Trump's conspiracy-mongering to please their base of voters.

In fact, Trump had built on a cynical media strategy that had helped keep Republicans dominant as the country's demographics changed. For many years the Republican base had been fed a news diet created by conservative talk-radio, cable, and digital media that stoked grievances, fabricated conspiracy theories, and encouraged deep distrust of the mainstream media, educational institutions, and the American political system.[82] Republican politicians who had long profited from this media system were eventually caught in its web. As Trump engaged in worse and worse behavior, they felt powerless to stand up to him. They could not defend democratic norms and speak out against Trump's corruption without risking their own political careers. And when Trump was finally caught red-handed using the powers of his office to smear his political rival, the members of his party fell meekly in line. If by this point many Republican politicians felt that they had no choice, it is because the ground for their incapacity had been prepared by years of short-term political strategies that hastened long-term constitutional rot.

G. The Bad News—and the Good News

That's the bad news. Here is the good news.

This is not the first time that the American political system has faced similar challenges. To be sure, it is the first time that all of the cycles I have described have lined up in this particular way. But it is not the first time that we have experienced the anxiety of an exhausted political regime and a gradual transition to a new one. It is not the first time we have experienced a cycle of polarization and depolarization. And, above all, it is not the first time that we have been through a cycle of constitutional rot and renewal—or faced the daunting challenges of rising economic inequality, rampant corruption, divisive propaganda, fake news, and political polarization.

Our current situation most resembles the Gilded Age, or what I would call the First Gilded Age, because I believe we are now in America's Second Gilded Age. As I describe it, you will see some of the parallels, and why I think it is a period with many similarities to our own.

The Gilded Age runs from around the middle of the 1870s to the beginning of the twentieth century.[83] It is a period of rapid technological progress and enormous economic growth.[84] It is a period in which a small number of people make huge fortunes, and hence it is also a period of increasing inequalities of wealth, which are leveraged into political power—and political corruption.[85] The new fortunes of the Gilded Age generate a great deal of corruption, so much so that government is effectively for sale, and people believe that senators and cabinet officials are effectively in the pay of the trusts—the large monopolistic enterprises of the late nineteenth century.[86]

The Gilded Age is also a period of great waves of immigration from around the world, changing people's ideas about what it means to be an American.[87] For the same reason, it is also a period of increasing nativism, racism, social unrest, violence, and rioting.[88] It is the period in which many of the achievements of racial equality in the First Reconstruction are eventually blunted and white supremacy is resurgent. The beginnings of Jim Crow and black disenfranchisement occur near the end of the Gilded Age, symbolized by the Supreme Court's blessing of Jim Crow in *Plessy v. Ferguson* in 1896,[89] and its refusal to do anything about black disenfranchisement in 1903 in *Giles v. Harris*.[90]

The Gilded Age is a period of severe political polarization between Democrats, the party of the South, Jim Crow, and white supremacy, and Republicans, who repeatedly wave the bloody shirt and label the Democrats the party of Rum, Romanism, and Rebellion. The Gilded Age is a period of resurgent populism—the People's Party forms during this period—and it is also a period of populist demagogues.

Journalism during the Gilded Age—which had long been highly partisan—began to focus more and more on scandal and exposure.[91] Plummeting revenues caused by technological change and cut-throat competition led newspapers to publish lurid and fabricated news accounts that often had little to do with the facts.[92] In fact, the term "yellow journalism" comes from the late Gilded Age. Hoping to grab reader attention and increase circulation, the competing Hearst and Pulitzer newspapers published sensationalist stories and political propaganda that encouraged the United States to go to war with Spain.[93]

If you had been living in the First Gilded Age, you might well have looked around you—at the increasing economic inequality, the corruption, the influence peddling, the effective control of government by the wealthy, the demagoguery, the racism, the social unrest, the fabricated news, and the violence—and wondered whether American democracy could or would survive.

And yet it did survive. The First Gilded Age gives way to the Progressive Era, a period of extensive reforms at local, state, and national levels, four constitutional amendments, and eventually to the New Deal.[94] By the turn of the twentieth century, there are progressive wings promoting government reform in both major political parties. American democracy bottoms out of its cycle of rot and begins a long process of democratic renewal and government reform. There are a series of mobilizations for good government, for public health, for workers' rights, for women's rights—and many far less savory mobilizations too. Political polarization eventually declines as well.

Of course, things will not happen in exactly the same way they did before. But my point is that constitutional rot, like polarization, does not have to get worse and worse. I not only believe that we can bottom out from a period of constitutional rot and experience a period of constitutional renewal, I know that it has happened before. Just as the First Gilded Age gave way to a Progressive Era, it is possible for this, our Second Gilded Age, to give way to a

Second Progressive Era, a period of reform and renewal addressing the urgent problems of our own time.

Our politics is the result of a series of overlapping cycles, which together have produced our political world. From this larger perspective, the emergence of a successful demagogue like Trump is a genuine problem for American democracy; yet it is merely a symptom of a much larger set of problems that festered long before he ran for president. Trump was only able to rise to power because the Reagan coalition is aging and falling apart, because his party's political strategies have contributed to increasing polarization and distrust among fellow citizens, and because the regime's commitments to policies that produce economic inequality have contributed to increasing constitutional rot. To be sure, President Trump has done his best to exacerbate both the polarization and the rot. But even if tomorrow President Trump resigned or was removed from office, and replaced by Vice President Mike Pence, the new president and the party he leads would face the same problems.

The Reagan regime is crumbling. It will eventually fall away, replaced by a new regime, probably in five to ten years. It is likely that the Democrats will be the dominant party in this new regime. According to this possible future, this regime will feature a new dominant coalition that will build on and further develop Barack Obama's 2008 and 2012 "coalition of the ascendant." Although insufficient in 2016—and perhaps even in 2020 if Trump wins re-election—that emerging coalition of voters will grow comparatively stronger, as parts of the older Reagan coalition age and die, as newer, younger voters emerge to replace them, and as educated professionals, women, and other whites defect to the Democratic Party. To be sure, it is also possible that a third party will emerge, like the Republicans did in the 1850s, to become the dominant party. But this is more difficult to achieve in the twenty-first century than it was in the nineteenth, and the Democrats, unlike the Whigs in the 1850s, do not seem ripe for dissolution. Still another possibility is that the Republican Party will break into separate parties. But it will take time for a breakaway party to achieve national dominance.

Whatever happens, the agendas of politics ten years in the future are likely to look very different from the politics that we are suffering through now. That is the message with which I will leave you: constitutional development doesn't move in straight lines. It goes in cycles. And there are multiple cycles at work. There is a cycle of constitutional rot and renewal. There is a cycle of polarization and depolarization. And there is the cycle of the rise and fall of political regimes.

When all of these cycles line up in a particularly unhappy way, the country moves into political darkness, an eclipse of democracy. But just like the eclipse on August 21, 2017, the darkness does not last forever. In fact, it lasts only a few minutes in the larger scheme of things. You may not see that now, but I promise you, this eclipse is purely temporary.

PART II
THE CYCLES OF JUDICIAL REVIEW

6
Judicial Review in the Cycles of Constitutional Time

In Part I of this book I described American constitutional history in terms of three cycles: a cycle of the rise and fall of political regimes, a cycle of polarization and depolarization, and a cycle of constitutional rot and constitutional renewal. We are near the end of a political regime, near the peak of a cycle of political polarization, and (hopefully) near the low point of a cycle of constitutional rot.

What role does the federal judiciary, and in particular, the US Supreme Court, play in this story? In Part II, I explain how these three cycles affect the work of the judiciary.

How does the cycle of the rise and fall of regimes affect the federal judiciary? For the most part, the rise and fall of regimes shapes partisan attitudes about the exercise of judicial review. How people feel about judicial activism and judicial restraint depends on where they are in political time, and which party tends to control the Supreme Court and the lower federal courts.

When a new regime begins, politicians from the newly dominant party may not control the federal courts and the Supreme Court and the courts may be hostile to their political program. They may also face decades of judicial doctrines that reflect the old regime's values and that block political reforms. As a result, the newly dominant party and its intellectual allies tend to be skeptical of the federal judiciary; they argue that courts should defer to the political branches and exercise judicial restraint. As the dominant party gains control of the courts, however, these skeptical views begin to change. The dominant party and its associated legal intellectuals start to recognize the advantages of judicial review in protecting and promoting the party's values and commitments.

The two parties' positions are mirror images of each other. As the regime proceeds, the dominant party relies more and more on judicial review to achieve its goals, while the opposition party, which eventually loses control of the courts, becomes increasingly skeptical of judicial review. Increasingly, the opposition party advocates judicial restraint—although neither party ever fully abandons the idea of using judicial review to advance its policies. As the

The Cycles of Constitutional Time. Jack M. Balkin, Oxford University Press (2020). © Jack Balkin 2020.
DOI: 10.1093/oso/9780197530993.001.0001

cycle moves from the beginning of a regime to its final days, the parties—and the legal intellectuals allied with them—gradually switch positions. The party of judicial restraint becomes the party of judicial engagement, and vice-versa. The effect, however, is generational; older people may stick with their hard-won lessons about the courts, while younger generations, who have very different experiences, take contrary positions.

How does the cycle of polarization and depolarization affect the judiciary? Increasing or decreasing polarization tends to affect the political supports for judicial review: that is, why politicians either put up with or actively support judicial review. Politicians support judicial review for somewhat different reasons when politics is relatively depolarized and there is relatively greater elite consensus than when politics is sharply polarized and elites are even more polarized than the rest of the country. When politics is depolarized, politicians find it convenient to let judges handle certain questions because it allows politicians to fight over other issues. Judicial review also tends to enforce the values of national political elites, especially against state and local governments. When the country is polarized, however, political elites disagree about everything, so judicial review cannot do the same work. Instead, judicial review allows polarized political elites to win victories they can no longer win in the political process. As legislative politics is mired in polarization, the judiciary becomes a more efficacious method of policymaking.

How does the cycle of rot and renewal affect the judiciary? Increasing constitutional rot also affects the political supports for judicial review: the reasons why politicians like or accept judicial review. As I explained in chapter 5, constitutional rot stems in part from increasing economic inequality and political polarization, which tend to exacerbate each other. They are two of the four horsemen of constitutional rot. In periods of advanced constitutional rot, judicial decisions become especially polarized. Judicial majorities tend to reach decisions that increase economic inequality, shrink the electorate, and help maintain political oligarchy. Members of the dominant party—who by this point in a regime tend to control the federal judiciary—want judges to help them stay in power, to support politicians' self-entrenching behavior, to defend and protect politicians from charges of corruption, and to enrich their financial supporters. In short, during periods of constitutional rot, the judiciary tends to be part of the problem rather than part of the solution. Politicians attempt to gain control of the judiciary in order to ratify policies that increase income inequality or help entrench the dominant party in power.

Ordinarily, the US Constitution relies on the judiciary to protect democracy and republicanism, and to prevent political corruption and self-entrenching behavior. But in periods of heightened or severe constitutional rot, judicial independence itself is compromised. That is not because the judges themselves are especially corrupt, although they can be. Rather, it is because of the strategy of partisan entrenchment. In periods of constitutional rot, the judiciary is not the solution to constitutional rot, and is more likely to be part of the problem. The judiciary cannot bring the country out of constitutional rot by itself; only sustained political mobilization and demands for reform can do this.

Each of the three cycles affects the judiciary in different ways, and their effects are cumulative. I begin with how judicial review interacts with the cycle of regimes and the cycle of polarization, and then explain how it interacts with constitutional rot. Although as I noted in Part I, we are on the cusp of a change in regimes, our greatest challenge today is the conjunction of high political polarization with pronounced constitutional rot. Unfortunately, the two phenomena feed off of each other: polarization leads to rot, rot encourages polarization.

In our constitutional system the judiciary is designed to be insulated from constitutional rot, and in ordinary times, an independent judiciary is an important safeguard against constitutional rot. But as polarization proceeds and constitutional rot becomes pronounced, it threatens even the federal judiciary. At some point, the federal judiciary stops being a protector of democracy and begins to participate in the forces that produce constitutional rot. That is because the federal judiciary is drawn from legal elites who are subject to the same forces of polarization as politicians. In a period of strong polarization, the federal judiciary is more likely to exacerbate rot than protect us from it.

I begin with three important ideas that ground our discussion. The first is judicial time; the second is the political supports for judicial review. The third is partisan entrenchment.

A. Judicial Time

Within each regime, dominant parties have tended to control the Supreme Court. Table 6.1 shows that the dominant party in a regime tends to have many more opportunities to appoint new Justices.

One must take these numbers with a grain of salt. Justices have remained on the Court for varying lengths of time; for example, several of the early Federalist Justices stayed on the Court only briefly. Even so, the numbers suggest that the dominant party has considerably more influence over the composition and direction of the Supreme Court than the opposition party does.

Table 6.1 Opportunities for Supreme Court Appointments

Name	Years	Appointments by Dominant Party	Appointments by Opposition Parties
Federalist	1789–1800	Federalists (14)	Jeffersonians (0)
Jeffersonian	1800–1828	Democratic-Republicans (7)	Federalists (0)
Jacksonian	1828–1860	Democrats (12)	National Republicans; Whigs; Republicans (2)
Republican	1860–1932	Republicans (36)	Democrats (7)
New Deal/ Civil Rights	1932–1980	Democrats (16)	Republicans (10)
Reagan (Second Republican)	1980–?	Republicans (9)	Democrats (4)

Source: Paul Brest, Sanford Levinson, Jack M. Balkin, Akhil Reed Amar, and Reva B. Siegel, Processes of Constitutional Decisionmaking 1734–53 (7th ed. 2018). I do not count the elevation of Justices Harlan F. Stone and William Rehnquist to Chief Justice.

Moreover, opposition presidents have tended not to appoint strongly ideological representatives of their parties' positions. This has made the dominant party's influence even greater than the numbers might otherwise suggest. During the New Deal/Civil Rights Era, for example, many of the Republicans' ten Supreme Court appointments—by Eisenhower, Nixon, and Ford—turned out to be quite moderate or even liberal. Earl Warren and William Brennan were key members of the Warren Court's liberal coalition; Harry Blackmun and John Paul Stevens were moderates who ended their careers as liberals. During the first Republican regime, several of Grover Cleveland's appointments (Melville Fuller, Edward White, and Rufus Peckham) were from the business-friendly wing of the party. One of Woodrow Wilson's appointments, James Clark McReynolds, turned out to be more conservative than several of his Republican colleagues.[1]

Because judges have lifetime tenure, the partisan composition of the federal judiciary and the Supreme Court is a lagging indicator of where we are in political time. Therefore we can speak of the gap between *political time* and *judicial time*. Judicial time is the change, over time, of the partisan composition of the federal judiciary, and how it harmonizes with or fails to harmonize with the dominant political party in a regime.[2] If judicial time lined up perfectly with political time, then the dominant party would always dominate the composition of the federal judiciary and it would always maintain majority support on the US Supreme Court. As politics got more or less polarized, we would also see a matching polarization or depolarization among federal judges. But judicial time rarely matches political time, because federal judges have life tenure.

So there can be a time lag or a mismatch between where we are in political time and the composition of the federal courts and the Supreme Court.

Here are two examples. When the New Deal/Civil Rights regime began in 1932, most of the federal judges and Supreme Court Justices had been appointed by Republicans, and many of them were hostile to Franklin Roosevelt's New Deal reforms. The time lag between the ascendance of a new dominant party and the party's control over the federal judiciary led to the famous constitutional struggle over the New Deal. It was only fully resolved after Supreme Court vacancies began to open up near the end of 1937. Within five years, Roosevelt was able to replace almost everyone on the Supreme Court and also stock the lower federal courts with judges who supported the New Deal.[3]

The opposite effect occurred in the transition between the New Deal/Civil Rights regime and the Reagan regime. The Burger Court, which began in 1969, had begun to move the Supreme Court to the right over a decade before the end of the New Deal/Civil Rights regime.[4] This happened because President Lyndon Baines Johnson made crucial errors in his appointments strategy. He attempted to nominate a political ally, Justice Abe Fortas, to succeed Earl Warren as Chief Justice. Fortas was soon embroiled in scandal and had to resign; this gave Richard Nixon two Supreme Court appointments to replace Fortas and Warren. Two years later, in 1971, John Marshall Harlan and Hugo Black retired, giving Nixon a third and fourth appointment. In 1975, Nixon's successor, Gerald Ford, obtained a fifth Republican appointment, following the retirement of William O. Douglas. The last Democratic president in the New Deal/Civil Rights regime, Jimmy Carter, did not get a chance to appoint anyone to the Supreme Court. The result was that Republican presidents got all of the Supreme Court appointments from 1969 to 1992, thus beginning the Court's shift to the right earlier than the change in political regimes.

Polarization in the judiciary and polarization in electoral politics also may not line up. A key feature of the Reagan regime has been asymmetric polarization; the Republican Party became increasingly very conservative, while Democrats became a bit more liberal.[5] Because judges are appointed for life, and there are very few Supreme Court appointments in this era, the process of polarization occurred much more slowly in the federal judiciary. Many of the earlier Republican appointees (e.g., Blackmun, Stevens, Souter) came from the moderate wing of the party. They appeared increasingly liberal as the party became more ideologically coherent and shifted increasingly to the right.[6] George H. W. Bush's 1990 appointment of David Souter—part of a moderate Northeastern wing of the party that was rapidly growing extinct—further delayed the Court's polarization.

Only when John Paul Stevens retired in 2010, replaced by Elena Kagan, was the Court fully polarized. The liberal appointees were all appointed by Democrats and the conservative appointees were all appointed by Republicans.[7] However, one of the Republican appointees, Anthony Kennedy, occasionally voted with the liberals. With Kennedy's retirement and replacement by Brett Kavanaugh in 2018, the Supreme Court is strongly polarized like the rest of the country.

B. The Political Supports for Judicial Review

The political supports for judicial review are the reasons why politicians support judicial review, even though it gives judges the power to strike down their laws and decisions.[8] These are medium- to long-term calculations by politicians that having judicial review will do more good for them and for their party than curtailing it or getting rid of it.

Politicians support judicial review and construct it in certain ways because judicial review performs important tasks and manages problems for politicians over the long run, even if they disagree with particular decisions.[9] That is why politicians do not regularly strip the courts of federal jurisdiction, why they often expand federal causes of action, and why they continually add new life-tenured federal judges to the system.[10] Put another way, politicians have historically constructed judicial power and the opportunities for judicial review in order to make it serve politicians' and political parties' medium- to long-term interests. The federal courts have grown increasingly powerful during the country's history, and especially following the Civil War. They have taken on more and more tasks, and been given more and more things to do. This did not happen despite politicians' wishes. It happened because of their political and strategic calculations.[11]

The reasons that politicians support judicial review are not the same as the reasons that judicial review is a desirable feature of constitutional design. Constitutional designers might want judicial review to keep politicians from overreaching, limit corruption, protect democracy, and defend human rights. Politicians, by contrast, want to be re-elected; they want to avoid deciding hard issues that might cause them to lose an election or split their party's coalition; they want courts to defend their values and interests; and they want to achieve policy victories without having to take the political heat for doing so or expending unnecessary political capital.

If the political supports for judicial review mesh well with the reasons why judicial review is a desirable feature of constitutional design, this is clearly an advantage for a constitutional democracy. But if the political supports are misaligned with the reasons why judicial review is a good thing, the practice of judicial review will tend to be driven by the political supports, and not by reasons of good design. Politicians will structure judicial review in ways that benefit them, and they will pick judges who serve their interests more than the interests of constitutional democracy. That is because politicians write the jurisdictional statutes and pick the judges, and they tend to pick the kinds of judges who will give them what they want from judicial review.[12] As I will explain in more detail in chapters 9 and 10, this potential gap between what politicians want and what serves constitutional democracy becomes especially troublesome in times of constitutional rot and high political polarization.

The political supports for judicial review, and what politicians want judges to do for them, can change over time as the party system evolves, and as we go through the cycles of political regimes, political polarization, and constitutional rot. The political supports of judicial review also change because of the long-term secular trend toward an ever more powerful judiciary. The Supreme Court in 1803 that decided *Marbury v. Madison*,[13] in the shadow of a Jeffersonian putsch of the lower federal judiciary, had different political supports than the Supreme Court in 2000 that was so powerful that it was asked to decide a presidential election in *Bush v. Gore*.[14] In 1803, the Court was weak. The newly ascendant party, the Jeffersonians, was not sure how much judicial review it needed, or whether it even wanted a truly independent judiciary. By 2000, when the Court decided *Bush v. Gore*, politicians had spent two hundred years building up the federal judiciary's power and learning how to make use of it. The early twenty-first century Court is strong and politicians of both parties find it useful to rely on it.

So why *do* politicians put up with or even prefer judicial review? Here are a few reasons:

(1) In a federal system with separation of powers, national politicians want the judiciary to settle disputes between federal and state governments and between the president and Congress. (Because presidents appoint federal judges, however, the judiciary often tends to support the executive branch in these disputes, which is an additional reason why presidents in particular support judicial review.)

(2) Judicial review can set basic ground rules of politics that limit the boundaries of political struggle so that politics doesn't spin out of control.

(3) Some difficult issues would split party coalitions if politicians had to decide them. Handing off these issues to judges gives politicians plausible deniability.[15] For example, some moderate and suburban voters are able to

vote Republican because the Supreme Court currently protects abortion rights. If *Roe v. Wade*[16] were overturned and Republican politicians had to take difficult votes on whether to outlaw abortion, this might undermine the Republican coalition in moderate and swing states. Perhaps paradoxically, the pro-life Republican Party can form a larger coalition with *Roe* than without it.

(4) Politicians want courts to legitimate their actions by declaring them constitutional and lawful.[17] And politicians want courts to defend laws and actions they like in later years when the opposition party takes power.[18]

(5) Conversely, politicians want courts to strike down or narrowly interpret laws passed by their political opponents.[19] Although reasons (4) and (5) appear to point in opposite directions, they are actually connected. Courts can't legitimate laws unless they can also strike down laws.[20] Moreover, preemptive presidents and oppositional parties may look to courts as the only source of potential assistance in a hostile political environment.[21]

(6) Politicians want courts to enforce their values nationally by striking down contrary state and local laws, and overturning state judiciaries that disagree with these values.[22]

(7) Finally, politicians want courts to further their party's policy positions through statutory and constitutional interpretation.[23] Especially in times of strong polarization or when the political process is gridlocked, courts can achieve policy victories that politicians can't.

Some readers might object to this account of the political supports of judicial review on the grounds that judges are supposed to apply law, not do the work of politicians. As Chief Justice Roberts tells us, judges are supposed to be umpires who do not intervene in the game but just call balls and strikes.[24] Whether this is a plausible account of what judges actually do, it is orthogonal to the question I am interested in—why politicians support the institution of judicial review even when judges sometimes decide cases in ways they oppose. We must consider *that* question from the perspective of politicians who must regularly stand for election.

Historically, asking courts to deliver policy victories for politicians and achieve things that politicians can't or won't dare do is a task devoutly wished by politicians on both the left and the right, and from every political party, much as politicians may deny it in public—often quite sanctimoniously. The fact that courts perform these tasks—whether or not judges understand their role in this way—is one of the key political supports for judicial review. So the next time you hear a politician blather on about rogue judges who are imposing their personal preferences, imagine what that same politician would say if the courts went his or her way. He or she would sing the praises of an independent judiciary and demand that the other party stop complaining about the decision and respect the law. Courts can't and won't do everything politicians would like, mind you—they can only decide cases in which they have jurisdiction and they can only issue opinions and judgments.[25] But for many politicians, that is plenty.

C. Partisan Entrenchment: Judicial Review and the Party System

The third idea, which I have already alluded to is, partisan entrenchment.[26] An important driver of constitutional change is partisan entrenchment in the federal judiciary. Political parties attempt to place their ideological allies in the federal courts, where the latter will enjoy life tenure. The idea is that judges will still be around to protect the party's values and interests long after the politicians who appointed them are gone or out of power. Accordingly, presidents tend to appoint judges and Justices who are aligned with their political and policy views.

This means, among other things, that where a party is internally divided over an issue—for example, race—judges and Justices are more likely to support the president's position within the party, unless, of course, the president has struck a deal with copartisans. Kevin McMahon has shown that Franklin Roosevelt appointed many Justices and lower court judges who were racial liberals, despite opposition from the Southern wing of his party.[27]

Over time, partisan entrenchment can help generate major changes in constitutional law, and that is one reason why parties often care a great deal about judicial appointments.[28] A major cause of the Supreme Court's shift to the right in the fifty years between 1969 and 2019 is that Republicans made many more Supreme Court appointments than Democrats did. During this period there have been fourteen Republican appointments—not counting William Rehnquist's elevation to Chief Justice—and only four Democratic appointments.[29] In addition, the later Republican appointments have generally been more conservative than the earlier ones. Of the first nine Republican appointments, only two—William Rehnquist and Antonin Scalia—could be classified as movement conservatives. Since Clarence Thomas, all of the Republicans' Supreme Court appointments have been movement conservatives, and one expects that this pattern will continue for a long time.

Partisan entrenchment is an imperfect tool. Presidents do not have unfettered discretion to appoint whoever they like. The Senate must advise and consent to appointments; when the Senate is controlled by the opposite party, presidents must temper their ambitions and pick candidates who are perceived as more moderate or otherwise more acceptable to the opposition.[30] Moreover, Senators of both parties have traditionally had considerable influence in shaping appointments to the lower federal courts in their states.[31]

Presidents often make appointments for reasons other than ideology.[32] They may want to please demographic or geographical constituencies. They may want to reward favors. Or they may want to deal with political rivals or otherwise troublesome politicians by kicking them upstairs and placing them on the federal bench.

Generally speaking, and especially in times of increasing political polarization, presidents view ideological compatibility as quite important—especially on what the administration regards as the key issues that may soon come before the courts. But presidents may guess wrong about their appointees, about the most important issues, or about both. Presidents tend to focus on the short to medium term. But judges hold office for long periods of time. The key constitutional issues that arise years later may be quite different than presidents expected. The political valence and importance of certain issues may change because political conditions have changed.[33]

Presidents may also care only about a handful of issues that are highly salient at the time of appointment, but become less important later on. Franklin Roosevelt chose his Justices primarily to uphold New Deal programs. But very soon afterward the central issues before the courts involved civil liberties, and his appointees disagreed strongly among themselves.[34] Richard Nixon made appointments to limit court-ordered busing and get tough with criminals. He did not have abortion or gay rights in mind.[35] When the Court decided *Roe v. Wade*[36] in 1973, three of Nixon's appointees supported abortion rights, while only one dissented.

Political parties may change their ideological complexion over time, and the Justices may not move with them. As a result, a president may stock the courts with people who are well within the mainstream of the party at the time of appointment, but as time goes on, their views may start to diverge from where the party is heading. As noted previously, this happened with several Republican-appointed Justices as the party moved to the right. It also happened with Democratic Justices such as Felix Frankfurter and Byron White, who appeared more conservative as the Democratic Party's values changed.

Even given its limitations, politicians generally like partisan entrenchment. The ability to install like-minded judges on the bench is one of the most important political supports of judicial review. Viewed from the standpoint of politicians, partisan entrenchment serves several functions.[37] First, it helps ensure that the courts will defend the party's commitments of ideology and interest when the party loses power. Second, it helps ensure that courts will legitimate and uphold the party's political program against constitutional attack. Third, it helps ensure that courts will enforce the party's constitutional values and interests against states and local governments controlled by people who think very differently. Fourth, politicians have constitutional values as well as policy goals, and partisan entrenchment is one of the most important ways for parties to change the Constitution outside of Article V amendment.

In our work on constitutional change, Levinson and I have noted the historical connection between constitutional change and partisan entrenchment. Appoint enough like-minded judges, and constitutional doctrine will start to change.[38] There are three reasons why this happens.

First, partisan entrenchment often shifts the location of the median Justice(s)—the Justice or Justices in the middle of the Court's ideological spectrum. In the most ideologically charged cases, the Justices in the middle usually decide the outcome.[39]

Second, in the modern period, access to the Supreme Court is a very scarce resource, and the Justices effectively choose their own docket.[40] A conservative majority will choose different cases to hear from the lower courts and the state courts than a liberal majority. Thus, partisan entrenchment changes the mix of cases that get decided in the first place.

Third, changing the composition of the Court affects the kinds of novel constitutional claims that a majority of the Justices will be most sympathetic to. Change the composition of the Justices, and the majority will be more sympathetic to the claims of different kinds of political and social movements. For example, the Warren Court and the early Burger Court were sympathetic to novel claims brought by African Americans, left-wing dissenters, and advocates of birth control. As the Court moved to the right, it became more sympathetic to equal protection claims brought by whites opposed to affirmative action, to Christian conservatives seeking religious exemptions, and to First Amendment claims made by drug companies, advertisers, labor union opponents, and corporations.

At any point in time there are many different social and political movements offering novel interpretations of the Constitution, each seeking to move doctrine in different directions. Partisan entrenchment affects the environment in which these claims will flourish or die.

For example, partisan entrenchment affects the likelihood that novel constitutional claims will succeed in the lower federal courts. These courts are important because they tee up claims for consideration by the Supreme Court.[41] The ideological composition of the Supreme Court affects the choice of the vanishingly small class of cases considered each term, which have an enormous effect on the direction of American constitutional law. Partisan entrenchment thus affects which groups' claims are likely to attract the Court's attention and make their way onto its very exclusive docket.

Each of these features of partisan entrenchment has cumulative and self-reinforcing effects. A conservative Court emboldens conservative social movements and conservative legal intellectuals to push the envelope with novel claims. As novel claims are incorporated into the law, they create an intellectual space for more novel claims that can move the law even further to the right, and so on.

In short, partisan entrenchment affects not only the identity of the median Justices, and the specific decisions of the Supreme Court. It also affects the entire legal environment in which constitutional claims are made and considered. Partisan entrenchment is one vehicle—among many others—for moving constitutional claims from off-the-wall to on-the-wall.[42] It is a method of translating constitutional politics into constitutional law.

Levinson and I have distinguished between two different kind of constitutional politics. "High politics" involves debates and struggles over important constitutional principles, visions, and values. "Low politics" is the struggle for naked partisan advantage.[43]

Judges will inevitably engage in fights over high politics: the balance between federal and national power, the scope of judicial review, and the meaning of basic principles of equality and liberty. What they should not do is engage in low politics—decide cases primarily in order to help their "team," or to advantage their preferred political party, interest group, or constituency.

The distinction between high and low politics is important for the Court's sociological legitimacy. But it comes under increasing stress in periods of high polarization and constitutional rot.

7
How the Rise and Fall of Regimes Affects Judicial Review

Over the course of a little more than a century, American liberals (or, in an earlier period, progressives) and conservatives have switched positions on judicial review, judicial restraint, and the role of the federal courts—not once, but twice.[1]

At the beginning of the twentieth century, progressives grew increasingly skeptical of judicial review, while conservatives embraced judicial review to limit federal and state regulation and protect property rights.[2] After the New Deal, these positions gradually flipped. By midcentury, liberals in both parties had begun to defend strong courts and judicial review, while conservatives began to denounce judicial activism and preach judicial restraint.[3]

But this arrangement, too, slowly reversed itself. By the first decade of the twenty-first century, liberals—who were now almost all Democrats—had become deeply concerned about how conservative majorities on the Rehnquist and Roberts Courts used judicial review. They attacked judicial supremacy and increasingly argued for judicial restraint. Conversely, conservatives—who were by now almost all Republicans—emphasized the importance of courts in protecting federalism, religious liberty, and other important conservative constitutional values. Some conservatives, in fact, have recently called for "judicial engagement" to protect important constitutional structures and rights, including economic rights.

There are several reasons for these long-term shifts.[4] One is the composition of the Supreme Court's docket. The relatively small number of cases the Supreme Court takes and decides each year are the most salient—and among the most important—exercises of judicial review in American politics. Even though the vast majority of cases are decided by the lower federal courts, the Supreme Court's work has a disproportionate impact on how politicians and legal intellectuals think about judicial review.

Much of what people think of as activism and restraint—and which Justices are doing which—is driven by the composition of the Supreme Court's docket. If the Supreme Court accepted nothing but abortion and gay-rights cases, liberals and Democrats would appear to be firm advocates of judicial

The Cycles of Constitutional Time. Jack M. Balkin, Oxford University Press (2020). © Jack Balkin 2020.
DOI: 10.1093/oso/9780197530993.001.0001

engagement, and conservatives would appear to be defenders of judicial restraint. Conversely, if the Court accepted nothing but commercial-speech, campaign-finance, and federalism cases, conservatives and Republicans would appear to be aggressive judicial activists, and liberals defenders of a modest, deferential judiciary. There are many other issues in which the Justices might strike down or uphold laws, but if those cases never come before the Court, people are less likely to consider them in their positions on judicial review.

The identity of the litigants also matters. In the heyday of the Warren and early Burger Courts, the Supreme Court took race cases in which the petitioners who complained of racial discrimination were mostly black or Latino. In the Rehnquist and Roberts Courts, the Court took more and more cases in which the plaintiffs complaining of racial discrimination were white.[5] In the Warren and early Burger Courts, the Justices were primarily interested in the religious claims of relatively smaller religious sects with little political power;[6] in the Rehnquist and Roberts Courts, the Justices' docket has expanded to include the religious claims of Evangelicals, Catholics, and other conservative Christians.[7]

Behind the composition of the Supreme Court's docket lies a deeper explanation for the shift in attitudes about judicial review: the judicial appointments process. Because the Supreme Court mostly controls its own docket,[8] the kinds of cases the Court takes depend on who enjoys a working majority on the Supreme Court. All other things being equal, a working majority of liberal Justices will choose a different set of cases to hear than a working majority of conservative Justices. Who sits on the Court affects the kinds of cases in which the Court exercises judicial review, and thus the way that the public understands the political valence of judicial review and judicial restraint. The Roberts Court has taken a series of cases protecting commercial advertisers and challenging public-sector unions largely because the conservative Justices on the Court have wanted to hear those kinds of cases.

Liberals have not had a working majority on the Supreme Court since 1969. For this reason, and although there are important exceptions, the long-term development of constitutional doctrine, and the use of judicial review in a wide range of areas, has tended to reflect and promote conservative values more than liberal ones.

Thus, an important reason why liberals and conservatives have switched sides on judicial restraint and judicial engagement is partisan entrenchment in the judiciary. From the earliest days of the republic, the political parties have used the judicial appointments process to stock the courts with ideological allies. And from the earliest days of the republic, political parties have understood that judicial review can be a useful tool for defending and advancing a party's commitments of ideology and interest.

For much of the twentieth century and into the twenty-first, the Republican Party, as a whole, has been more conservative than the Democratic Party as a whole. When politics was less polarized, both parties had liberal and conservative wings. As a result, Republican presidents sometimes nominated moderate and progressive Justices, while Democrats sometimes nominated moderate and conservative Justices. Ideological differentiation between the two parties became stronger with the rise of the modern conservative movement and the departure of conservative Democrats into the Republican Party. At least since the 1980s, the Republican Party has been a movement party driven by the policy agendas of movement conservatives. This has affected the composition of the federal judiciary. Republican politicians have sought to control the federal courts and the Supreme Court in order to change constitutional doctrine and restore what conservatives believe to be the correct interpretation of the Constitution. Since 1980, Republican presidents have successfully appointed nine new Justices, Democratic presidents only four.[9] Since 1991, when Justice Thomas joined the Court, the Supreme Court has had a strong conservative majority with three movement conservatives. Since 2006, four of the Court's five conservatives were movement conservatives, and since 2018, all of the members of the Court's conservative majority are movement conservatives.

Partisan entrenchment in the judiciary offers a deeper explanation for liberal and conservative shifts concerning the role of the courts. Partisan entrenchment affects the kinds of cases the Supreme Court takes, the kinds of litigants the Justices are most interested in vindicating and protecting, and hence how judicial review is deployed.

In fact, there is an even deeper explanation for the long-term change in attitudes about judicial review. Behind both the composition of the Court's docket and the judicial appointments process is the slowly changing structure of national party competition in the United States. This is the cycle of regimes—one of the cycles of constitutional time.

Generational shifts in views about judicial activism and judicial restraint mirror the rise and fall of political regimes. The kinds of issues Justices select, and how the Justices exercise their powers of judicial review, reflect where the country is in political time—whether it is early in the regime, in its middle years, or in its later days. For this reason, the rise and fall of regimes shapes partisan (and ideological) attitudes about the exercise of judicial review.

Early in a regime, the newly dominant party faces opposition from judges appointed by the old regime and obstacles from the constitutional jurisprudence those judges created. Hence its supporters tend to be more skeptical of judicial review. As the dominant party gains control of the courts, however, its followers increasingly recognize the importance of judicial review to promote and protect the party's commitments of ideology and interest.

The positions of the two parties are symmetrical: as time goes on, one party relies ever more heavily on judicial review to further its goals, while the other party increasingly preaches judicial restraint—although neither party entirely gives up on using the courts to promote its favored policies. As the political regime moves from its beginning to its conclusion, the positions of the two parties gradually switch, and so too do the views of legal intellectuals associated with the parties. The effect, however, is generational, and not everyone changes sides: older legal intellectuals may cling to their long-held beliefs about judicial review, while younger thinkers adopt a different perspective.

A. Three Questions About Judicial Review

To understand how the cycle of regimes affects judicial review, consider the following three questions about the judicial role:

(1) Do you currently support how the courts are using their power to interpret the Constitution and strike down laws, or do you think that there should be greater judicial restraint? (This is a question about *judicial restraint*.)

(2) Do you think that Supreme Court Justices are deciding cases according to the Constitution and the law, or do you think that they are just making things up and imposing their own political preferences under the guise of following the law? (This is a question about the proper methods of *judicial reasoning*.)

(3) Do you think that it is important for the Court to uphold constitutional principles in order to check overreaching by the political branches, or do you think that the courts have become elitist and undemocratic and that they should stop interfering with democratic decision-making and let the political branches do their jobs and represent the people? (This is a question about *majority rule*.)

How people feel about these three questions—judicial restraint, judicial reasoning, and majority rule—is often affected by which party they most identify with. Perhaps even more interestingly, it is affected by where that party is in political time. The rise and fall of political regimes has important effects on how the dominant and opposition parties think about judicial restraint, about the legitimacy of methods of judicial reasoning, and about majority rule.

At any point in time, supporters of the dominant party and the opposition party will tend to take mirror-image positions on these questions. However, these positions will change as political time moves forward and the regime rises and falls, so that by the end of the regime the parties will have effectively switched positions on judicial review and judicial restraint.

Not everyone will change their positions, of course. As the regime proceeds, some members of the coalition and some legal intellectuals will change their minds, while others will not.[10] Those least likely to change their minds about the courts will be older generations; they will regard younger people's views about judicial power as foolhardy, forgetting important lessons learned the hard way. The younger generation of partisans and legal intellectuals, however, will not feel bound to agree with the views of older members of the coalition. And most elected politicians, who focus on the short to medium term, may shift positions with little concern about consistency. Their flip-flops on judicial review and judicial restraint may be amusing or outright hypocritical, but most people will not notice them.

Put differently, these shifts in views about judicial review are often generational, they occur gradually, and they may create significant divisions within each party's coalition. And all of this will occur despite the fact that politicians from all parties generally support judicial review as a basic feature of the system.

Moreover, as I pointed out earlier, there is a long-term secular trend in which politicians of both parties rely more and more on judicial review as the judiciary becomes more powerful.[11] So when we talk about how the cycle of regimes affects partisan attitudes about judicial restraint, we can say only that one party is *relatively* more supportive of judicial restraint than the other party, and this attitude, in turn, depends a great deal on the Supreme Court's docket, which is mostly constructed by the Justices.

B. Judicial Review in the Life-Cycle of a Political Regime

That's the big picture. Now let's see how the changes occur as we travel through the life cycle of a political regime. It's important to note that the effects I describe become most important in the twentieth century—the period of constitutional modernity. During the First Gilded Age at the turn of the twentieth century, the Supreme Court struck down the federal income tax,[12] limited the antitrust laws,[13] and began to develop the police power jurisprudence now associated with *Lochner v. New York.*[14] Earlier in the history of the republic, the Supreme Court was less powerful and exercised judicial review in less politically salient ways, although more frequently than people generally assume.[15]

Put another way, in the early Republic politicians had not yet constructed judicial review in its modern form. That really began after the Fourteenth Amendment and the creation of federal question jurisdiction made a wide range of state and local laws vulnerable to constitutional challenges, and the federal government began to produce more economic regulation in the late nineteenth century.[16] For this reason, the beginnings of modern judicial review lie in the late nineteenth and early twentieth centuries. Alexander Bickel's notion that the federal courts faced a countermajoritarian difficulty[17] is also a twentieth-century conception. Therefore, although I will give a few examples of earlier regimes, the effects are less pronounced, and I will focus primarily on the twentieth century and afterward.

My two central examples will be the rise and fall of the New Deal/Civil Rights regime, in which the Democrats were the dominant party and the Republicans were in opposition, and the Reagan regime, in which the Republicans have been the dominant party and the Democrats have been in opposition.

Let's imagine that the previous regime has collapsed and a new regime is just beginning. This would be the years 1932 to 1940 in the case of the New Deal /Civil Rights regime, and 1980 to 1988 in the case of the Reagan regime.

The previously dominant party has been cast into the political wilderness and is now the new opposition party, while a new dominant party and political coalition is ascending. But the new dominant coalition faces a problem. What is now the opposition party—precisely because it was dominant for so long—probably got to appoint most of the federal judges in the previous regime. It probably still controls the majority of the federal courts, and it may have a working majority on the Supreme Court. Perhaps more to the point, judges from the old regime may have produced a lot of constitutional jurisprudence that members of the newly dominant party oppose, either because that jurisprudence is inconsistent with their policy views or because it threatens to block needed reforms.

Because politicians in the newly dominant party don't yet control the federal courts, or because they must contend with lots of constitutional decisions that may take years to overturn, they are likely to be skeptical of the federal courts and of judicial review. Members of the new political coalition and their allies among legal intellectuals are likely to regard much of the previous jurisprudence as anti-majoritarian and anti-democratic.

Moreover, they are likely to see that jurisprudence as stemming from improper forms of judicial reasoning that have mangled the meaning of the true Constitution. The judges who represent the values of the old regime misapplied the Constitution and made things up. They imposed their personal or political values under the guise of interpreting the law. The representative judges of the old regime are misguided, smug, arrogant, antidemocratic, and out of touch with social realities and with the values of the public. They are acting as an elite corps of platonic guardians who think they know better what the Constitution means and what the American people want.[18] It is time to return the Constitution to the people and restore its correct meaning.

Conversely, members of what is now the opposition party (Republicans in 1932, Democrats in 1980)—and the legal intellectuals associated with them—are likely to take the opposite view about the federal courts. They want to protect their constitutional values and policy commitments—which they think are correct and just—from the radicals who have just won major political victories. Those same radicals threaten to tear down the valuable institutions, doctrines, and laws they have carefully built over many years. Defenders of the old order want to protect the existing jurisprudence developed by judges in the previous regime. They fear that the newly dominant party will destroy the Constitution and undermine its central principles. Now more than ever, they believe that it is important for judges to defend the Constitution from misguided majorities in order to protect established rights and freedoms. There is much to be concerned about, because the new regime's lawyers and legal intellectuals are promoting dangerous ideas about constitutional interpretation and judicial review. Robust judicial review and fidelity to the real Constitution is the only thing that can preserve the republic.

It follows that the newly ascendant party is more likely to preach judicial restraint and argue for a more deferential judiciary, while holdovers from the old regime are more likely to support judicial review and the constitutional jurisprudence of the old regime. Defenders of the old regime want to protect precedents that articulate the Constitution as they understand it, while the new regime's lawyers want to chip away at these precedents in order to free up democratic energy and renew the country. Politicians in the newly dominant party don't control the judiciary yet, and they have been subjected to years of judicial review by the other party's judges. So they preach judicial restraint and tend to be critical of judicial review.

Keith Whittington points out that reconstructive presidents—those who begin a new regime—are the most likely to make "departmentalist" claims.[19] Departmentalism holds that each branch of government is an equally authoritative interpreter of the Constitution and that within its own sphere each branch is entitled to interpret the Constitution as it sees fit. Reconstructive presidents tend to engage in departmentalist talk, Whittington explains, because they usually do not control the federal courts when their presidencies begin.[20] As a result, they cannot rely on the courts to support their reconstruction of American politics. Therefore, it may be politically more useful, as Franklin Roosevelt did, to treat the courts as an adversary blocking necessary reforms. Or, as Reagan and movement conservatives did, it may be politically advantageous to denounce the courts for having abandoned the Framers' values.

How great a struggle develops between the courts and the new administration depends on the configuration of the courts and the Supreme Court when the new regime begins. Roosevelt and Reagan faced different situations. In 1933, when Roosevelt took office, Republicans had controlled the White House for twelve years. Therefore Republican presidents had appointed most of the federal judges. Conservatives also enjoyed a working majority on the Supreme Court that included seven Republican appointees and a conservative Democratic ally, James C. McReynolds. To be sure, some of the Republican appointees were moderates or progressives—that describes Herbert Hoover's three appointments of Charles Evans Hughes, Benjamin Cardozo, and Owen Roberts. But even the Court's more progressive Justices were wary of departing too much from the old regime's jurisprudence of national power—that is one reason why the Court unanimously struck down the National Recovery Act in the *Schechter Poultry* case.[21] Because Roosevelt was shut out of any Supreme Court appointments until 1937, a collision over the New Deal was predictable, if not inevitable.

Imagine, however, that one of Woodrow Wilson's appointments, John H. Clarke, did not resign in 1922 to campaign for the League of Nations, or that Wilson picked a more progressive candidate instead of the irascible and reactionary McReynolds.[22] Or imagine that one of the conservative Four Horsemen retired early in Roosevelt's first term. This actually might have happened if Congress had not stupidly slashed the Justices' retirement pensions in half in 1932. Although the pension amounts were soon restored, the episode frightened Justices Sutherland and Van Devanter during the middle of the Great Depression, and convinced them not to resign.[23] If either or both had left the Court early, progressives might have enjoyed a majority on the Hughes Court, and the transition to the New Deal might have gone much more smoothly.

In contrast to Roosevelt, when Reagan assumed office in 1981, Republican appointees already had a majority on the Burger Court, because, as noted previously, Lyndon Johnson badly misplayed his hand and Jimmy Carter got no Supreme Court appointments. That meant that the conservative judicial revolution began before the Reagan regime itself. Imagine, however, that history turned out a little differently. Suppose that Johnson had not tried to elevate Fortas and had appointed a liberal Democrat to replace Earl Warren; and either William O. Douglas (who left the Court in 1975) or Hugo Black (who died in 1971) retired before Johnson left the White House. Then Richard Nixon and Gerald Ford together would have gotten only two appointments. Imagine further that Jimmy Carter was able to replace Potter Stewart with another liberal Democrat.[24] Then Reagan would have faced a phalanx of five and possibly six staunchly liberal Justices, who would have spent the previous decade building on and expanding the Warren Court's liberal jurisprudence. In such a scenario, Reagan, like Roosevelt, might have faced serious conflicts with the Supreme Court.

In any case, even though Reagan faced a friendlier Supreme Court than Roosevelt did, the New Deal/Civil Rights regime had produced many years of accumulated jurisprudence. In 1981, movement conservatives objected to Warren and Burger Court decisions in many areas, including reproductive rights, criminal procedure, church–state relations, and federalism.[25] *Roe v. Wade*[26] was only the most obvious example. Like the New Deal progressives before them, Reagan's movement conservatives were skeptical of judicial power and they were especially critical of the reasoning by which courts reached these liberal decisions.

As presidents from the dominant party begin to appoint new judges and Justices, judicial review becomes increasingly useful to the regime's dominant party. The newly installed judges are more likely to uphold the party's program and relax some of the constitutional restraints in the old regime's jurisprudence. Legal intellectuals who support the regime's commitments begin to rationalize and celebrate the new decisions, while the legal intellectuals on the opposite side criticize and bemoan them.

Slowly but surely the positions of the dominant and opposition parties begin to shift. The dominant party and its affiliated legal intellectuals increasingly see the value of strong judicial review to protect regime commitments, while members of the opposition party and their associated legal intellectuals become increasingly skeptical of judicial review.

But this process takes a very long time, and it is complicated by many factors. One is the degree of ideological coherence within the parties. Different factions of the party may disagree about legal issues, with some wanting courts to be more active and others wanting it to be more deferential. Good examples are the fierce disagreements within the Democratic Party during the New Deal/Civil Rights regime about race, and especially about

Brown v. Board of Education.[27] Southern conservatives did not want the federal courts ordering desegregation of schools and other institutions. Northern liberals supported *Brown*. In addition, Southern Democrats were often critical of liberal decisions on criminal procedure and free speech. Conversely, many Southern Democrats were skeptical of Congress's powers to pass civil rights statutes and the Voting Rights Act and wanted the courts to intervene to protect state's rights. Northern liberal Democrats, by contrast, believed that the New Deal settlement applied: courts should defer to Congress just as they should in other kinds of economic and social legislation.

A second, related, factor is the degree of polarization between the parties. If there are liberal Democrats and liberal Republicans, as there were during the New Deal/Civil Rights Regime, the parties will not have coherent views about when courts should exercise judicial review or engage in judicial restraint. Rather, liberals, regardless of party, are more likely to agree with other liberals and conservatives with other conservatives. The liberal Warren Court was actually a coalition of liberal Justices appointed by presidents of different parties who enforced the commitments of the New Deal/Civil Rights regime.[28] Two of the most important liberal stalwarts on that court, Chief Justice Earl Warren and Justice William Brennan, were Eisenhower appointees. Although Eisenhower is supposed to have said that they were two of his mistakes as president,[29] these appointments made perfect sense in the context of the politics of the time, in which Eisenhower wanted to demonstrate his bipartisanship and moderation.[30] Neither of these appointments were out of line with the moderate politics of his administration, or the moderate liberal politics of his Attorney General, Herbert Brownell.[31]

The story is a bit less complicated after the parties begin to divide more strongly by ideology in the Reagan Regime. Democrats were increasingly liberals, as Southern Democrats left the party; Republicans became very conservative. Republicans achieved a working conservative majority on the Supreme Court in 1991, when Clarence Thomas succeeded Thurgood Marshall. At that point, the Rehnquist and Roberts Courts began to expand the use of judicial review for conservative ends. Yet as Thomas Keck explains, the presence of Justices O'Connor and Kennedy on the Court meant that the liberal Justices could form occasional majorities as well. The most important examples concern abortion and gay rights: *Planned Parenthood of Southeastern Pennsylvania v. Casey*,[32] which reformulated the abortion jurisprudence of *Roe v. Wade*, and the Rehnquist Court's landmark gay rights decisions, *Romer v. Evans*[33] and *Lawrence v. Texas*.[34] The result was a Supreme Court that employed judicial review both for liberal and conservative causes,[35] although the general tenor was largely conservative.

The list of conservative uses of judicial review is far too long to catalog, but examples include the Rehnquist Court's federalism revolution in the 1990s and early 2000s, which limited state liability for damage suits under federal statutes, held that states could not be required to enforce federal programs, and limited Congress's powers to enforce the Reconstruction Amendments against the states;[36] the Roberts Court's decisions in *District of Columbia v. Heller*[37] and *City of Chicago v. McDonald*,[38] recognizing Second Amendment rights; the 2007 *Parents Involved*[39] decision striking down voluntary desegregation plans; the 2013 decision in *Shelby County v. Holder*[40] striking down parts of the 1965 Voting Rights Act; and a series of First Amendment cases—including *Citizens United v. FEC*[41]—which struck down restrictions on campaign finance and commercial speech.[42] Following Justice Kennedy's retirement in 2018, the solidly conservative Roberts Court majority will likely find new ways to exercise judicial review in a conservative direction.

C. The Causes of Change

Why do the parties' positions on judicial review shift? There are multiple reasons, but the most important ones are partisan entrenchment and the reconstitution of the Supreme Court's agenda. As the regime proceeds, the dominant party is able to appoint a larger share of judges and Justices. When that happens, judicial review becomes increasingly useful to politicians in the dominant party, or at least, the presidential wing of the dominant party.[43] (As noted earlier, during the New Deal/Civil rights regime, Northern liberal Democrats often disagreed with Southern conservative Democrats.) Federal courts can help the dominant party in three different ways: (1) by upholding its preferred laws, policies, and programs; (2) by striking down or narrowly interpreting disfavored laws or laws that benefit political adversaries; and (3) by enforcing the party's values nationally against state and local governments.

To achieve these goals, it is not enough for courts simply to stay their hands. Rather, courts must actively exercise their powers of judicial review to further the constitutional values and policy commitments of the party (or the presidential wing of the party). And because the Supreme Court controls much of its own docket, the Justices can pick the cases that best further these values and commitments, making judicial review even more valuable to regime politicians and affiliated legal intellectuals.

As a result, as soon as presidents from the dominant party have been able to appoint a majority of Supreme Court and lower court judges—usually within a decade or so after the regime begins—these judges and Justices start to defend and promote the regime's commitments through striking down laws and executive actions as well as through upholding them and exercising judicial restraint.

In order for judges and Justices to defend the regime's commitments, it will usually not be sufficient to defer to the political branches in every case. Judges must also strike down, narrowly construe, or hobble laws and executive actions that are inconsistent with the regime's values. Judicial assertion is especially important in the case of state and local governments, which may be controlled by the opposition party.[44] In addition, as political time proceeds, the Supreme Court's agenda gradually changes. The Justices pick a different set of cases, creating opportunities for what members of the conservative movement now call "judicial engagement."[45]

The increasing use of judicial review to protect and promote the constitutional and policy values of the dominant party leads to repeated charges of "judicial activism" by members of the opposition party (and, in the nonpolarized New Deal/Civil Rights regime, also by conservative and Southern Democrats). Critics increasingly charge that the federal courts and the Supreme Court have gotten out of control, are imposing their political preferences in defiance of settled law, and are mangling the Constitution. Progressives during the *Lochner* Era, conservatives during the New Deal/Civil Rights regime, and liberals during the Reagan era have all complained about judicial activism by courts promoting regime commitments of ideology and interest.

One of the most interesting features of the Reagan Regime, however, is that liberal Democrats are not the only ones who have complained about judicial activism. Even as the Supreme Court has used judicial review aggressively in the service of conservative values, conservative politicians have continued to pretend that the Warren Court is still in business; they continue to denounce the evils of liberal judicial activism, even though the "activism" is increasingly in a conservative direction.[46] The most likely reason is that Justices Kennedy and O'Connor occasionally voted with the liberals on culture war issues, which are highly salient to the Republican Party's conservative base.[47]

The increasing usefulness of judicial review to the dominant party slowly causes attitudes about judicial review to shift. Politicians and legal intellectuals affiliated with the dominant party begin to argue that strong judicial review is a good thing—and even necessary—when judges reason in the right way about the Constitution.[48] Continuing to adhere to bromides about judicial restraint makes less and less sense. It may have made sense in the past, but that was because the old jurisprudence was based on a defective vision of the Constitution and defective forms of constitutional reasoning.

Once again, these changes are generational; younger intellectuals are quicker to embrace judicial review, while older ones remain skeptical—remembering the lessons of the past.[49] (There may also be lack of consensus if the parties are depolarized.) Elected politicians care far less about intellectual consistency; they simply change their rhetoric from case to case, hoping that nobody notices.

Now consider attitudes about judicial review among members of the opposition party—in particular, conservative Republicans in the New Deal/Civil Rights regime, and liberal Democrats in the Reagan regime. Their views about judicial review tend to be a mirror image of changes occurring in the dominant party.

After a new regime begins, members of the opposition party may continue to support strong judicial review for a long time, because they believe that judicial review is necessary to defend important values and commitments. They may even hold out hope that they will soon regain control of the federal courts, and things can return to the way they were before. But as the dominant party takes over the courts, a new generation of judges doesn't seem to be doing what judges should be doing—that is, respecting and protecting the prior regime's values and commitments. The Supreme Court and the lower federal courts are increasingly using judicial review to *undermine* these important values and commitments.

Opposition politicians and legal intellectuals increasingly face a quandary—their rhetoric about the importance of judicial review no longer seems to match reality. At some point, perhaps midway through the regime, oppositional leaders and intellectuals realize, in Sanford Levinson's phrase, that "the Warren Court has left the building."[50] The Supreme Court majority is simply not on their side, and probably won't be for years to come. The content of the Supreme Court's docket has changed, and in these new kinds of cases, opposition politicians and legal intellectuals will usually be arguing for deference to the political branches or judicial restraint.

Again, these effects are also generational, and many opposition leaders and intellectuals will still cling to the old-time religion. Moreover, because of the long-term secular trend of a more powerful judiciary supported by both parties, there will still be issues in which opposition leaders and intellectuals believe that judicial review is necessary to protect the commitments of the opposition party. In the Reagan regime, the most obvious examples involve criminal procedure, reproductive rights, and gay rights. These cases follow the pattern of the end of the New Deal/Civil Rights regime—liberals want courts to step in, while conservatives want them to stay out. Perhaps even more to the point, liberals want courts to preserve older, liberal jurisprudence, so they become defenders of stare decisis, especially for decisions like *Roe v. Wade*.

As a political regime progresses, jurisprudential accomplishments build up, and arguments that were once off-the-wall become on-the-wall. Judicial creativity and ambition appear to increase because earlier decisions have already laid important groundwork, and because social movements and litigation campaigns can make increasingly ambitious arguments for reinterpreting or changing the law. This acceleration in judicial creativity and ambition is most likely to occur in the middle of the regime. The judicial creativity of the Warren Court and the first few years of the Burger Court is an example; so too is the work of the post-1995 Rehnquist Court and the Roberts Court.

Near the end of a regime, the dominant party finds it difficult to accomplish its ideological goals through the political branches. This makes control of the judiciary increasingly important. That is not because people know that the regime is about to end; rather, it is because the judiciary is simply in a better position to achieve political and ideological victories when the political branches are stymied. Judicial appointments are important throughout the life of a regime, but they become increasingly important late in the regime. Senate Majority Leader Mitch McConnell has devoted a great deal of his energies during the Trump administration to stocking the courts with as many strong conservatives as he can. That is not because McConnell knows that the Reagan era is about to end—indeed, he hopes that it will last for many years to come. Rather, it is because McConnell recognizes that conservatives will get more mileage out of judicial appointments when their legislative agenda is effectively stalled.

Once a regime is over, and the dominant party has lost power, much depends on whether the party has already lost control of the courts—this was the Democrats' fate in 1980—or still maintains majority control, as Republicans did in 1932. In the latter situation, it may seem that judicial ambition is going into overdrive. An example is the conservative majority that faced off with FDR during the struggle over the New Deal.[51] What is really happening is that the new regime is starting to enact its political program. Judges representing the values of the old regime feel that they must be especially vigilant to preserve the old regime's interests and constitutional values in the face of a newly ascendant party with contrary values.

An interesting example is the Chase Court in the first years of the post–Civil War Republican regime. Suddenly, the Court became very active. Mark Graber explains that this was because the Court still had a group of Jacksonian Democrats, who were defending the values of the previous regime. When the Jacksonians controlled Congress or the White House in the previous

Table 7.1 Judicial Review in the Cycle of Regimes

Views about judicial review (relative to the other party)	Dominant Party	Opposition Party
Early in Regime	Judicial restraint	Judicial engagement
Middle of Regime	Disagreements emerge (especially if party system is depolarized); generational shift to judicial engagement	Disagreements emerge (especially if party system is depolarized); generational shift to judicial restraint
Late Regime	Judicial engagement	Judicial restraint

N.B. The long-term secular trend is increasing reliance on judicial review by both parties.

regime, they successfully blocked laws they regarded as unconstitutional aggrandizements of federal power; but once Republicans gained control of both Congress and the presidency in 1861, Jacksonian judges were the only remaining defense against what they viewed as assaults on the Constitution.[52]

We can summarize the way the cycle proceeds in Table 7.1.

D. Judicial Review on the Cusp of a New Regime

If, as I have argued, we are nearing the end of a cycle, what does this analysis hold for the future? President Trump and Senate Majority Leader McConnell have solidified a conservative Republican majority on the Supreme Court, and they are trying to appoint as many conservative Republicans as possible to the lower federal courts. If the dominant party in the next regime is the Democrats, this would make the most likely scenario similar to that faced by FDR in 1937. The new regime will begin with the old regime having appointed most of the federal judiciary and a majority on the Supreme Court.

By contrast, imagine that President Obama had managed to appoint Merrick Garland to replace Antonin Scalia. Then the Roberts Court would be a little like the early years of the Burger Court after Richard Nixon's four appointments. The Roberts Court would have had a moderately liberal Supreme Court majority *before* the new Democratic regime began. This is analogous to the situation that Ronald Reagan faced in 1980, when the Burger Court's moderately conservative majority was already in place.

That, however, is not what happened. McConnell successfully held Scalia's seat open, and Trump obtained not one but two Supreme Court appointments, and many lower federal court appointments, solidifying conservative control. As a result, if the Democrats are the new dominant party, we are likely to see a series of confrontations with the federal judiciary as the Democrats try to enact their policy program. As those confrontations happen, liberal Democrats will be increasingly hostile to judicial review. Yet at the same time, because of the long-term trend mentioned earlier, Democrats will be unwilling to give up completely on the powers of judicial review. They will want to defend liberal precedents such as *Roe v. Wade* and *Obergefell v. Hodges*.[53] The Democratic position will probably be more complicated than the strong progressive critique of judicial review in the 1920s and 1930s.

Earlier I noted that attitudes about judicial review begin to change as the new regime gets control of the Supreme Court. Roosevelt did not obtain a Supreme Court appointment until 1937, four years into his presidency. In the present case, it may take the Democrats considerably longer to obtain a new liberal majority. Most of the members of the current Republican Supreme Court majority are still fairly young, and two of the Democrats on the Court are very old. If President Trump wins re-election, he may be able to replace both Justice Ginsburg and Justice Breyer with conservative Republicans. Then the Supreme Court would have a phalanx of seven conservative Republicans, who would defend the values of the Reagan regime for many decades into the future. For this reason, some Democrats and allied progressive intellectuals have been toying with the idea of a new court-packing plan that would increase the size of the Court to create a Democratic majority. I discuss the pitfalls of this approach in chapter 11.

8

The Role of Constitutional Theory in the Cycle of Regimes

In 2004, Barry Friedman noticed that constitutional theory ran in cycles.[1] In response to the Rehnquist Court's federalism revolution and *Bush v. Gore*,[2] liberal legal scholars had started to become skeptical of judicial power after many years of defending strong judicial review.[3] We can connect Friedman's insight to the cycle of the rise and fall of regimes.

I begin, however, with a few caveats.

First, constitutional theories—at least those generally offered by academics and other commentators—tend to focus almost obsessively on the Supreme Court, rather than on the lower federal courts or the state courts.[4]

Second, constitutional theories are shaped by the living memory of the theorists who create them. For example, liberal constitutional theorists who came of age during the constitutional struggle over the New Deal tended to view later developments through that lens. This led older liberal thinkers to be deeply suspicious of Warren Court jurisprudence.[5] Theorists who came of age during the civil rights era, by contrast, had different views about judicial review. In this sense, constitutional theorists are often "fighting the last war," which is a major source of intergenerational disagreements.

Third, constitutional theories purport to offer general views about constitutional interpretation and the judicial role. But because they are produced in historical circumstances, they tend to focus on the canonical cases of their era (for example, *Brown v. Board of Education* or *Roe v. Wade*), and on relatively recent Supreme Court decisions. Constitutional theories may pay relatively little attention to how judicial review operates in wide swaths of doctrine because recent decisions have not made these areas of doctrine particularly salient.[6]

Thus, constitutional theories are often strongly influenced by the Justices' control over their own docket, which is a contingent feature of judicial politics. For example, when a conservative Court constructs the docket, this will eventually create the illusion of a general liberal preference for judicial restraint. But if liberal Justices constructed the Supreme Court's docket, they would pick a different set of cases involving a different set of plaintiffs. Then

The Cycles of Constitutional Time. Jack M. Balkin, Oxford University Press (2020). © Jack Balkin 2020.
DOI: 10.1093/oso/9780197530993.001.0001

questions about judicial review and constitutional interpretation might look very different to liberal theorists. The same points apply to conservative theorists. Conservatives will be very skeptical of judicial review when liberals control the docket and liberal public interest firms make most of the novel constitutional claims. Their views will shift once conservative public interest firms bring different kinds of novel claims and conservative Justices construct the Supreme Court's docket.

Fourth, it follows that academic theories of constitutional interpretation have little to say about the work of lower federal courts, which cannot choose their own cases, and which must follow existing Supreme Court precedents—regardless of what the constitutional theories of the day say that courts should do.[7]

Fifth, constitutional theory is affected by the long-term secular trend toward more powerful courts and by the political construction of judicial review by political parties over two centuries. Regardless of their rhetoric about judicial activism, which varies from case to case, contemporary politicians from both parties support judicial review to protect their interests. By the early twenty-first century, it is simply not plausible for politicians on either side to take as strong a position in favor of judicial restraint as progressives once did in the 1920s and 1930s.

When liberals and conservatives flip positions on judicial restraint in successive cases depending on whether the substantive issue is (for example) abortion rights or gun rights, same-sex marriage or the constitutionality of the Voting Rights Act, we must take contemporary arguments for judicial restraint with a very large grain of salt.[8] Thomas Keck has called the modern approach "bipartisan judicial activism." He argues that it makes far more sense of what both politicians and the public want and expect from the federal judiciary than most academic constitutional theories would suggest.[9]

Sixth, the views of legal intellectuals, whether liberal or conservative, are not monolithic. People's views about constitutional law are shaped by background and experience—including age, race, gender, immigrant status, educational training, and many other factors. My claim is that in general, as we move through political time, judicial review will look different to successive generations of legal intellectuals.

In contrast to politicians, legal intellectuals resist changing their minds and flip-flopping on these questions. Most will continue to preach the lessons of their youth. To be sure, like Saint Paul on the road to Damascus, a few members of the older generation may have a conversion experience about judicial review mid-career. But if legal intellectuals have more than one conversion experience in their careers, they start to look unserious and more like simple partisans. Instead, changes in theoretical perspective usually come from the next generation of legal intellectuals. This creates perpetual tensions and conflicts within groups of liberal or conservative legal intellectuals.

With these six caveats in mind, consider the two major schools of modern constitutional theory I mentioned in chapter 1—living constitutionalism and originalism. The relationship of both of these theories to judicial review and judicial restraint has cycled with the rise and fall of political regimes.

A. The Cycle of Regimes and Living Constitutionalism

The idea of a living Constitution emerged at the turn of the twentieth century.[10] The idea of a constitution that evolved in response to changing conditions soon developed into the idea that the Constitution's application should change with changing circumstances, which in turn was adapted to progressive criticisms of the Supreme Court's work in the *Lochner* era. Progressives criticized decisions of the *Lochner*-era Supreme Court that limited federal regulatory power and protected freedom of contract from economic regulation. The Constitution, progressives argued, should evolve to meet changing social and economic circumstances; it must adapt to a world very different from that of the founding.[11]

Thus, in its early incarnation, living constitutionalism was an argument for judicial restraint that criticized how conservative judges exercised judicial review in the then-existing (Republican) regime.[12] Living constitutionalism attacked the status quo with respect to all three questions of the judicial role: judicial restraint, legal reasoning, and majoritarianism. First, the early version of living constitutionalism was a theory of judicial restraint.[13] It argued that judges should uphold reforms that sought to deal with new social realities. Second, advocates of a living Constitution argued that conservative judges were engaged in formalist reasoning that was out of touch with the world they lived in. These judges were imposing their laissez-faire economic views on the country in the guise of interpreting the Constitution; they were mangling the Constitution and betraying its true spirit.[14] Third, advocates of a living Constitution argued that judges should defer to the will of democratically elected majorities, who wanted social and economic reform.[15]

The early version of living constitutionalism corresponds to the views of an opposition party near the end of an old political regime, and of a newly dominant party at the very beginning of the successor regime. FDR argued that the Court was imposing a "horse-and-buggy" vision of the Constitution on a modern nation.[16] The country needed, in Franklin Roosevelt's words, "members of the Court who understand . . . modern conditions, . . . who will not undertake to override the judgment of the Congress on legislative policy, . . . [and] who will act as Justices and not as legislators."[17] This version of living constitutionalism made sense of the judicial role in the early years of the new regime, when the political branches and the Supreme Court were sharply in conflict.

By the end of the 1940s, however, Democratic presidents had appointed all of the Supreme Court's Justices. New issues confronted the Court, including civil rights and civil liberties. Justice Frankfurter and his followers continued to advance the idea of living constitutionalism as a theory of judicial restraint. Eventually, however, legal intellectuals allied with the New Deal/Civil Rights regime began to employ the idea of a living Constitution in a different way. Now living constitutionalism became an argument for active judicial protection of civil rights and civil liberties.

The Supreme Court's footnote four in *United States v. Carolene Products Co.*[18] suggested how this might come about: the Court should intervene when democracy or the Bill of Rights were at stake.[19] The New Deal Justices began to disagree among themselves about how and when to exercise judicial review. A famous early example was the 1943 decision in *West Virginia State Board of Education v. Barnette*,[20] which overturned the 1940 decision in *Minersville School District v. Gobitis*.[21] *Barnette* held that the State could not require Jehovah's Witness schoolchildren to salute the flag, arguing that the First Amendment and other fundamental rights should be "beyond the reach of majorities and officials,"[22] while Justice Frankfurter's dissent continued to preach the virtues of judicial restraint.[23]

The Supreme Court's 1954 decision in *Brown v. Board of Education*[24] marked a crucial turning point. Although all of the Justices—including Frankfurter—supported the decision, Chief Justice Earl Warren's opinion invoked the idea of a living Constitution as a justification for judicial review, not judicial restraint: "We cannot turn the clock back to 1868 when the [Fourteenth] Amendment was adopted," Warren explained.[25] "We must consider public education in the light of its full development and its present place in American life throughout the Nation. Only in this way can it be determined if segregation in public schools deprives these plaintiffs of the equal protection of the laws."[26]

Writing in 1963 in the Harvard Law Review, Yale Law Professor Charles Reich, in a tribute to Justice Hugo Black, argued that the growth of government power following the New Deal meant that courts had to be vigilant in protecting civil rights and civil liberties in compensation.[27] The living

Constitution, Reich argued, required judges to be active, not passive, in defense of these rights and liberties, and to read constitutional liberties broadly in order to meet contemporary versions of the problems they were designed to prevent. This "concept of 'faithful adherence' keeps the Bill of Rights alive and capable of growth along with the rest of the Constitution."[28] Although Reich attributed these ideas to Justice Black, he was actually articulating the views of many liberal legal intellectuals who wanted courts to protect civil rights and civil liberties.

In 1966, in *Harper v. Virginia Board of Elections*,[29] Justice William O. Douglas took these ideas one step further. He argued that the Supreme Court could and should recognize new rights not specifically mentioned in the text. Virginia could not impose a poll tax that disenfranchised its poorest citizens because there was an unenumerated guarantee of an equal right to vote under the Fourteenth Amendment's Equal Protection Clause.[30] "In determining what lines are unconstitutionally discriminatory, we have never been confined to historic notions of equality, any more than we have restricted due process to a fixed catalogue of what was at a given time deemed to be the limits of fundamental rights," Douglas proclaimed. "Notions of what constitutes equal treatment for purposes of the Equal Protection Clause *do* change."[31] His erstwhile ally, the liberal originalist Justice Hugo Black, dissented vigorously, arguing that the Equal Protection Clause meant no such thing.[32] The previous year, in *Griswold v. Connecticut*,[33] the Court, in another opinion by Douglas, recognized an unenumerated right of marital privacy that protected the purchase and use of contraceptives. Once again, Black dissented.[34]

By the 1960s and 1970s, the concept of a living Constitution had mutated from a Progressive-era *critique* of how the *Lochner* Court had engaged in judicial review to a liberal *justification* of judicial review to protect important rights and liberties—whether or not explicitly mentioned in the Constitution's text. By the mid-1970s, liberal legal scholars had swung decisively toward strong judicial review as necessary to protect liberty and equality.

The change was generational, with different thinkers taking different positions over the years. Liberal legal process scholars like Herbert Wechsler (b. 1909) were skeptical of the Warren Court's innovations, and continued to argue for judicial restraint and adherence to "neutral principles" of constitutional law that would prevent the courts from appearing political.[35] Frankfurter's mentee, the great Yale constitutional theorist Alexander Bickel (b. 1924), tried to take a middle position. He supported *Brown* and wanted the Court to protect civil rights and civil liberties, but argued that in a large number of cases the Court should employ the "passive virtues" and avoid exercising judicial review in order to conserve its political capital for the cases that mattered most.[36] As the Court and the Democratic party moved further to the left, Bickel became disillusioned and grew more conservative. In his 1969 Holmes Lectures, *The Supreme Court and the Idea of Progress*,[37] he warned that the Warren Court's aggressive use of judicial review would backfire.[38] Bickel's intellectual odyssey reflects the intellectual strains on mid-regime legal intellectuals who experience an increasing dissonance between the regime's changing ideological commitments and their settled views about the judicial role.

John Hart Ely (b. 1938) dealt with the tension in a different way. He sought to confine the scope of judicial review to the protection of the political process, while maintaining the progressive theory of judicial restraint elsewhere.[39] Expanding the theory of *Carolene Products*, Ely argued for strong judicial review to protect democracy, free speech, and the rights of criminal defendants, but stopped short of endorsing the Court's reproductive rights decisions, and famously criticized *Roe v. Wade*.[40] Other scholars, like Ronald Dworkin (b. 1931), Owen Fiss (b. 1938), Paul Brest (b. 1940), and Laurence Tribe (b. 1941), offered full-throated defenses of judicial review in defense of liberal rights jurisprudence.[41]

By the 1970s, the Frankfurterian vision of judicial restraint had been eclipsed in the younger generation of liberal legal intellectuals. The progressives' ideas of judicial restraint and majoritarianism were now taken up by political conservatives and conservative legal intellectuals—primarily in the Republican Party—who objected to liberal judicial decisions in the New Deal/Civil Rights regime.

B. The Cycle of Regimes and Originalism

The story of originalism has a similar structure, and takes up where the story of living constitutionalism leaves off. In the 1970s, Robert Bork and Raoul Berger adapted the progressive critique of *Lochner* to conservative ends.[42] They connected progressive ideas about judicial restraint to the philosophy of original intention, just as the liberal Justice Hugo Black had in his dissent in *Griswold v. Connecticut*.[43] (In fact, Black's *Griswold* dissent makes virtually every argument for judicial restraint that conservative originalists would eventually adopt.) Conservatives used originalism to criticize the liberal jurisprudence of the Warren and early Burger Courts, including criminal procedure and First Amendment decisions, *Griswold v. Connecticut*, and *Roe v. Wade*.[44]

The idea of using originalism as a critique of the status quo did not begin with conservatives. Franklin Roosevelt had defended the New Deal as a return to the Framers' flexible vision of a national government that was able to meet the crises and challenges of the future.[45] The Warren Court had used originalist arguments in many of its famous civil rights and civil liberties cases.[46] Criticizing the Warren Court's use of history, Alfred Kelly noted that the Warren Court often used appeals to the Founding as a "precedent-breaking" device that allowed judges to sweep away old doctrinal structures and put new ones in their stead under the guise of preserving continuity.[47] This is, in fact, a familiar use of a return to origins: it allows a critic to delegitimize existing practices and start over again by appealing to an even older authority and a deeper fidelity.[48] Now that liberals had established a new status quo, conservatives employed originalist rhetoric to attack it as well.

This early version of originalism was primarily a criticism of judicial activism by liberal judges. Keith Whittington explains that like much constitutional theory, "originalism was largely oriented around the actions of the U.S. Supreme Court," so that "originalism's agenda was whatever was on the Court's agenda."[49] Hence, the early version of originalism was primarily a way of critiquing the Court's civil rights and civil liberties decisions.[50]

Like living constitutionalism before it, conservative originalism criticized the status quo on grounds of judicial restraint, legal reasoning, and majoritarianism. First, like early versions of progressive living constitutionalism, conservative originalism was a theory of judicial restraint.[51] Courts should not expand rights or recognize novel rights claims against governments. Second, like their progressive forebears, conservative originalists argued that liberal judges in the New Deal/Civil Rights regime had engaged in a defective form of legal reasoning.[52] Their decisions had no basis in the Constitution's text, history, or structure, and merely substituted their personal ideology for the law. This betrayed the true meaning and spirit of the Constitution. The liberal theory of a "living Constitution" was nothing more than a cover for the belief that unelected judges could decide for themselves what was best for the country.[53] Channeling progressive-era rhetoric, Robert Bork argued, for example, that *Griswold v. Connecticut* was no better than *Lochner v. New York*.[54]

Third, like progressive living constitutionalists, conservative originalists argued that judges should defer to the will of democratically elected majorities.[55] Liberal jurists were just like the members of the Old Court that opposed FDR.[56] They were elitists who were out of touch with the public's values and views. Originalism was necessary to restrain judges from imposing their personal preferences, and to maintain the separation of law from politics.[57]

Once again, these kinds of attacks made perfect sense for conservatives in the last years of the New Deal/Civil Rights regime and the first years of the new Reagan regime. Although Richard Nixon had moved the Court to the right, Republican presidents had not yet thoroughly reshaped the federal courts, and there was still a considerable amount of liberal jurisprudence to object to. Accordingly, Reagan's second Attorney General, Edwin Meese, announced that the Reagan administration was committed to a jurisprudence of original intention,[58] and the Reagan Justice Department's Office of Legal Policy began compiling lists of cases that should be overruled because they were inconsistent with originalist principles.[59]

By the 1990s, however, the political situation had changed. The Supreme Court had a conservative majority. Its docket reflected a conservative policy agenda. A reflexive posture of judicial restraint increasingly made less sense. The question was no longer what courts should not do. It was what the courts should do.[60]

In the meantime, conservative litigators and conservative public interest firms began bringing a series of federalism and rights claims that promoted conservative values and attacked liberal laws and policies.[61] As Steve Teles has explained, conservative public interest lawyers discovered an important structural bias in public interest lawyering in the United States—one that was already known to liberal lawyers in the previous generation.[62] In general, there are greater rewards for bringing cases that *challenge* government discretion and authority than for bringing cases that *defend* it.[63] Put another way, claims that promote liberty and seek to limit government discretion tend to work better for public interest firms than claims that hope to buttress government power. First, funders for public interest litigation are more impressed by challenges that succeed in striking things down or halting government policies; second, governments already have a group of lawyers to defend their actions.

This structural feature of public interest work produced a bias toward libertarian rights claims and away from traditional conservative defenses of government authority. For example, lawyers representing Christian conservatives tended to make rights claims under the Free Speech and Free Exercise Clauses rather than defend municipal governments from Establishment Clause claims.[64] The result is that conservative litigators did what liberal litigators had done decades before: they began producing a series of rights claims that required courts to use judicial review to vindicate.

The Supreme Court's conservative majority now began to use judicial review energetically, to protect the rights of states, commercial advertisers, and conservative Christians; to limit liberal civil rights laws, and to strike down liberal affirmative action programs and campaign finance regulations.[65] These decisions, Thomas Keck explains, "created what we might think of as a 'policy feedback' effect, with the Court's protection of conservative rights claims fostering the development of organized conservative interests committed to defending judicially enforceable rights, and with those interests, in turn, demanding ever more active judicial protection."[66] As the Court's docket changed, originalism took on a new role. It was no longer enough to justify judicial restraint against liberal rights claims; now originalism had to explain and justify an increasingly active use of judicial review to protect conservative rights and values.[67]

By the turn of the twenty-first century, originalism had largely shed its role as a theory of judicial restraint and majoritarianism. Instead, originalism had become a theory that held that courts should actively protect important rights, structures, and interests from interference by the political branches. Its central rationale was no longer majoritarianism but judicial duty to confront unconstitutional laws and executive actions.[68] Conservative judges and Justices now used originalism to argue that they were required to strike down laws and ignore majority will when the Constitution's original meaning—or the basic structural assumptions of the Constitution—required it. (At the same time, primarily because of abortion and gay rights, conservative politicians continued to pretend that Earl Warren was still Chief Justice, and warned the public against elitist judges legislating from the bench.)

Conservative intellectuals sought to create a new vocabulary to explain the transformation. A few conservative intellectuals attempted to rehabilitate the concept of "judicial activism" in defense of original meaning and limited government.[69] Others distinguished between judicial *activism* (now seen as a misleading term) and judicial *engagement* (to protect individual liberty and limited government);[70] between judicial *passivism* (bad as a general principle) and judicial *restraint* (in appropriate cases);[71] or between judicial *deference* (often bad) and judicial *constraint* (i.e., being constrained by the Constitution's original meaning).[72]

Once again, the shift from originalism as a theory of majoritarianism and judicial deference to originalism as a defense of judicial engagement was gradual and generational, with many intermediate positions. The oldest group of conservative originalists, which included Raoul Berger, (b. 1901), Robert Bork (b. 1927), Lino Graglia (b. 1930), Edwin Meese (b. 1931), and Antonin Scalia (b. 1934), generally argued for judicial restraint in controversial cases—except, of course, for affirmative action, which conservative originalists believed was unconstitutional but never quite squared with originalism. Meese, Berger, and Graglia claimed that the Warren Court's incorporation of the Bill of Rights against state governments was inconsistent with originalism.[73] Movement conservatives would later abandon that position—which was not well supported historically.[74] Moreover, the notion that the Bill of Rights did not bind state and local governments made little sense strategically as the focus shifted from the Warren Court's criminal procedure decisions to conservative constitutional challenges to state and local restrictions on commercial speech, land use, and gun rights.

In its early incarnation, originalism was closely linked to majoritarianism and the rejection of liberal rights claims.[75] Scalia's 1989 Taft Lecture, *Originalism: The Lesser Evil*,[76] argued that a central reason to adopt originalism was that it forced judges to restrain themselves and respect majority will.[77] As the Supreme Court's docket changed, however, the central cases before the Court involved conservative requests to exercise judicial review, in cases brought by conservative public interest firms and litigators and supported by conservative amicus briefs written by conservative law professors and think tanks.[78] Fidelity to original meaning was often (but not always) a justification.

Conservative legal intellectuals increasingly argued that the courts should exercise judicial review to strike down unconstitutional laws and policies, cheering on the Rehnquist and Roberts Courts when they did so. Scalia himself joined or wrote many of these opinions. Like many conservative jurists, he retained the older rhetoric of judicial restraint and majoritarianism primarily for prominent "culture war" cases, especially those involving abortion and gay rights.[79] Justice Clarence Thomas (b. 1948) adopted even more forceful originalist rhetoric, arguing in 1995 for rolling back substantial parts of the New Deal settlement.[80] Thomas, even more than Scalia, became a hero to the younger generation of conservative legal intellectuals who sought to use the courts to advance conservative constitutional principles.

As with liberals, the transition between generations was gradual rather than sharp. The older generation of conservative originalists like Bork, Scalia, and Graglia, essentially accepted the New Deal settlement and the progressive theory of judicial restraint that came with it. In the 1980s, libertarian intellectuals like Bernard Siegan and Richard Epstein proposed that courts once again protect economic liberties under the Fourteenth Amendment.[81] But most of the older generation of originalists disagreed; they had absorbed the progressive critique of the Old Court and were not about to change their minds: *Griswold, Roe* and *Lochner* were equally illegitimate.[82]

By contrast, younger generations of conservative legal intellectuals were far more willing to question the New Deal and reject the nostrums of judicial restraint—which, they correctly understood, had been borrowed from their political adversaries, the progressives.[83]

A Federalist Society debate in 2013 between Judge J. Harvie Wilkinson, III (b. 1944) and Georgetown University Professor Randy Barnett (b. 1952) symbolized the evolution of conservative theories about the Constitution.[84] The debate was entitled "RESOLVED: Courts are too Deferential to the Legislature," a proposition that would have come as a shock to the first generation of conservative originalists like Bork, Berger, and even the early Scalia.

Wilkinson, who supported the Rehnquist Court's federalism revolution, took a position roughly analogous to John Hart Ely's attempt at a middle way. In his view, originalists could and should use judicial review to protect the Constitution's structural guarantees, but not to adjudicate substantive disputes.[85] This approach distinguished modern conservative originalists from the activism of the *Lochner* Court and the Warren Court.[86] Wilkinson rejected the idea that originalists should use the Fourteenth Amendment to protect new rights, including economic liberties.[87] This was no better than the liberal judicial activism that conservatives had long criticized. [88] In his 2012 book *Cosmic Constitutional Theory: Why Americans Are Losing Their Inalienable Right to Self-Governance*,[89] Wilkinson described the Court's decisions in *Heller* and *McDonald*, which recognized an individual right under the Second Amendment, as nothing more than judicial activism, and even compared them to the *bête noir* of constitutional conservatism, *Roe v. Wade*.[90]

In one respect, Wilkinson's position was consistent with familiar originalist themes: disputes over hot button social issues should be left to majorities to decide, and the federal courts should not reach out to recognize novel constitutional rights claims. His views, however, were increasingly out of step with the conservative movement's constitutional vision. During the 2013 Federalist Society debate, the room, filled with younger conservatives, was mostly on Barnett's side.[91]

Barnett, who represented a younger generation of libertarian conservatives—most of them younger than himself—had helped develop the constitutional arguments against Obamacare.[92] He argued that the concept of "judicial restraint" was a snare that kept courts from enforcing the Constitution.[93] Barnett would eventually assert that *Lochner v. New York*—the central target of Robert Bork's early originalist arguments—was actually correctly decided.[94] He was not alone: George Mason Law Professor David Bernstein (b. 1967) wrote a 2011 book entitled *Rehabilitating Lochner: Defending Individual Rights against Progressive Reform*.[95]

Meanwhile Chief Justice Roberts (b. 1955), who was three years younger than Barnett, had not gotten the memo: in his 2015 dissent in the same-sex marriage case, *Obergefell v. Hodges*, he accused the majority of behaving just like the Justices in *Lochner v. New York.* It was not meant as a compliment. For Roberts, *Lochner* was the very symbol of what judges should not do.[96]

Similar developments occurred in administrative law. During the early years of the Reagan administration, conservatives argued for deference to administrative agencies. Justice Scalia offered a famous defense of the *Chevron* doctrine[97]—which requires courts to defer to reasonable agency interpretations of the statutes administrative agencies enforce—in the *Duke Law Journal* in 1989, the same year as his majoritarian defense of originalism.[98] By the 2010s, Barack Obama had demonstrated how liberals could use administrative agencies to advance their policy goals in areas ranging from environmental law to immigration. Conservatives, who had never been all that happy with the administrative state in the first place, began to turn against judicial deference to administrative agencies. *Chevron,* once defended by conservatives, was now a conservative target.[99]

C. The Return of Liberal Skepticism About Judicial Review

While all this was going on, liberal legal intellectuals' views on the courts were evolving in almost a mirror image. Liberals were frustrated by the Rehnquist Court's federalism revolution and by the conservative majority's increasingly assertive use of judicial power.[100] For many liberal legal intellectuals, the 2000 decision in *Bush v. Gore* seemed like the last straw—only it wasn't, because the Supreme Court continued to grow even more conservative after Justice Alito replaced Justice O'Connor in 2006. As Barry Friedman pointed out in his article on the cycles of constitutional theory, "All of a sudden, the talk among *progressives* is of complaints about judicial supremacy and the hegemony of the Supreme Court. We have come full circle: the early 2000s are the early 1900s all over again, and one might as well forget that the Warren Court happened in the middle."[101]

In fact, the early twenty-first century was different from the twentieth century in one important respect. The long-term trend of both parties investing in judicial review tempers the cycling of positions between judicial review and judicial restraint. This secular trend is one aspect of Skowronek's concept of the "institutional thickening" of politics over time.[102]

In the early twenty-first century, American politicians and legal intellectuals depend so heavily on the federal judiciary for so many things that it is almost unthinkable that they would willingly renounce judicial review as a tool of policy advancement.[103] For example, it is difficult to believe that most liberal constitutional theorists will wholly abandon judicial review and simply adopt the progressive critique of judicial review from the 1920s and 1930s. Even given today's deep disillusionment with judicial review in the hands of a conservative judiciary, liberal legal intellectuals continue to defend a large number of liberal civil rights and civil liberties precedents—for example *Roe* and *Lawrence*—and there are still other precedents they would like to extend further. (Similarly, after decades of conservative judicial hegemony, conservative legal intellectuals will continue to have strong interests in preserving their own favored set of precedents and doctrines—for example, *Heller* and *Citizens United*.) In short, liberal intellectuals in the late twentieth and early twenty-first centuries have been skeptical of judicial power and judicial supremacy, but not quite as skeptical as their progressive forebears.

Liberal theorists have taken a variety of approaches to criticize the conservative decisions of the Reagan regime. The first strategy was popular constitutionalism, which has many variations. Mark Tushnet (b. 1945) argued that judicial review was by nature hopelessly conservative, and in a 1999 book, he argued for "taking the Constitution away from the courts."[104] Larry Kramer (b. 1958), dean of the Stanford Law School, advocated popular constitutionalism as a counterweight to the Court's conservative elitism.[105] Robert Post (b. 1948) and Reva Siegel (b. 1956) argued that courts should be informed by legislative interpretations of the Constitution—as part of their larger theory of "democratic constitutionalism."[106]

A second strategy offered new variations on progressive ideas of judicial restraint. Cass Sunstein (b. 1954) revived Alexander Bickel's ideas about prudentialism. But instead of focusing on Bickel's passive virtues, Sunstein offered a theory of "judicial minimalism," in which courts would refrain from deciding too much, and would offer rationales that could command assent from a broad spectrum of public opinion.[107]

A third strategy was preservationist—explaining why the achievements of liberal constitutionalism in the previous New Deal/Civil Rights regime had been legitimate and why they should not be disturbed by conservative courts. Precisely because judicial review had become so important to both parties by the end of the twentieth century, preservationist strategies had important differences from progressive arguments of the 1920s and 1930s for judicial restraint. Because older precedents should be preserved, courts should continue to strike down laws and executive actions that violated the constitutional principles of the previous (liberal) regime. Bruce Ackerman's (b. 1943) project sought to show that Americans had amended their constitution outside of Article V through a series of "constitutional moments," and that conservatives had so far failed to create a new constitutional moment that would justify deviating from the New Deal and the Civil Rights revolution.[108] David Strauss (b. 1951) argued for a common law theory of constitutional interpretation, which, he argued, was superior to originalism.[109] Courts should avoid sudden shifts in doctrine (for example, to the right) and respect liberal precedents.

A fourth strategy was to borrow a page from Hugo Black and the Warren Court and reinterpret originalism as a liberal theory of interpretation. Akhil Amar (b. 1958) and yours truly (b. 1956) argued for liberal versions of originalism that were tied to a narrative of democratic progress (in Amar's case) or constitutional redemption (in mine).[110]

Liberal legal intellectuals (with the exception of Amar and myself) also attacked originalism in much the same way that progressives had attacked the formalism of the Old Court and movement conservatives had attacked living constitutionalism. They argued that originalism was an incoherent philosophy of judging that allowed conservative judges to impose their personal and ideological predilections into the law.[111] Sunstein labeled the conservative Republican-appointed judges "Radicals in Robes."[112] Mitchell Berman (b. 1966) declared that "Originalism is Bunk."[113] Eric Segall (b. 1958) argued that modern originalism is little more than window dressing for conservative policies and that originalist judges conveniently jettisoned originalism whenever it got in the way of their preferred results.[114]

D. Looking Ahead

The 2016 election and the appointment of Justices Gorsuch and Kavanaugh supercharged liberal discontent with the Supreme Court. If we are near the end of the Reagan regime, it would make sense that legal intellectuals affiliated with the current opposition party (the Democrats) would engage in a version of the progressive triptych: advocating judicial restraint; criticizing the reasoning of the current conservative majority as political, incoherent and arbitrary; and demanding deference to democratic decision-making. And if, as I expect, the Democrats create the next constitutional regime, *relative* skepticism about judicial review will continue until Democrats regain control of the Supreme Court and the lower federal courts through new appointments. That will change both the Court's personnel and, equally important, the selection of cases on its docket.

However, given the Trump administration's energetic attempts to flood the judiciary with young conservative jurists, that transformation may take some time. As a result, Felix Frankfurter's star may rise again among liberal legal academics, and we are likely to see new rounds of theoretical arguments for judicial restraint.[115] Only when a liberal Supreme Court majority is firmly in place and the docket of the Court has been fully transformed will a new cycle of liberal constitutional theories justifying strong judicial review emerge.

Even so, liberals today are in a very different position than progressives in the 1930s. They are heirs to a considerable liberal jurisprudence that protects civil rights and civil liberties and requires judicial review to defend it. Although we should probably expect more liberal theories that attack judicial supremacy and advocate judicial restraint in the face of a conservative judiciary, each of these theories will have to deal with this inheritance. They will have to contend with how—and how much—they wish to preserve previous liberal precedents such as *Roe v. Wade* and the gay rights decisions.

Conversely, the current generation of conservative and libertarian legal intellectuals, who have spent so much time and intellectual capital defending judicial engagement, will not soon abandon their views about judicial review. They will continue to argue that the Supreme Court should embrace judicial engagement to vindicate their constitutional values. Eventually, the ideological character of the courts will change. Yet like liberals in the 1980s, conservative legal intellectuals may still hold out hope that conservatives can once again obtain a Supreme Court majority and that the rightward march of constitutional jurisprudence can continue unabated. Some years later, a newer generation of conservative intellectuals will gradually recognize—to vary Sanford Levinson's metaphor—that Clarence Thomas and Antonin Scalia have left the building.[116] At that point, the slow, generational transformation of positions on judicial review will begin again.

9

How Cycles of Polarization and Depolarization Shape the Exercise of Judicial Review

I now turn to the cycle of polarization and depolarization in American politics. This cycle affects judicial review in four different ways. First, it alters the political supports for judicial review. Second, it undermines one of the important justifications for judicial review. Third, greater polarization increases the urgency of fights over judicial appointments. Fourth, and for the same reason, it encourages the parties to engage in constitutional hardball. To understand how polarization and depolarization affect judicial review, I'll start with a very famous case, *United States v. Carolene Products Corp.*[1] In my introductory course on Constitutional Law, *Carolene Products* is one of my favorite cases to teach.

Most law students know this case for two reasons. First, it was decided right after the Court's capitulation to FDR in the constitutional struggle over the New Deal. *Carolene Products* announces a new standard for judicial review of social and economic legislation. Instead of the federal courts closely scrutinizing laws that interfered with economic liberty, the Court announced that it would uphold social and economic legislation if it had a rational basis—that is, if it could be justified on any conceivable basis.[2] Second, after announcing this new highly deferential test, the Court dropped a footnote—the famous footnote four of *Carolene Products*.[3] That footnote put down a marker. The Court would not defer to the political branches in three different situations. First, it would not defer if explicit constitutional guarantees like those in the Bill of Rights were at stake. [4] Second, it would not defer if the political branches tried to undermine or skew democratic processes like voting, public discussion, and representation to keep themselves in power.[5] Third, the Court would not defer if the political branches targeted "discrete and insular minorities" such as religious and racial minorities; that is because majorities might scapegoat them in ways that would prevent them from defending themselves in ordinary democratic politics.[6]

The Cycles of Constitutional Time. Jack M. Balkin, Oxford University Press (2020). © Jack Balkin 2020.
DOI: 10.1093/oso/9780197530993.001.0001

Carolene Products is famous for its articulation of the rational basis test and for footnote four. But if we look past its doctrinal importance, we can see that it is important for another reason. It tells us what the job of courts is in the constitutional order—and particularly what the job of courts is in a *depolarized* constitutional order.

A. The Judiciary in a Depolarized World

In the depolarized world imagined by *Carolene Products*, the job of courts is settle basic rules of constitutional democracy—which might include federalism, the separation of powers, and the rules of democratic competition. Everything else is a matter for politicians to fight about. Mark Graber calls these last issues the "spoils of government."[7] He argues that once American politics began to depolarize at the turn of the twentieth century, it made increasing sense to think of courts as playing this kind of role.[8] The bitter party clashes that characterized much of the nineteenth century—and had even led to civil war—began to fade away, and politics began to look very different. In this new dispensation, courts should set down the basic rules of fair political combat, leaving everything else to be worked out in political struggle.

Of course, what fell into these two categories—the background rules of political combat and the "spoils" of successful politics—could still be deeply and bitterly contested. For example, conservative Republicans thought that federalism and liberty of contract meant that many federal labor laws were off the table, while progressives disagreed. But what both sides had in common was the belief, or the faith, if you will, that courts could be left to work out these basic rules, leaving politicians to fight over what they wanted to fight over, which is money, property, and political power.[9]

In this respect, the theory of *Carolene Products* is a mid-twentieth-century liberal answer to the question of how courts should settle the basic rules of political combat. It is a special case of a more general approach, one possible answer among many possible answers to how courts should behave in a depolarized world.

Graber calls this new dispensation of judicial and political power "the long state of courts and parties."[10] How long did it last? It begins as depolarization commences in the beginning of the twentieth century and it ends when the parties are fully repolarized, sometime in the middle of the Reagan regime. For convenience, we can pick the early 1990s as the conclusion. Between those two endpoints, it was really possible for many people to believe that courts were supposed to set up the basic rules of the game, get out of the way, and let the players play the game.

What may seem remarkable is that this account arises at the same time as American legal realism, which rejected legal formalism and understood judging as ineluctably political. But if one believes that the Constitution, like other legal materials, gives judges abundant discretion, it is but a short step to try (unsuccessfully, as it turned out) to cabin judges' role to a limited set of questions, while leaving most issues to politics.[11] This vision clearly influences the Legal Process School that emerged after World War II, including Henry Hart and Albert Sacks's idea of "institutional settlement,"[12] and Herbert Wechsler's idea that judicial decisions should be premised on "neutral principles of constitutional law."[13] Unfortunately for Wechsler, he found himself unable to square his theory with *Brown v. Board of Education*.[14]

Yet even advocates of the civil rights and civil liberties revolution of the 1960s who disagreed with Wechsler could understand the Court's role as the elucidation of basic principles (although younger generations of thinkers, to be sure, did not). An example is Ronald Dworkin's vision of the Supreme Court as the "forum of principle."[15] Dworkin would eventually argue that judicial review was justified in order to protect fundamental rights and liberties in an expansive "constitutional conception" of democracy.[16]

In the alternative, liberals could argue that judicial review was necessary to make the political system work fairly and the processes of representation more democratic. John Hart Ely's *Democracy and Distrust*, published in 1980, in the twilight of the New Deal/Civil Rights regime, made precisely this case for the Warren Court's rights revolution.[17] That revolution, Ely argued, was perfectly justified given the proper role of courts in a democratic system—enforcing the basic ground rules of politics and then getting out of the way. The Warren Court's activism was nothing more than the federal courts fulfilling their basic structural purpose: to protect democratic processes. All the Warren Court did, Ely insisted, was to finally live up to the promise of the *Carolene Products* footnote.[18]

In his judicial confirmation hearings in 2005, Chief Justice Roberts, who had graduated from the Harvard Law School in 1979—two years before I did, and a year before Ely published his famous book—compared the work of a judge to an umpire.[19] The umpire is supposed to call balls and strikes, but not otherwise interfere in the game. He is supposed to stay in the background and not be the focus of attention.[20] Roberts's comparison of judges to umpires was admittedly difficult for many people to accept.[21] By the time Roberts spoke, American politics was as polarized as it had been in many years, and it was about to get even more polarized. Control of the federal courts—and particularly the Supreme Court—had become one of the greatest "spoils of government."[22]

What Roberts was doing, in fact, was harking back to the world in which he grew up and attended law school, a world in which it was still possible to believe in a depolarized vision of politics, in which courts set the basic rules of the game, and the parties fought over money, government programs, and political power. It was a conservative spin on the same vision of courts and democracy that had motivated Ely. Of course, what Ely regarded as just making the game of politics fairer, movement conservatives regarded as the courts arrogantly stepping into the game and changing the score on behalf of their favorite team.

Indeed, one of the great ironies of Roberts' remarks about judges as umpires is that Roberts himself was a foot soldier in the Reagan Justice Department and the conservative movement. Like other conservative legal intellectuals, he strongly believed in the separation of law from politics. Yet he was part of the very movement that had helped undermine this vision of courts and politics. That may seem puzzling at first, because conservatives regularly blamed liberals for the original sin of hijacking the Constitution and destroying the law/politics distinction (just as progressives had blamed an earlier generation of conservative jurists before the New Deal). But liberals had operated in a bipartisan, depolarized legal world. Ironically, it was the very success of the conservative movement that had made American law and politics increasingly polarized, and thus helped make Roberts's vision of courts as neutral umpires seem increasingly naïve.

The depolarized world in which both John Roberts and I grew up was captured in important works of political science. One example is the work of the great Yale political scientist Robert Dahl. Dahl argued that the Supreme Court is essentially a majoritarian institution that enforces the values of national political majorities—or, more precisely, the values of national political elites.[23] The great Harvard political scientist Robert McCloskey offered a similar analysis, arguing in his famous phrase that "the Court [has] seldom strayed very far from the mainstreams of American life."[24] Dahl's and McCloskey's account of the Supreme Court as a fundamentally majoritarian institution was a lesson that a generation of political scientists—and law professors influenced by political science, like me—took to heart.[25] One purpose of this book is to rethink these assumptions—assumptions that I myself long held—in a world of high polarization and increasing constitutional rot.

A depolarized politics has important consequences for the political supports of judicial review. In a depolarized party system, politicians of both parties find judicial review useful for three central reasons. First, as the discussion of *Carolene Products* implies, courts are expected to settle the basic constitutional ground rules of politics and leave fighting over the "spoils of government" to politicians. Second, given that there is an overlapping elite consensus at the national level, courts can help discipline local and regional outliers who depart from that national elite consensus.[26] Third, courts are useful to decide difficult issues that would otherwise split a party's electoral coalition.[27] That matters especially in a depolarized politics in which political parties may not be ideologically coherent.

These political supports for judicial review presuppose that political and legal elites have a lot in common and tend to agree about many things that might divide the general public. Judges, and especially Justices, tend to be chosen from this group of national political elites. They travel in elite networks and are socialized into this elite consensus. In terms of Lawrence Baum's theory of the audiences for judges, national political elites form an important peer group or "audience" for federal judges and Supreme Court Justices.[28]

Of course, what elites agree on can change over time. In the 1890s, elites believed in scientific racism, so it's no surprise that in 1896 the Supreme Court gave its blessing to Jim Crow laws in *Plessy v. Ferguson* by a vote of 8–1.[29] Following World War II, national elite views on race had changed considerably, and in 1954, *Brown v. Board of Education*, which overruled *Plessy v. Ferguson* in the area of elementary and secondary education, was decided 9–0.[30]

The notion that Democratic and Republican political elites—and therefore Democratic and Republican appointed-Justices—could share so many common assumptions about the world and about public policy seems positively bizarre to us in our currently hyperpolarized world. But it helps explain why sexual revolution-era cases like *Griswold v. Connecticut* and *Roe v. Wade* were decided by bipartisan majorities of Democratic and Republican-appointed Justices. Elite values generally supported contraceptive rights and viewed abortion as a public health issue.[31] Our contemporary culture-war framing of these cases was several years away.

Perhaps even more remarkably, a year before *Roe v. Wade*, in 1972, a bipartisan coalition of Justices decided *Furman v. Georgia*,[32] temporarily halting the death penalty in the United States, an unthinkable proposition only ten years later. *Furman* reflected the then-existing elite consensus that something had to be done about the criminal justice system and the death penalty. All of this happened, however, as the New Right was emerging—and what we now call the culture wars had begun to heat up. But in 1976, none of the Justices, save possibly William Rehnquist, had very much of a connection to the powerful conservative movements that would soon dominate American politics.

As is so often true of the Supreme Court, the Burger Court Justices were a lagging indicator of the direction of American politics.

The fact that Justices were usually selected from a pool of legal and political elites who, in turn, shared many common assumptions, helps us better understand Dahl's arguments about the Supreme Court and judicial review. A group of Justices repeatedly selected from this pool *would* be unlikely to stray very far from the center of national elite opinion (or from the dominant national coalition, which might involve politicians in both parties). And if the Court did get out of line, new judicial appointments would soon take care of the problem, recalibrating the Court's membership—and the median Justices—to better match the center of elite opinion. In 1957, Dahl's statistics showed that presidents rarely had to wait very long to get a Supreme Court appointment,[33] and begin moving the Supreme Court in their preferred direction. FDR's problem, Dahl explained, was that he had to wait more than four years to get his first appointment—which, according to Dahl, was a very rare occurrence. If FDR had been just a bit more fortunate, the New Deal conflict would have gone much more smoothly.[34]

Dahl's assumption of regular appointments, of course, was eventually undermined. Before the middle of the twentieth century, Justices lived shorter lives, and it was not uncommon for Justices to retire early. Charles Evans Hughes resigned to run for president in 1916 (he later rejoined the Court as Chief Justice); Justice John H. Clarke retired to campaign for the League of Nations; Justice Arthur Goldberg retired to become UN Ambassador; Justice James F. Byrnes retired to run FDR's Office of Economic Stabilization, which effectively made him the nation's chief domestic policy advisor.[35] It was very common for judges to be drawn from the ranks of politicians and political advisors, and sometimes to return to those ranks. This reinforced their connections to the views of other political elites.

Beginning in the 1980s, Justices began to live much longer, and almost all of them were selected from state or lower federal courts.[36] This created a more professionalized scheme for judicial selection. It also meant that presidents got fewer opportunities to select new Justices. As a result, there were many fewer opportunities to adjust the Court's center.

In a depolarized model of politics, the median Justice—or Justices—serve two different functions that are often confused. First, they cast the deciding votes in the most contested cases. Second, they also tend to reflect the center of popular opinion, and where popular and elite opinion diverge, the median Justices tend to reflect the center of elite opinion.

In a strongly polarized politics, the median Justices still cast the deciding vote in the most contested cases. But there is no longer a guarantee that the median Justices' views will be close to the center of either popular *or* elite opinion. For example, Anthony Kennedy remained largely on the right as popular opinion moved to the left on many issues. With Kennedy's retirement, the median Justice became John Roberts, a movement conservative who is far to the right of the center of the country.

Perhaps more important, in a polarized world, the very idea of an *elite* consensus dissolves; elite opinion becomes bimodal—so that it has, strictly speaking, no center to it.

B. The Changing Audience for Judges

Strong polarization upsets many of the background assumptions about judicial review in a depolarized world. Consensus among national political and legal elites gradually vanishes. Bipartisan agreement about key social issues becomes the exception rather than the norm. And because judges continue to be selected from legal and political elites, they mirror this growing divide.

In a depolarized era, elite education and socialization helped guarantee convergence on a wide range of issues and values. But in a highly polarized era, the more educated you are, the more you are likely to disagree sharply with elites from the other party, and engage in motivated reasoning about facts.[37] Media consumption habits exacerbate these divisions. The conservative movement now has its own media, which portray the world quite differently than the "mainstream" media consumed by liberal elites.[38]

Elite social networks no long narrow differences and maintain a rough conformity in elite opinion. Quite the opposite: in a polarized world, social networks of elites exacerbate polarization and help keep politics polarized. Legal and political elites now are organized in distinctive peer groups of liberal Democrats and conservative Republicans.[39] Legal and political elites no longer share a single audience or peer group whose opinion they respect or care about.

In their 2019 book, *The Company They Keep: How Partisan Divisions Came to the Supreme Court*,[40] Neal Devins and Lawrence Baum drew out these consequences of political polarization for Supreme Court decision-making. In an earlier work, *Judges and their Audiences*, Baum had pointed out that judges are especially influenced by their "audiences."[41] These are the people whose good opinion judges care about most, and before whom judges "perform." In most cases, the audience for judges is a collection of several different audiences, which include family, friends, social networks, and professional colleagues.

For Supreme Court Justices, who sit at the top of their profession, and who strongly identify with it, the most important audiences are political and legal elites, especially other prominent members of the legal profession, members of the Supreme Court Bar, and parts of the legal professoriate.[42] In other words, the most important audience for Supreme Court Justices is other elite legal professionals and legal intellectuals.

That is not altogether surprising. Judges and Justices are selected from groups of elite professionals and likely value professional status and influence over mere income. In fact, federal judges and Justices forego large sums of future income to achieve their power and status.[43] It is therefore likely that they especially value being held in esteem by fellow members of the elite groups from which they are selected.[44] This fact offers yet another reason why, in a depolarized politics, the Supreme Court is unlikely to stray very far from the views of national political and legal elites.

I've already pointed out that elite opinion is not static, but changes over time, and that judicial perspectives gradually change with it. What happens when politics polarizes? The answer is that elite opinion also polarizes, and judicial opinion as well.[45] Instead of a distribution of elite opinion organized around a common center reinforced by elite education and socialization, we get a bimodal distribution, with liberals agreeing with liberals and conservatives agreeing with conservatives, and an increasingly pronounced abyss between the two groups.

In fact, elites may tend to polarize earlier than the rest of the country does. That is because political activists tend to drive party polarization, and they include many highly educated people who either influence elite opinion or are part of political and legal elites themselves.[46]

As I noted previously, one of the key features of the Reagan regime is asymmetric polarization: Republicans moved farther and faster to the right than Democrats moved to the left. The development of elite institutions reflected these changes. The conservative movement believed that it was being unfairly shut out of cultural and legal power by a liberal hegemony. As a result, movement conservatives created their own counterinstitutions, including conservative media like Fox News (begun in 1996), conservative think tanks like the Heritage Foundation (founded in 1973), and conservative elite networks like the Federalist Society (begun in 1982).[47] These counterinstitutions produced and nurtured a set of conservative elites who became the new reference group for Republican-appointed judges and Justices.[48]

The result was a sharp bimodal distribution of elite opinion, with liberal Justices paying attention to (what used to be called) the "mainstream" of center-liberal elite opinion, and conservative judges and Justices paying attention to their cohorts in the world of conservative elite opinion. One of the ironies of conservative rhetoric during the Reagan era was its repeated assertion that liberal judges are elitists—that is, that they are influenced by liberal elites. Whether or not that is the case, conservative judges were no less influenced by elites—just by a different set of elites!

During the twentieth century, judicial candidates from both parties were vetted by the American Bar Association, a mainstream professional organization. Movement conservatives distrusted the ABA, thinking that it was controlled by the very liberal elites they sought to displace.[49] Instead, conservatives have turned to conservative policy networks like the Federalist Society and think tanks like the Heritage Foundation to identify and vet judicial candidates.[50] The Federalist Society is officially nothing more than a society for debating and discussing legal issues, and does not make official recommendations on either policy or personnel. Instead, all of the ideological work is done by individuals and groups who are important leaders within or are otherwise connected with the Federalist Society. The Federalist Society operates as a networking and credentialing organization, helping fellow conservatives find each other, engage in joint projects, and nurture young lawyers.[51]

The Trump administration effectively made official what was already the unofficial practice. While campaigning for the 2016 presidential nomination, Donald Trump pledged to nominate Supreme Court justices from a list preapproved by people affiliated with the Federalist Society and the Heritage Foundation.[52] Once in office, Trump administration officials worked with Leonard Leo, the executive vice president of the Federalist Society, to pick the administration's judicial nominees.[53]

Today, conservative jurists are picked from a peer group of fellow conservative legal elites. Conservative legal intellectuals have their own organizations, think tanks, and conferences; they are part of a larger set of conservative intellectual, professional, and political networks. These conservative social networks are the central audience for conservative judges' performances as judges.[54] This means that conservative judges really don't care all that much about what liberal elites think, much less about the views of the general public. They care far more about what other conservative elites think.

A signal advantage of these counterinstitutions is that conservatives can be more confident that properly vetted candidates will remain reliably conservative throughout their careers.[55] For this reason, it is far less likely that Justices like Sam Alito, Neil Gorsuch, or Brett Kavanaugh will drift to the center or the left the way that Harry Blackmun, David Souter, or Sandra Day O'Connor did. The newer Justices are firmly ensconced in elite networks of conservative lawyers and legal intellectuals, who constitute their most important audience and their most important source of professional and social validation. If their thinking evolves, it may be because conservative legal thought has evolved as well.

Because polarization has been asymmetric, the story is a little different for liberal judges and Justices. Unlike conservatives, liberals did not have to create counterinstitutions. Instead, they simply remained connected to mainstream institutions and elite professional networks, and to the American legal academy, which, by the middle of the Reagan regime, had long since ceased being a conservative institution, and had become overwhelmingly liberal. Eventually, in response to the success of the conservative movement, liberal legal elites began to create mirror image organizations like the American Constitution Society (ACS). But because liberals didn't have to retreat from the mainstream to create a counterestablishment, ACS and liberal think tanks never have had the same importance or the same credentialing functions that the Federalist Society and the Heritage Foundation possess.[56] The audience for liberal judges, therefore, is a more diffuse set of mainstream center-left institutions, and elite professional networks of lawyers and legal academics. But the bottom line is much the same: elite views are polarized. Liberal judges also don't care very much what conservative elites think about their work. They care far more about the good opinion and respect of liberal legal, political, and policy elites.

C. The End of Elite Consensus

In a world of strong political polarization, it no longer makes sense to say that the Supreme Court does not stray very far from the views of national political elites. Constitutional law does not develop in accord with an elite consensus, because elite opinion is bimodal and the center has been vacated. For the same reason, one must reevaluate Dahl's notion that the Supreme Court usually stays in touch with the center of the national political coalition. There is no bipartisan "national political coalition." There are only partisan coalitions that succeed each other, with very different views.

In many legal questions that do not touch on the major issues that divide the two parties, the work of the Justices continues as before. There are many unanimous opinions, and voting often cross-cuts liberal and conservative coalitions of Justices.[57] On the other hand, the Justices become increasingly predictable on ideologically salient issues that divide the two parties.[58] This effect is overdetermined. It happens in part because these cases draw the most media attention and are thoroughly vetted in elite legal networks. In addition, these cases may also generate a large number of amicus briefs from liberal and conservative elite lawyers and political networks. Amicus briefs not only offer the Justices materials they can use in writing their opinions; they also offer an additional signal to the Justices about what their respective audiences think.[59] In high-profile cases that generate the most press coverage and the greatest number of amicus briefs, cross-cutting majorities are most likely only for issues on which the two major political parties are not yet strongly divided.

In a depolarized world, the appointments process tended to keep Justices in line with national elite opinion. But now that elite opinion is bimodal, this moderating function of partisan entrenchment is hardly guaranteed, and any moderating effect may be accidental. At most, we can say that the Justices appointed by the dominant or opposition party reflect the center of that party's coalition, which may be far from the center of national popular opinion. For example, following Brett Kavanaugh's appointment, John Roberts became the new swing Justice. He is not a moderate. In fact Anthony Kennedy, the prior swing justice for many years, was not a moderate either. Kennedy is a conservative libertarian, voting with conservatives on most issues, and with liberals on a few.[60]

When the ideological distance between the most moderate liberal Justice and the most moderate conservative Justice is great, successive appointments can cause the Court's center to swing wildly from very liberal to very conservative (or back) with a single appointment. Mark Graber calls this phenomenon the "constitutional yo-yo,"[61] and although it can happen in a depolarized world, the effect is likely to be most striking when liberal and conservative elites are very far apart.[62] For example, when Justice Scalia died in February 2016, the Court had four liberals and four conservatives. Adding Obama's nominee, Judge Merrick Garland, would have produced a very different Court than adding Donald Trump's nominee, Judge Neil Gorsuch.

In 2016, the widening gap between liberal and conservative Justices was well understood by politicians of both parties. For that reason, Senate Republicans believed that they had an enormous stake in preventing President Obama from successfully making a Supreme Court appointment, and they refused to schedule any hearings for Judge Garland. Their gamble paid off when Donald Trump won the presidency.

D. The Breakdown of the *Carolene Products* Model

I noted previously that in a depolarized world there are three major reasons why politicians support judicial review. First, courts can set up the basic ground rules of democratic politics and leave politicians to fight over other matters. Second, judges can enforce national elite values against regional outliers in state and local governments. Third, courts can take on especially divisive issues that would split electoral coalitions. In a polarized world, these justifications increasingly make less sense. A different set of political supports for judicial review gradually replaces them.

In a polarized politics with a polarized judiciary, the distinction between the basic ground rules of constitutional democracy and the subjects of everyday political struggle—what Graber calls the "spoils of government"[63]—becomes increasingly untenable. In particular, the *Carolene Products* model—in which judges devote themselves to protecting fundamental rights and protecting the integrity of democratic processes while leaving other issues to ordinary political contest—breaks down. It becomes difficult for judges appointed by polarized parties to agree on when judges should intervene to protect democratic structures and minority rights and when to leave these questions to ordinary democratic struggle. This distinction, which lies at the heart of the *Carolene Products* model, was always tenuous even in a nonpolarized politics, but it becomes unworkable in a strongly polarized politics.

The problem is not that this approach is no longer necessary. The problem is not that when politics is polarized, parties no longer try to entrench themselves in power, cripple their political adversaries, suppress the voting rights of their opponents, target minority groups as scapegoats, or engage in zero-sum status politics. Quite the contrary: each of these bad behaviors may actually *increase* in a polarized world. As partisan conflict becomes increasingly bitter, and partisans try every trick in the book to gain power or stay in power, democratic structures may be increasingly at risk. Rather, the problem is that when both politics and the judiciary are so strongly polarized, it becomes very difficult to get judges with different political priors and different understandings of the world to agree on what judicial interventions are necessary to protect democracy or vulnerable minorities—or even agree on who the vulnerable groups are.

The parties begin to disagree about what democracy actually is, which minority groups actually suffer discrimination, and what interventions would actually help them. The parties develop liberal Democratic and conservative Republican conceptions of democracy, which tend to correspond to Democratic and Republican constituencies, and to the reforms that help Democrats and Republicans gain power or stay in power.

For example, Republican elites tend to believe that limitations on campaign contributions and corporate expenditures restrict freedom of speech, censor important voices, entrench powerful interests, and therefore undermine democracy; that voter impersonation fraud is real and pervasive and threatens democracy; that voter identification laws are necessary to prevent fraud and do not discriminate against minorities or the poor; that when Republican-controlled legislatures gerrymander districts to maximize Republican victories they are not discriminating against racial minorities; that there are no judicially administrable standards to prevent partisan gerrymandering—which may be a good thing; and that the Federal Voting Rights Act is an unreasonable interference in the right of states and local governments to organize elections. Democratic elites believe the opposite on all of these questions.

Similarly, Democratic and Republican elites disagree strongly about which minorities need protection in the democratic process and how best to protect them. Republican elites argue that whites, males, and conservative Christians have been unduly singled out and harmed by antidiscrimination laws and affirmative action. Swift enforcement of the death penalty is necessary to vindicate victims, many of whom are members of minority groups. The most vulnerable group of all is unborn children, who have been slaughtered in a holocaust caused by liberal abortion rights. Contraception and abortion rights and transgender rights are not sex equality issues. Protecting these rights may discriminate against and oppress conservative Christian religious dissenters. Protecting gays from discrimination in public accommodations and requiring private businesses to recognize same-sex marriages oppress people who regard homosexuality and same-sex marriage as sinful; moreover, these laws unfairly target conservative Christians as intolerant and bigoted.

Democrats disagree on virtually all of these issues of minority rights. They argue that courts should protect gays and transgender people from discrimination. They view reproductive rights as deeply connected to women's equal citizenship status and race-conscious affirmative action as necessary to secure equality. They argue that the criminal justice system and the system of mass incarceration pursued by politicians of both parties are tainted with racism and must be reformed. And they argue that allowing religious people to discriminate against gays is no more acceptable than allowing religious people to discriminate against blacks.

In short, in a polarized world, each party develops its own views about fundamental rights, fundamental structures, democracy, and the basic rules of politics.[64] Each party has a vision of what it means to protect democracy and minority rights that is a mirror image of the other party with few areas of overlap in the most salient controversies.

Equally important, the distinction between judicially enforceable democratic structures and the spoils of government begins to dissolve. Partisans may think that questions about voting rights, campaign finance, religious liberty, group status, and minority protection (or nonprotection) are key goals of political struggle. Status conflict is not something to limit and manage but something to openly advocate as a way of pleasing constituents and showing them that you are standing up for their interests and values. Put another way, polarization expands the class of things that politicians view as the spoils of political victory. Because polarization in the Reagan regime has been asymmetric, Republicans are a leading indicator of these changes, and Democrats a lagging indicator.

E. The Collapse of the Distinction Between High and Low Politics

In our 2001 article on partisan entrenchment, Levinson and I distinguished between "high politics"—basic constitutional values and principles—and "low politics"—the pursuit of partisan advantage.[65] We argued that it was naïve to doubt that judges would further their visions of high politics in constitutional controversies, but that it was inappropriate for them to engage in low politics—that is, to decide cases to benefit their favored political party. Our criticism of *Bush v. Gore* was precisely along these lines: we argued that the majority of the Republican-appointed Justices adopted legal positions designed to ensure that the Republican candidate, George W. Bush, won the election.[66] What was suspicious was that these legal positions conflicted with those Justices' usual views about "high politics": in particular, their considered views about equal protection, federalism, originalism, and judicial restraint.[67]

As politics polarizes, however, high and low politics may not push in different directions as they did in *Bush v. Gore*. When all of the conservatives are Republican appointees and all of the liberals are Democratic appointees, and when the two parties line up on opposite sides of almost every issue, it is likely that many of the parties' favored principles and policies will also enhance their electoral chances and undermine the electoral chances of the other party. Voting rights are a good example. Republicans defend partisan gerrymandering and voter identification laws while attacking the Voting Rights Act. All of these positions help Republicans electorally.[68] What helps Republicans electorally is increasingly what promotes their constitutional values.

As a result, when Justices on a polarized Court promote their appointing party's constitutional values, they may also be helping that party entrench itself politically. The danger is not cases like *Bush v. Gore*, in which high and low politics pushed in different directions. Rather, it is cases like *Shelby County v. Holder*,[69] which struck down section 4 of the voting rights act; *Rucho v. Common Cause*,[70] which held that federal courts had no power to consider claims of partisan gerrymandering; or *Janus v. AFSCME*,[71] which employed the First Amendment to defund public sector unions that normally vote Democratic. (Campaign finance law is another area in which this can occur.)

F. Disciplining Outliers Makes Less Sense

A second reason why politicians may support judicial review is that it allows national elites to discipline outliers in state and local governments. This idea, too, makes less sense in a polarized world in which political elites disagree strongly and the courts are ideologically polarized.

First, because elites disagree, it is more difficult to identify genuine outliers from a national consensus. Instead, there may simply be opposed sides in a national dispute, with legal elites in the two parties taking opposing positions.

Second, the idea of disciplining outliers is often connected to a story about the inevitable direction of constitutional development. For example, David Strauss calls the process of bringing outlier jurisdictions into line with national values "modernization."[72] That term strongly implies that the outliers are behind the times. They are simply slower to catch up with the rest of the country, and the Justices simply apply the final shove to bring them in line.[73] But as the two parties polarize, it becomes more difficult to predict the direction of history. If a few states move refuse to go in the direction of others, or actively move in the opposite direction, they could be the leading edge of a countertrend.[74] These states could be indicating that the "modernization" movement is not progress, but has gone too far, or in the wrong direction.[75] The breakdown of elite consensus means that there is no clear direction of either history or "progress."

G. The Federal Judiciary as Policy Vanguard

Politicians generally want courts to decide cases consistent with politicians' constitutional and policy values. Yet at the same time, they may also want courts to decide and resolve problems that threaten to split their party's coalition—no matter which way the courts decide. In a nonpolarized world, this second purpose—protecting electoral coalitions—is often as important as the first.[76] In a polarized world with conflict extension, the first purpose—furthering politicians' policy values—dominates the second. There are two reasons for this.

First, when the parties are strongly polarized and there is conflict extension, party coalitions tend to be less divided internally, so there are fewer issues that threaten to split coalitions apart, and more issues in which politicians (and highly polarized elites) simply want policy victories. (Again, because of asymmetric polarization, this effect may be felt more by Republicans than by Democrats, who still have many moderate and even conservative voters in their coalition.)

Second, periods of high polarization are also often periods of political gridlock at the national level, and it may be difficult for politicians to push their policy agendas through legislation. When this happens, it is less important for courts to take on issues that might fracture a party's coalition, and more important for judges allied with the party's values to achieve policy victories for constituents—victories that politicians can't achieve themselves through the political branches. In periods of sustained gridlock, the executive will continue to try to govern though administrative regulations, but these are subject to judicial review and they may also exacerbate gridlock and polarization.[77] The result is that, as politics polarizes and gridlock becomes the norm, the courts become ever more important to achieving a party's policy goals. In saying this, it is important to remember that courts police only a small segment of the national policy agenda, and there are many areas of policy that courts can't and don't touch.[78] But when politics is gridlocked, politicians will take what they can get.

Developing constitutional doctrine is only one aspect of what courts can do for gridlocked parties. Ideologically allied courts are also valuable to politicians in cases involving statutory interpretation, interstitial lawmaking, and review of administrative agency action. Gaining control of the federal courts allows politicians to push the party's commitments of interest and ideology on many different fronts simultaneously. It offers an end run around the gauntlet of bicameralism, the Senate filibuster rules, and the presidential veto.

Periods of high polarization and gridlock are usually also periods of intense party competition. Because judges shape the ground rules of political competition—both at the federal level and in the states—control of the courts becomes crucial to polarized parties, and especially so for a political party that fears that its coalition is vulnerable or fraying. Courts friendly to the dominant party can tilt the playing field in the party's favor—or help lock in existing advantages for the party—and help it stay in power.

Third, in periods of high polarization and gridlock, ideologically allied judges can perform other valuable functions. In those state governments that are not gridlocked, courts can uphold and legitimate even more radical policy changes. And, just as in nonpolarized times, courts can serve as crucial veto points to opposition party policies—whether these policies come from state and local governments controlled by the opposite party, or from administrative agencies and the White House.

In sum, in a strongly polarized world hobbled by political gridlock, judges do not serve as umpires of the political process; rather, they become a *policy vanguard*, especially for the party that controls the courts.[79] A vanguard is a force that is out in front. The courts become a policy vanguard not because they can do all that much, but because they can continue to do their work effectively when politicians can't. They can also intervene in highly charged areas of political contention. This creates the illusion that they are out in front—that is, a vanguard. Justices Scalia and Thomas, for example, became political heroes to conservative Republicans because they could often promote the Republican agenda better than Republican politicians could.

Politicians almost always want judges to do some of their work for them: that is the whole point of partisan entrenchment. But in the later stages of a regime, when the dominant party controls the federal courts, its politicians may find the role of judges as policy vanguards especially attractive. First, ideologically allied judges have been slowly building up a series of precedents that can support ever more daring innovations. Second, near the close of a political regime, ordinary politics is most likely to be dysfunctional, either because of partisan gridlock or because the dominant party is simply unable to move its agenda. Federal courts are not subject to this kind of gridlock or dysfunction. They continue to hear cases, and thus continue to achieve policy victories in an aging regime, furthering the dominant party's commitments of interest and ideology. Moreover, as noted earlier, in their decisions about the structure of the political process—campaign finance and voting rights—friendly courts can also help lock in partisan advantages.

The last ten years show how effectively national Republicans have made use of a conservative majority on the Supreme Court. Republicans could not easily repeal the McCain-Feingold campaign finance legislation. But the Roberts Court took care of the problem for them, striking down multiple provisions in successive litigation.[80] Republicans could never have gotten rid of the Voting Rights Act, one of the crown jewels of the Second Reconstruction. But the Roberts Court took care of it for them, by striking down the preclearance formula, hobbling the act, and allowing Republican-controlled state and local governments to change voting rules to their political benefit.[81] Republicans could never have rewritten the 1925 Federal Arbitration Act to limit the rights of employees and consumers, but the Roberts Court took up the task in a series of cases.[82] Congressional Republicans could not knee-cap class actions[83] or defund public sector unions through legislation. But, once again, the Roberts Court did it for them.[84]

What makes judges a policy vanguard is *not* that they are especially "activist" in these periods. It is that they are able to act when politicians can't, *and* that they actively promote the values of a highly polarized party. Once again, the feeling that judges appear to be "out in front"—that is, as a vanguard—is a framing effect of political polarization and dysfunction. Because of partisan entrenchment, judges often promote a regime's values and policy commitments, even in nonpolarized times. For example, during the 1960s and early 1970s the Supreme Court furthered the policy commitments of liberal Democrats and Republicans in the New Deal/Civil Rights regime. Conservative Democrats and Republicans complained about the "judicial activism" of those years. They argued that the Justices were behaving like politicians in robes. But there are three important differences between courts in a depolarized and polarized politics.

First, both the liberal Supreme Court majority and its critics during that period were bipartisan. And because the Supreme Court operated in a relatively depolarized party system, many kinds of deals were possible between the two parties. (The civil rights acts were bipartisan achievements, for example.) Today, the members of the conservative judicial majority are Republicans appointed by Republican presidents. Aside from the omnibus bills necessary to keep the government running, most major legislative initiatives are passed either by Democrats or Republicans, with relatively few cross-cutting votes.

Second, during the 1960s and early 1970s, the Supreme Court decided its cases in the midst of far larger reforms by the political branches. During those years Congress was also very active and passed lots of important legislation. Courts worked alongside of Congress and advanced many liberal policy goals, but they were not the central vehicle of policy development.[85] Much of what the federal courts did in this period was to police state and local governments, enforcing the Bill of Rights and the Equal Protection

Clause in the states.[86] Even in periods of divided government—for example, the Nixon administration—Congress was not gridlocked, and continued to churn out important legislation on a regular basis. Not so today. Late in the Reagan regime, Congress is relatively inept and inert. The executive branch compensates through executive orders and administrative regulations. In this world, the courts—even with their limited reach—are increasingly important players in policy development.

Third, an important element of the Warren Court's work involved upholding and legitimating new congressional enactments: the Civil Rights Acts and the Voting Rights act are the primary examples.[87] Today, in the polarized politics of the Reagan regime, there is much less federal legislation for the Supreme Court to legitimate because Congress achieves far less.

H. The Stakes of Judicial Appointments in a Polarized World

Polarization affects each party's strategy for judicial appointments. As we saw earlier, as politics polarizes, the audiences of elites that judges look to for validation also become polarized. This, in turn, helps keep judges from straying ideologically. As a result, in a polarized politics partisan entrenchment is more effective and has more predictable effects than in a depolarized politics. That makes appointing judges especially valuable and important when a party is strongly polarized. This is especially true of contemporary Republicans, who are a social movement party.

Because polarization has been asymmetric, and because Republicans are a social movement party, they have been especially focused on maximizing the number of strongly and reliably conservative judicial appointments.[88] Moreover, as noted earlier, the creation of counterinstitutions and a conservative elite culture helps produce a cadre of dependably conservative lawyers and helps reinforce conservative movement ideas. Democrats in the Clinton and Obama administrations, by contrast, have viewed judicial appointments as ways of pleasing demographic constituencies.[89] Because Democrats are a collection of various interest and demographic groups, with many moderates and even conservatives in the party, Democratic presidents have focused on increasing representation of various demographic groups—and especially on appointing more women and minorities to the bench.[90] This strategy does not put a premium on maximizing judicial appointments or on ensuring ideological conformity. It produces liberal appointments, but not necessarily strongly liberal appointments. There is nothing like the vetting and networking process of the Federalist Society and other conservative counterinstitutions.

We can see the results of asymmetric polarization in Supreme Court appointments. Beginning with Clarence Thomas, the Republican appointees (Thomas, Roberts, Alito, Gorsuch, Kavanaugh) have been "among the most conservative Justices to sit on the Court in the modern era," while "there are no strong liberals on the current Court."[91]

As noted earlier, in a gridlocked politics, judges become an important policymaking force, especially for the dominant party. Hence, in a polarized political system, political elites want ideological loyalty from judges above all. A judge who strays from the party line in a case is a lost opportunity for a policy victory.[92]

The incentives for ideological loyalty are defensive as well as offensive. If a party loses control of the courts, it stands to lose a great deal. Not only will it lose many policy fights, but a judiciary controlled by ideological opponents may strike down the party's achievements or interpret them narrowly. And because of life tenure, longer lifespans, and the modern disinclination of judges to retire early, losing control of the Supreme Court and the lower federal courts means that a party's political opponents may enjoy the upper hand for a long time.

Given these stakes, fights over the judiciary become especially heated in periods of increasing polarization. The Bork hearings in 1987—a relatively nonpolarized era—were a harbinger of more bitter battles to come. A strongly polarized politics creates incentives to engage in ever increasing rounds of constitutional hardball. It is no accident that many historical examples of constitutional hardball involve the federal judiciary. In 1863, Republicans increased the size of the Supreme Court to ten members to counteract the remaining Democrats on the Taney Court. Then, after Lincoln's assassination, they shrunk it to seven to prevent Democrat Andrew Johnson from appointing any Supreme Court Justices.[93] Following Ulysses S. Grant's election in 1868, Congress increased the size of the Court to nine members so that Grant could make new Republican appointments.[94] It is worth noting that FDR's court packing plan took place during a depolarized politics, and it failed in part because FDR faced resistance from within his own party.[95] Successful constitutional hardball, in other words, usually requires a unified and polarized party.

In the Reagan regime, constitutional hardball over the judiciary ramped up slowly and accelerated during the George W. Bush administration. Democrats were angry about how the Republican-controlled senate had treated President Bill Clinton's nominees, and filibustered several of George W. Bush's circuit court appointments in 2003.[96] Staring with the confirmation of Chief Justice John Roberts in 2005, Supreme Court Justices, once routinely confirmed by overwhelming margins, are now conformed largely on party line votes.[97] As political polarization proceeded, the parties have become more intransigent and unwilling to cooperate with each other on judicial appointments, and become ever more daring in breaking norms.

After Senate Majority Leader Mitch McConnell stalled President Obama's judicial nominations—including those to the DC Circuit—Democrats eliminated the filibuster for all appointments in the executive and judicial branches other than the Supreme Court.[98] Not to be outdone, after Justice Scalia died in 2016—opening up a seat that would give liberal Democrats a working majority—McConnell refused to allow any hearings for President Obama's pick, DC Circuit Judge Merrick Garland. McConnell's exercise in constitutional hardball paid off when Donald Trump won the 2016 election. After Democrats threatened to filibuster President Trump's first Supreme Court nominee, Neil Gorsuch, McConnell eliminated the filibuster for Supreme Court appointments, completing the elimination of the filibuster in judicial nominations.[99] In some sense, this development was inevitable in a polarized world, because neither party trusted the other to cooperate any longer. Given the role of federal judges and Justices in a period of polarization and gridlock, it is easy to see why.

After Justice Kennedy's retirement, both parties pulled out all the stops in the bitter battle over Brett Kavanaugh's confirmation.[100] Democrats accused Republicans of preventing a full investigation of allegations of sexual misconduct by Kavanaugh when he was a young man. Republicans, in turn, accused the Democrats of a smear campaign. The nominee himself, in an unprecedented tirade before the Senate Judiciary Committee, hurled angry invectives against the Democratic Senators and warned them, ominously, that "what goes around comes around."[101]

With the political polarization of both the parties and the United States Supreme Court essentially complete, constitutional hardball was no longer a rarity. It had become fully normalized. Some Democrats, enraged by the Kavanaugh nomination and by Senator McConnell's refusal to afford even a hearing to Merrick Garland, began to propose packing the Supreme Court as Reconstruction Republicans had during the 1860s.[102] McConnell, for his part, understood that his most important task was not to pass legislation but to confirm as many conservative judges as possible to the federal courts.[103] McConnell has used every stratagem available to him to speed the appointments process.[104] He recognizes that Republicans may not be in power forever, and therefore it is crucial to stock the federal courts with young, reliable conservative jurists. These judges can support the Trump administration and future Republican administrations, and they can check future Democratic ones.

We can summarize the lessons of this chapter in Table 9.1.

In general, a nonpolarized politics has a more stable conception of the division between law and politics, or—in Levinson's and my terms—between high politics and low politics. Members of both parties have greater confidence that the Supreme Court can be trusted to enforce the law in a principled fashion. In a world of high polarization, this degree of trust breaks down: partisans increasingly fear that the judges appointed by the other party can't be trusted to enforce the Constitution properly or according to law.

Table 9.1 Judicial Review and the Cycle of Polarization

	Depolarized World	Polarized World
Elite views	Consensus/convergence	Bimodal distribution
Audience for judges	Well-educated legal and political elites	Distinctive, separate groups of ideological/partisan elites
What is the relationship of the Supreme Court to elite/public opinion?	The Supreme Court never strays far from the center of the national political coalition/ elite opinion; median Justices keep the Court tethered to the political center	There is no necessary relationship between the median Justice and the center of public opinion; the Justices reflect the bimodal distribution of American politics
The role of courts in protecting the democratic process (*Carolene Products* model)	Possible, because of greater agreement among elites about what democracy requires	Implausible, because elites disagree strongly about what democracy requires
Distinction between high and low politics	Holds (in most cases)	Collapses
Judicial review of state and local governments	Courts protect national elite values, and police and discipline outliers	Concept of outliers makes less sense when there is no national elite consensus
Political supports for judicial review	Set the basic rules of the road, leaving politicians free to fight about other things	Serve as a policy vanguard
The "spoils of government"	Money, control of bureaucracy and government programs	Everything, including issues of status politics and ideological control over the federal judiciary
Stakes of judicial appointments	Modestly high	Extremely high
Judicial confirmations	Easy in many cases, often with bipartisan support	Intensely partisan, bitter, and difficult
Constitutional hardball	Less frequent	More frequent, especially about judicial appointments

Political gridlock exacerbates the problem of trust, because politicians view courts as a policy vanguard and engage in increasingly bitter fights over judicial appointments. When this happens, it becomes increasingly difficult to separate law from politics. The judiciary appears as the central prize of politics, and therefore not really separate from it. This increases distrust in the federal courts, and, in turn, exacerbates constitutional rot, as I will discuss in the next chapter.

10
Law in the Time of Constitutional Rot

In the last three chapters, I described how the cycles of regimes and polarization affect the federal courts. In this chapter, I explain the effects of constitutional rot.

Because political polarization usually accompanies constitutional rot, we already have a fairly good sense of how judicial review responds to the cycle of constitutional rot and renewal. The more pressing question, and the one I take up in this chapter, is what role, if any, the judiciary plays in protecting the nation from constitutional rot and pushing it in the direction of constitutional renewal. We can restate this inquiry as a series of related questions:

(1) Can the Supreme Court act as a counterweight to growing constitutional rot? Will the Supreme Court protect democracy and republicanism long enough until politics has enough time to correct itself?

(2) Once constitutional rot has set in, will judicial review counteract the slide into further political corruption, or the accelerating loss of democracy and republicanism?

(3) Once constitutional rot is advanced, will the Supreme Court help pull the country out of its death spiral and serve as the basis of renewal?

Sadly, the answer to each of these questions is no. In times of constitutional rot, coupled with high party polarization, courts are usually not the solution. They are more likely part of the problem. Courts will not drag us out of a period of constitutional rot; they will either do little to help or actively make things worse. Perhaps equally important, in periods of constitutional rot, the courts are a special prize of politics. Politicians are likely to engage in ever more outrageous hardball tactics to entrench their power in the courts. This, combined with the disappointing performances of Supreme Court Justices, compromises public trust in the federal judiciary and the Supreme Court.

Consider the last two periods of pronounced constitutional rot in American history: the years just before the Civil War, dominated by the Slave Power, and the Gilded Age, dominated by what Teddy Roosevelt called "the malefactors of great wealth."[1] In neither age was the US Supreme Court the great protector

The Cycles of Constitutional Time. Jack M. Balkin, Oxford University Press (2020). © Jack Balkin 2020.
DOI: 10.1093/oso/9780197530993.001.0001

of democracy and republicanism. Quite the contrary, the Supreme Court reflected the tenor of the times in both periods.

In the first period, the Supreme Court's most famous decision was *Dred Scott v. Sandford*,[2] which attempted (futilely, as it turned out) to lock in political advantages for the Slave Power, by declaring all federal territories open to slavery and prohibiting black citizenship forever.

The most famous decisions of the second period do not show the Court in a very good light either. They include *Pollock v. Farmers' Loan & Trust Company*,[3] which struck down the federal income tax; the *Civil Rights Cases*,[4] *United States v. Harris*, [5] *Plessy v. Ferguson*,[6] and *Berea College v. Kentucky*,[7] which gave the Court's blessing to Jim Crow; *Giles v. Harris*,[8] which punted on the question of black disenfranchisement; the *Sugar Trust Case*, [9] which attempted to cripple the use of the new antitrust laws against business monopolies; and *Adair v. United States*,[10] which hindered the organization of labor as a counterweight to capital.

The corruption of an age rubs off on the courts of that age. In a period of constitutional rot, the Supreme Court will be sullied as well.

A. Courts and Party Politics in an Age of Constitutional Rot

Why are the federal courts likely to be part of the problem rather than part of the solution in periods of constitutional rot? First, periods of constitutional rot are usually also periods of high political polarization. Political elites from different parties are increasingly unwilling to trust or cooperate with each other; they increasingly regard the other party as enemies of the republic.

National politicians pick federal judges and they attempt to entrench jurists who are most likely to be sympathetic to their values and interests. As we saw earlier, federal judges are usually drawn from well-educated elite classes, who have adapted to and even benefited from the political and economic circumstances that generated constitutional rot. They tend to share many of the assumptions of elites of similar age and background. And because periods of rot are usually periods of high polarization, the federal courts and the Supreme Court may be as polarized as other political elites, and engage in similar forms of motivated reasoning. As chapter 9 described, judges and Justices look to fellow members of political and legal elites as their primary audiences. As a result, their worldviews, their constitutional values, and their understanding of facts are likely to be highly polarized as well.

The regime's dominant party—Jacksonian Democrats during the heyday of the Slave Power, Republicans in the Gilded Age, and Republicans in the Reagan regime—sets the basic tone and agenda of politics. The dominant party also picks most of the regime's federal judges, and it appoints most of the Supreme Court Justices as well.

Because the dominant party is the regime's most important political power, it is also the primary enabler and driver of constitutional rot. The dominant party's politicians are likely to try to keep the party in power through increasingly aggressive and corrupt tactics. These tactics exacerbate constitutional rot. They undermine the political culture of representative democracy and the norms of mutual tolerance and institutional forbearance necessary to maintain republican government.[11] Members of the dominant party, however, will not see the dangers. Their mistrust of the opposition party has grown so great that they feel they cannot afford to surrender power, and that their tactics are necessary and justified. Members of the judiciary who were selected by the dominant party, and who owe their high-status positions to that party, will be more likely to accept their copartisans' view of the world. As a result, they are likely to acquiesce in—or even support—policies and actions that hasten constitutional rot.

B. Polarization Limits Judges' Abilities to Recognize and Halt Constitutional Rot

Because polarization encourages motivated reasoning by judges and Justices, it is more difficult for them to recognize and hold accountable political overreaching when it is performed by the party most closely allied with their elite networks. Judges and justices are likely to be influenced by the ideas, opinions, and factual understandings circulating in those elite networks. They are also more likely to look to and trust amicus briefs written by members of those networks. Thus, it is not at all necessary for judges and Justices to be consciously partisan or corrupt for them to acquiesce in or even accelerate features of constitutional rot. Constitutional rot does its work even if they are lawyers of the highest professional skill. In a strongly polarized system, the distinction between constitutional principles and partisan advantage tends to melt away. All that judges and Justices have to do is forcefully defend a strongly ideological conception of high politics and they will probably also serve partisan interests.

Thus, in *Trump v. Hawaii*,[12] the Republican-appointed Justices upheld President Trump's travel ban. They did so not because they were especially supportive of Trump or because they agreed with his hostility to Muslims, but rather because they were predisposed by their judicial worldviews to give presidents the benefit of the doubt in national security cases. A five-Justice conservative majority also insulated partisan gerrymanders from judicial scrutiny in *Rucho v. Common Cause*;[13] it crippled the Voting Rights Act in *Shelby County v. Holder*,[14] and undermined public sector unions in *Janus v. AFSCME*.[15] These decisions reflected long-held views of conservative political elites about justiciability, federalism, the Voting Rights Act, and the First Amendment. It is likely that none of the Justices in the majority in *Trump, Rucho, Shelby County*, and *Janus* were primarily motivated by partisan considerations. No doubt they sincerely believed that they had the better of the legal arguments. Yet it is not purely accidental that their views about constitutional principles helped Republicans and hurt Democrats in the current political context. Moreover, the Justices' understanding of the facts and of the social consequences of their decisions were surely affected by their most important audience—conservative political and legal elites.

C. Judicial Decisions Can Exacerbate Constitutional Rot by Increasing Economic Inequality

Economic inequality is another driver of rot, and in periods of rot the dominant party often actively promotes policies that increase economic inequality. Supreme Court Justices, who reflect the values and worldview of polarized elites, may be more likely to decide cases in ways that increase economic inequality. This is what happened during in the First Gilded Age, and it appears to be happening again in the Second Gilded Age.

To be sure, judges do not appropriate revenue and they cannot pass tax legislation on their own.[16] They can only affect the distribution of income and wealth indirectly. Nevertheless, they can overturn redistributive legislation; they can limit or hold unconstitutional features of antitrust and competition law; they can weaken or hold unconstitutional government programs that benefit the working class and the poor; they can narrowly construe or overturn measures that protect employees and consumers from overreaching; they can interpret federal rules and statutes to limit class actions and restrict the jury trial rights of workers and consumers; and they can hobble intermediate institutions like labor unions that can effectively bargain for employee wages. Finally, judges can strike down or limit campaign finance rules that seek to limit the ability of wealthy individuals and corporations to shape the political process and direct the political agenda of politicians. When wealth has disproportionate influence over the political process—as it does in periods of constitutional rot—politicians beholden to wealth tend to pass laws (and political appointees tend to make administrative decisions) that make wealthy people and corporations even wealthier, increasing their financial and political power in the process. Money that could have been spent on public goods is redistributed upward. These results produce cumulative advantages that help accelerate the trend toward oligarchy. Judges may not be the most important contributors to increasing economic inequality, but as constitutional rot grows, they do their share of the work.

D. Rot Increases as Courts Become the Policy Vanguard

As polarization increases, legislation becomes more difficult to achieve. The federal judiciary becomes increasingly valuable to politicians as an effective way to achieve important policy goals, to reverse state and local policies they disagree with, and to overturn administrative actions that they oppose. Because legislation is blocked, sympathetic federal judges and Justices of the Supreme Court become a party's policy vanguard. That is not because judges and Justices see themselves as political actors. Quite the contrary: their professional self-conception is that they are firmly separated from politics. Rather, it is because judges and Justices tend to share the factual understandings of like-minded political and legal elites and tend to be sympathetic to their normative views. In a strongly polarized world, liberal judges and Justices tend to agree with the worldviews and factual assessments of liberal political and legal elites, while conservative judges and Justices tend to agree with the worldviews and factual assessments of conservative elites.

Of course, judges decide cases that further politicians' policy goals all the time: that is one of the purposes of partisan entrenchment. Judges only appear to become the vanguard of policy change when most other avenues to policy development are blocked. The notion of judges as a policy vanguard is not something to be celebrated—rather, it is a feature of a strongly polarized and dysfunctional politics.

The temptation to employ the courts as a policy vanguard in times of legislative gridlock grows as the federal judiciary has grown more powerful over time. Today, after a century and a half of political construction, the federal courts and the Supreme Court are as strong as they have ever been. The long-term secular trend of politicians making the federal courts ever more powerful means that today, in a period of legislative gridlock, advanced rot, and high party polarization, courts become especially important in furthering the parties' agendas—and especially the agenda of the dominant party; that is especially so if the party has a majority of sympathetic Justices on the Supreme Court.

When courts are relatively powerful and politicians are relatively impotent, it is especially important for politicians to control the composition of the federal judiciary, because courts are able to do what politicians can't. This makes the federal courts increasingly a central focus of policy development, rather than merely an adjunct or assistant, as they are in more depolarized periods.

Unfortunately, when politicians rely on courts so heavily to do their jobs for them, this makes claims about the separation of law and politics seem ludicrous; it also puts enormous strain on the distinction between high and low politics. This increases public distrust of both politicians and judges and exacerbates polarization; both of these, in turn, exacerbate constitutional rot. The total level of public trust in the courts may remain fairly high, but it becomes increasingly polarized, with partisans gaining or losing trust in the Supreme Court depending on how it rules in high-profile cases.

E. Rot Generates Constitutional Hardball, Which Further Undermines Trust in the Courts

In order to advance their policy agendas, politicians are tempted to engage in constitutional hardball to secure control of the courts and lock in their advantages for decades. Hardball tactics lead to reprisals, which increases mutual distrust and the desire to use even more extreme measures to control the courts—or to prevent the other side from controlling them.

As I noted in the last chapter, fights over the judiciary seem to be a recurring motivation for constitutional hardball. In periods of high polarization, breakdowns of norms of interparty compromise and forbearance tend to cluster around the judicial selection process because so much is at stake.[17] If a party loses the federal courts, and especially the Supreme Court, its members worry that they may lose a great deal. At the same time, constitutional rot undermines the judiciary's own authority to deal with hardball tactics by politicians, because the Justices themselves are increasingly seen as the unwitting tools of politicians and as the ideological representatives of parties.

Kevin McMahon has argued that the present period of high polarization has undermined McCloskey's assumption that the Supreme Court is a majoritarian body that will not "stray[] very far from the mainstreams of American life."[18] Two of the Court's nine Justices, Neil Gorsuch and Brett Kavanaugh, were nominated by a president who lost the popular vote by some three million votes.[19] And four of the nine Justices— Gorsuch, Kavanaugh, Clarence Thomas, and Samuel Alito—were confirmed in close confirmation votes by Senators who represented a minority of the American public.[20] Indeed, although Democrats have won the popular vote in six of the last seven elections going back to 1992, both they and the Republicans have appointed four Justices each. If we add to this the bimodal distribution of conservative and liberal legal elites, and the fact that Chief Justice John Roberts is now the median Justice, there is little reason to think that the Supreme Court will have much of a relationship to the values of a national majority.

From the standpoint of constitutional rot, however, the concern is of a different order. It is that the Republican strategy of partisan entrenchment, abetted by a strategies of constitutional hardball, will pay dividends that undermine republican (with a small "r") government. A minority party will have bootstrapped itself into disproportionate power in the national political process, and it will use those gains to bootstrap itself into even more power. In order to help the party achieve this bootstrapping and self-entrenchment, it is not necessary for judges and Justices to be consciously partisan. Because of motivated reasoning, judges and Justices will have a hard time identifying and preventing misbehavior and constitutional rot. Indeed, the problem runs even deeper than this, for reasons I shall now describe.

F. Courts Cannot Protect Democracy Because They Do Not Agree About What It Is

A further reason why we cannot expect judges and Justices to save the country from constitutional rot follows from the political polarization of elites. Judges and Justices who are selected from these strongly polarized groups of elites can no longer agree on the requirements of democracy, and thus about what is necessary to protect democracy.

Judges appointed by the dominant party are likely to view democracy through the lens of the ideological assumptions and factual understandings of elites in the dominant party. However, when constitutional rot is fairly advanced, the dominant party is probably pushing the envelope to entrench itself and stay in power, including, of course, appointing judges ideologically allied with the party. It follows that the judges who would be least likely to police the dominant party's strategies for entrenching itself in power are the very judges who have recently been appointed by the dominant party—and who have been carefully vetted by elite organizations and networks ideologically allied with that party.[21]

Thus, if elites in the dominant party believe that restricting corporate expenditures in political campaigns is a serious example of political censorship, and that a system of unregulated campaign finance actually promotes rather than undermines democracy, ideologically affiliated judges are unlikely to disagree. If political elites in the dominant party believe that voter fraud by impersonation is a very serious problem for democracy, but that partisan gerrymandering is not, judges appointed by that party are likely to give politicians the benefit of the doubt. If political elites in the dominant party view the federal Voting Rights Act as a meddlesome interference in local democracy rather than a crucial guardian of the franchise, judges vetted and appointed by the party's elites are likely to concur. And if political elites believe that the most serious form of racial discrimination today is the discrimination visited upon whites seeking college admissions, and the nation's most disempowered and despised minority is conservative Christians, judges connected to these political elites will probably have similar views.

Above all, judges appointed by the dominant party are unlikely to view that party's activities as especially corrupt, as unfairly entrenching itself in power, or as undermining democracy and republicanism. Surely, they will insist, both parties play at the same games—and, if anything, it is the opposition party that needs the most careful scrutiny. The dominant party and its politicians are not doing anything out of the ordinary; they are responding to perfectly ordinary policy concerns, which judges need not agree with in all respects in order to uphold. If there are any problems with democracy, elections, and representation, surely the political process can take care of itself, unless, of course, the political process produces reforms—like campaign finance laws or section 4 of the Voting Rights Act—that these judges believe clearly violate the Constitution.

G. Constitutional Rot Generates a Reverse-*Carolene Products* Effect

In a period of constitutional rot, the theory of *Carolene Products*—that judges can and should exercise judicial review to protect the democratic process and vulnerable minority groups—loses much of its force.

First, as we have seen, elites from the two parties profoundly disagree about what would violate the principles of democracy and minority protection.

Second, in the Reagan regime, conservative judges and Justices have been increasingly skeptical of the theory of *Carolene Products*, because it seems to invite judicial intervention in ways that conflict with the constitutional views of political conservatives. Affirmative action offers a good example. Whites are not a discrete and insular minority and legislatures elected by white majorities are unlikely to be significantly prejudiced against them. This might counsel a lower standard of scrutiny for race-conscious affirmative action programs than for laws that burden racial minorities. But this asymmetry conflicts with the conservative theory of colorblindness. In *Schuette v. BAMN*,[22] Justice Scalia derided the *Carolene Products* theory as nothing more than an "old saw."[23] He argued that the theory of footnote four was vague, tentative, incoherent, and wrong in several respects, and concluded that "we should not design our jurisprudence to conform to dictum in a footnote in a four-Justice opinion."[24]

Third, in a period of constitutional rot, judicial review may actually produce a "reverse-*Carolene Products*" effect, in which courts refuse to protect democracy when it is threatened, undermine fair democratic representation, and make it more difficult for minority groups to protect themselves.[25] Along similar lines, Nicholas Stephanopoulos has argued that the Roberts Court increasingly acts like an "anti-*Carolene*" Supreme Court, because the Court "declin[es] to intervene when American democracy is threatened . . . and prevent[s] non-judicial actors from curbing democratic abuses."[26]

One should not rush to blame these results on judicial corruption. To be sure, it is always possible that a deeply polarized system of judicial appointments will place a few party apparatchiks on the federal bench. But most judges will be well-respected legal professionals with excellent legal skills who have internalized the idea that judges should be isolated from politics. The same points apply to the Justices of the Supreme Court. The Justices do not understand themselves to be simply the ally or the adjunct of national political parties. They understand themselves to be above party politics. Their goal is to decide cases according to law.

Professionalism and legal skill, however, may not be enough to halt advanced constitutional rot. Because the judges and Justices appointed by the dominant party are likely to share the ideology, factual understandings, and worldview of elites in the dominant party, they are likely to do little to remedy democratic dysfunction. Indeed, they may even help undermine representative democracy by striking down laws that attempt to protect democracy and deferring to actions that actually harm it. Instead of acting as a necessary counterweight to political entrenchment, they may actually enhance political entrenchment. Thus, in *Rucho*, Chief Justice Roberts solemnly declared that even if partisan gerrymandering was "incompatible with democratic principles," unelected judges had no business interfering with competition between the two political parties,[27] while in *Shelby County* his scruples about unelected judges striking down the Voting Rights Act magically disappeared. During periods of constitutional rot, the Supreme Court may be a vanguard of partisan policy, but is unlikely to be a vanguard of democracy protection and constitutional renewal.

The Justices' sense of institutional obligation may lead them to curb the most egregious attacks on democratic norms. For example, in the Census case, *Department of Commerce v. New York*,[28] the Trump administration tried to depress participation in the census by immigrant households by adding a question about citizenship. Although such questions are sometimes directed to samples of the population, Secretary of Commerce Wilbur Ross wanted to ask each and every household. The government's own experts pointed out that doing this would scare away immigrants from participating, and produce an undercount of millions that would reduce federal funding to cities and would also affect the drawing of Congressional districts for areas with large immigrant populations.[29] Both results would help Republicans and hurt Democrats.[30]

Under oath, Secretary Ross testified before Congress in March 2018 that he added the question "solely" because the Justice Department asked him to, in order to better enforce the Federal Voting Rights Act.[31] This was not true, as documentary evidence soon confirmed. Ross had sought to add a citizenship question as soon as he took office and used the Justice Department as a fig leaf.[32] The central question in the case was whether the Supreme Court would allow the Trump administration to get away with lying to both Congress and the courts to cover up its attempt to use the Census to entrench the president's party in power.

When the cases were argued in late April 2019, Chief Justice Roberts and his four fellow Republican appointees signaled that they would defer to the executive and not look behind the official reasons given, just as they did in *Trump v. Hawaii*.[33] In May 2019, however, the challengers informed the Court about new evidence that seriously undermined Ross's claims. It showed that Thomas Hofeller, a Republican redistricting strategist who was the architect of the party's gerrymandering efforts, had played a key role in the Trump administration's decision to add the citizenship question, and that the question's purpose was to advantage whites and Republicans electorally. The evidence came on hard drives discovered by Hofeller's estranged daughter after his death in 2018.[34]

When the case came down in June 2019, Chief Justice Roberts broke with his four conservative colleagues. Roberts held that although Ross had the power to add the question, his stated purpose was pretextual: "We are not required to exhibit a naiveté from which ordinary citizens are free."[35]

One might draw two lessons from the Census case. The first is that the federal judiciary will still protect the political process in the most transparent cases of interference. The second conclusion is that the first conclusion is cold comfort. Had Hofeller's hard drives not been discovered in time, Roberts might not have changed his mind. One should not expect that a smoking gun will always appear at the last second to save the day.

Perhaps even more concerning, a smoking gun was not enough for Roberts's conservative colleagues. Even after the revelation that Secretary Ross and the administration had repeatedly misled Congress and the courts, four of the Republican-appointed Justices—all excellent lawyers—were still willing to look the other way. They argued that as long as the administration gave reasons for its actions, they would not inquire behind those reasons.[36]

Moreover, whether there even is a smoking gun may depend on the worldview of the observer. Justice Thomas, writing for himself and Justices Gorsuch and Kavanaugh, pronounced himself completely unimpressed with the evidence of Secretary Ross's deceit, viewing it as a nothing more than a liberal conspiracy theory.[37] If Republican elites do not see a threat to democratic norms, Republican-appointed judges, who are tightly connected to conservative elite networks, are likely to view the world through the same ideological lens.

Even so, one might point to the 1952 *Steel Seizure Case*[38] and the 1974 decision in *United States v. Nixon*[39] as cause for optimism. In *Steel Seizure*, Justices appointed by Franklin Roosevelt voted to prevent Roosevelt's successor, Harry Truman, from taking control of the steel industry. In *United States v. Nixon*, a unanimous Court—including five Justices appointed by Republican presidents, and three appointed by Nixon himself—ordered President Richard Nixon to surrender the Watergate tapes, leading to his resignation.

These are hopeful examples. But both of them occurred in a depolarized politics. Well into the 1970s, it was still possible for legal elites from different parties to agree about what was necessary to protect constitutional democracy, even when faced with insistent demands by the leader of one of those two parties. That was a very different world from the end of the 2010s.

Today well-educated legal elites disagree sharply about the nature of the world, about the facts of American politics, about the sources of political corruption, and, above all, about where the most serious threats to democracy may be found. If the facts of *Steel Seizure* or *United States v. Nixon* occurred in the middle of the Trump years, the outcome might well have been different in one or both cases.

Judicial review can sometimes serve as a safeguard to protect democracy and republican government. But judicial review performs this function best when the political system is already working fairly well in other respects; it is least dependable when the system is already working poorly.

This conclusion is a special case of a more general point: the federal judiciary as a whole, and the Supreme Court in particular, tend to reflect the injustices and ideological blindnesses of the times in which the judges live.[40] A Court appointed by slaveholders was unlikely to strike a blow against slavery in *Dred Scott v. Sandford*, and far more likely to defend it. A Court appointed by Gilded Age politicians was unlikely to dismantle the excesses of Gilded Age capitalism, and far more likely to defend those excesses.

In like fashion, one cannot expect that the Supreme Court or the federal courts as a whole will prove an effective counterweight against a deeply polarized politics and an advanced case of constitutional rot. Judges and Justices will either abdicate responsibility, look the other way, become part of the problem themselves, or arrive too late on the scene, offering remedies that are too little and too late. Sometimes the Supreme Court will rise above the times, and for that reason, one should never give up hope in the institution. But one should also not be surprised if that hope is not realized in a time of constitutional rot.

As this book went to press, the Supreme Court agreed to decide three cases in which President Trump sought to prevent both Congress and the Manhattan District Attorney from investigating his finances and gaining access to his tax returns. (Unlike every modern presidential candidate, Trump has refused to disclose his tax returns.) *Trump v. Mazars* and *Trump v. Deutsche Bank* concern congressional subpoenas, while *Trump v. Vance* concerns a state subpoena.[41] These subpoenas were not directed at the president or executive branch officials but to third parties—Trump's bank and accounting firm. He has intervened to try to keep these third parties from disclosing the information.

Current Supreme Court precedents—including *United States v. Nixon*—appear to offer little support for Trump's position.[42] The subpoenas are not directed at him or his advisors, and the materials are not protected by executive privilege.

Yet Trump has insisted that he is immune from investigation of his financial dealings—or indeed any criminal activity—while he is president. State prosecutors can do nothing to investigate any crimes he may have committed. And if Congress doesn't like it, they can threaten to impeach and remove him from office. But Trump's recent impeachment showed that he would also refuse to cooperate with any House impeachment investigation, and that he would face no accountability because his fellow Republicans in the Senate would refuse to remove him.

These cases will be an important test of how much the Supreme Court is willing to accede to the president's claims of complete immunity from investigation of potential illegal conduct. One might hope that the cases will be a replay of *United States v. Nixon*, and that the Court will easily rebuff Trump's most extreme arguments, either unanimously, as in *Nixon* itself, or by a wide margin. That is certainly my hope; in ordinary circumstances it would also be my prediction based on existing legal materials. But 2020 is a different world than 1974. We live in a deeply polarized legal culture in which legal elites view the world in very different ways. And their understandings of social reality and legal principle are likely to be most at odds when the values of low and high politics reinforce each other, as they do here. In a time of advanced constitutional rot we may not be able to depend on the judiciary when we need it most.

11
Judicial Politics and Judicial Reform

If history is any guide, the United States will come out of constitutional rot—if at all—through political action, and not through judicial decision, because judges are likely to be part of the problem and not the solution, at least for the foreseeable future. In the past, liberals have often looked to courts as engines of political reform. But the New Deal/Civil Rights era regime that produced *Brown v. Board of Education*, the reapportionment cases, and the civil rights revolution occurred during a time of low party polarization. That is not our world. We should not expect anything like the Warren Court to help get us out of this mess. The Taney Court or the Gilded Age Court are more likely analogies. Neither of these is particularly inspiring.

In this chapter, I describe how judicial politics will likely play out in the early years of the next regime. I also describe a series of judicial reforms for the long term.

A. Judicial Politics in the Next Regime

What role will the courts play in the next regime? In chapters 7 and 8, I explained that the Supreme Court and the lower federal courts will probably be controlled by conservative Republicans who have been vetted by conservative legal and policy networks. These courts will continue to develop conservative constitutional jurisprudence in a wide range of different areas, including federalism, religion, administrative law, the environment, business regulation, gun control, affirmative action, and reproductive rights. Because the Rehnquist and Roberts Courts have already developed a considerable amount of conservative jurisprudence, there is already a great deal to build on, and conservative judges will continue to break new doctrinal ground.

Conservative courts will not have to do this on their own. They will be ably assisted by conservative legal intellectuals, policy networks, and think tanks, who will generate new legal ideas and defend conservative positions; by conservative litigators who will tee up cases for the courts to decide; and by amicus briefs written by conservative lawyers and interest groups, who will

The Cycles of Constitutional Time. Jack M. Balkin, Oxford University Press (2020). © Jack Balkin 2020.
DOI: 10.1093/oso/9780197530993.001.0001

signal the views of conservative elites, and offer resources for writing conservative opinions.

Liberal Democrats will no doubt brand many of these new decisions as judicial activism. And if Democrats are able to pass important new legislation early in the next regime, the Supreme Court and the lower federal courts may strike some of it down. That might result in a replay of the struggles between the Court and the political branches in Franklin Roosevelt's first term.[1] Accordingly, liberal legal intellectuals will continue to argue for judicial restraint, while conservative legal intellectuals will come to the Court's defense. All this will eventually change, but because of the successful Republican strategy of appointing young conservative jurists, the turnover will be much slower than happened in the 1930s and 1940s.

While all of this is going on, however, one should not expect that the Supreme Court can or will do much to ameliorate constitutional rot. There may be exceptions, but they will probably be exceptional. That does not mean that lawyers should not continue to try to use the courts to protect democracy and restore republican government. But they should understand that the returns on their efforts will probably be limited, at least for the foreseeable future. Whenever the Justices take a step in this direction—no matter how modest—we should count it as an unexpected bonus.

Why do I offer such a pessimistic prediction? At most points in our history, the Supreme Court has been a lagging indicator of regime politics. This is the consequence of the divergence between political time and judicial time that I mentioned in chapter 6. Recall, for example, that the Supreme Court did not fully polarize until late in the Reagan regime. Given the long life expectancy of the Justices and the relative youth of the new conservative judiciary, the Supreme Court may not depolarize until many years into the next regime.

Even as the country as a whole starts to depolarize, the Justices, who were appointed many years before, will continue to fight the culture wars. Whether conservatives or liberals prevail in any particular controversy, a conservative Supreme Court will continue to shape its own docket in conversation with conservative litigators, conservative policy networks, and conservative public interest firms. It is therefore likely to continue to take and decide a series of hot-button issues that heighten polarization and exacerbate economic inequality rather than reduce them.

Moreover, in the early years of a new political regime controlled by liberal Democrats, a conservative Supreme Court may be the only institution in which conservative Republicans can score any significant policy victories and hold off the damage caused by liberal politicians. Hence, whether they want the role or not, the Court's conservative Justices (and conservative judges in the lower federal courts) are likely to continue to serve as a policy vanguard for conservative politicians who no longer control the national political process. These judges will comfort conservative causes and afflict liberal ones. They will be the last line of defense against Democratic presidents, who, like Barack Obama, will be viewed as tyrants by conservative legal intellectuals.[2]

Predictably, this will cause liberal Democrats to attack the Court ever more vehemently, further undermining its legitimacy at precisely the moment when public trust in the courts would be most valuable to stem constitutional rot. Liberal Democrats will likely use the Supreme Court as a foil in electoral politics—as Republicans did before them. They will argue that the conservative Justices are simply imposing their personal beliefs on the country, that they are mangling the Constitution to gain policy victories, and that their pious invocations of originalism are a sham designed to impose conservative political results. Many liberals have already started to argue for a twenty-first-century version of court-packing to regain the seat they claim was stolen from Judge Merrick Garland, and to avenge their inability to stop the appointment of Justice Brett Kavanaugh.

In short, we should expect that political renewal in the United States will occur in spite of the US Supreme Court, not because of it. Right now we are in an especially corrupt moment and the courts are unlikely to extricate us. They may even make things worse in the short run, because they will probably increase economic inequality at the margins, and because the two parties will disagree vehemently about what judicial interventions actually protect democracy.

Democrats may argue that the country needs to reform its voting procedures, and that judges need to prevent politicians from constricting the franchise to keep themselves in power. But conservative judges and Justices are likely to be unsympathetic to new voting rights legislation passed by Democrats. They will usually give Republican-controlled legislatures the benefit of the doubt when the latter pass new regulations that restrict the practical ability of people to vote. Moreover, conservative judges and Justices will continue to be deeply skeptical of campaign finance regulation, arguing that it is little more than political censorship.

The lesson of history seems clear enough: during a period of advanced constitutional rot and high political polarization, the federal courts are unlikely to be an instrument of constitutional renewal. We should not expect that courts will save us from constitutional rot. Only democratic mobilization can do that.

That does not mean that Americans should give up on judicial review. One should be guided by the nature of the times. Rather than oppose judicial review per se, one should simply not expect too much from courts, and endeavor to keep them from doing too much harm. Things will eventually change. In the meantime, it is best not to look to an institution that cannot do much to assist the country's renewal.

B. Reforming the Supreme Court

As I explained in chapters 7 and 8, there are good reasons to think that a general philosophy of judicial restraint will not prove lasting for either party in the early twenty-first century, as soon as that party gets control of the federal courts. Over the course of a hundred and fifty years, American politicians have constructed powerful federal courts, and both parties and both sides of the political spectrum will want to make use of them.

Reform of the judicial system, however, is another matter. In fact, I would argue that the next regime offers a good opportunity to push for good-government reforms of the judicial system, and especially the Supreme Court. Because of the current state of our politics, these reforms will probably not be possible immediately. But they may well be possible a decade from now.

To understand the kinds of judicial reforms we need, we need to recall several important features of constitutional rot: rot encourages polarization and it is exacerbated by polarization. Rot both produces and is caused by distrust in government institutions, especially the courts. Rot leads to ever more aggressive rounds of constitutional hardball; it causes politicians to believe that they should risk reprisals to force a victory now before the other side has a chance to force a victory on them.

Therefore, reforms to the judiciary should lower the stakes of judicial appointments rather than raise them. They should encourage bipartisan forbearance and turn-taking rather than successive rounds of constitutional hardball.

It follows that attempting to increase the size of the Supreme Court to ensure an ideological majority is a bad idea, even if it could be accomplished. Packing the Supreme Court by increasing its membership does nothing to promote public trust in the courts or the political branches. It encourages constitutional hardball by the other side. It is likely to increase polarization. It will lead the losers in the struggle over Court packing to view the winners as enemies of the Constitution and the republic. Court packing may make liberal Democrats feel better, but it will not address the deeper causes of rot in our constitutional system.

Instead, consider four different kinds of reforms that might lower the stakes of judicial appointments: (1) instituting regular and predictable Supreme Court appointments; (2) creating a practical equivalent of term limits for Supreme Court Justices; (3) giving the Supreme Court less control over its own docket; and (4) using sunrise provisions that will encourage bipartisan reform.

1. Instituting regular and predictable Supreme Court appointments. Congress should begin by regularizing judicial appointments and requiring Congress to act on presidential nominations within a specified period of time.[3]

Congress could provide that on the first day of February of every odd numbered year, the president shall nominate a new Justice of the Supreme Court. The Senate will be required to vote on the nomination within ninety days.

Because the Senate must take a vote, the party in power will face strong pressure to hold hearings. If they turn down the nomination, the president will nominate some else promptly and they will have to take another vote. Indeed, the proposal could allow the president to name more than one candidate at the outset, so that the Senate understands the consequences of voting no.[4] If the Senators turn down the first pick, the clock immediately begins running on the second nominee, and so on. The proposal could even require that the second and subsequent votes must take place in less time—sixty days or even forty-five days—to discourage the Senate majority from trying to run out the clock. It is important to remember that long periods of consideration for Supreme Court Justices are a relatively new phenomenon tied to our polarized politics. In the first part of the twentieth century, votes often followed nominations quickly.[5]

Of course, if Supreme Court Justices are nominated every two years, soon there will be more than nine Justices holding commissions. This brings us to the next reform, which is designed to create the effective equivalent of Supreme Court term limits and create incentives for earlier retirements.

2. *Creating a practical equivalent of term limits for Supreme Court Justices.* Congress has the power to choose both the number of Justices and the quorum for the Court to decide cases.[6] It should provide that the quorum for deciding Supreme Court cases shall be the nine Justices most junior in service. Because presidents get to appoint a new Justice every two years, this means that after eighteen years, the most senior Justices will no longer be part of the regular quorum for deciding Supreme Court cases.

That does not mean that the more senior Justices have nothing to do. First, senior Justices can still pinch-hit if a more junior Justice is recused, dies, or retires. (In order to prevent junior Justices from manipulating their choices to recuse themselves, Congress can require that fill-ins will be chosen by lottery from among the senior Justices on a case-by-case basis.) Second, senior Justices can also help select cases for the quorum to decide.

Third, and perhaps most important, Congress should provide that senior Justices will continue to decide cases in the lower federal courts. This last rule would create virtuous incentives for the Justices. It will lead them to reveal why they enjoy being federal judges. If they only stay on because they want to be at the apex of judicial power, they now have incentives to retire after eighteen years. But if they like being a federal judge because they like deciding cases, they can stay on and work in the lower federal courts.

When Justice Scalia died suddenly in 2016, Senate Majority Leader Mitch McConnell refused to consider anyone President Obama nominated. As a result, the Court had only eight Justices for over a year. In the new system McConnell would not have that option.

First, by 2005, Scalia would no longer have been in the quorum for deciding cases. By 2016, his replacement would already have been on the Court for eleven years. Thus, the new system makes appointments far more regular and predictable; and it makes it much less likely that a crucial opening will be created because a Justice dies suddenly.

Second, even if Scalia had been in the quorum when he died, his place immediately would have been filled by senior Justices David Souter and/or John Paul Stevens. The Court would have had a full complement of nine Justices until a new Justice was appointed in 2017. Because there would be nothing that members of either party could do until after the election, there would have been no exercise of constitutional hardball.

Because of the new system, the partisan composition of the Court will usually depend far less on luck and far more on the results of presidential elections. One-term presidents would not get four appointments like Warren Harding, or none at all like Jimmy Carter.[7] Every presidential term would have two appointments, one in each odd-numbered year. The more often a party won the presidency, the more Justices it would be able to appoint.

This system does not end partisan entrenchment in the Supreme Court. Rather, it regularizes it, makes it more predictable, and thus reduces incentives for constitutional hardball to achieve it.

These changes do not require a constitutional amendment. The Constitution gives Congress the power to organize the Supreme Court and the lower federal courts.[8] Congress not only has the power to decide the number of Justices and the size of the quorum for deciding cases, but also the power to give federal judges the ability to sit by designation in other federal courts.[9]

This system lowers the stakes for judicial appointments for two reasons. First, both parties know that Justices will do most of their work in their first eighteen years on the bench. If Senators guess wrong about a Justice, the consequences are limited. They need no longer fear appointments like William O. Douglas (if you are a conservative) or Clarence Thomas (if you are a liberal) who will continue to wreak havoc for thirty to forty years. Second, because Justices will have fewer years to shape doctrine, parties have fewer incentives to choose younger "stealth Justices" about whom relatively little is known. They can consider older, more experienced candidates with long records of public service, in the hope that these appointments will inspire trust and confidence in other lawmakers and in the public.

3. *Giving the Supreme Court less control over its own docket.* Yet another way to reduce the stakes of judicial confirmations is to change the Supreme Court's docket.

One might think that the best way to rein in the Court is to further reduce the number of cases that it hears each year. Historically, whenever members of Congress have become angry at the Court's decisions, they have threatened to shrink the Court's jurisdiction by taking certain kinds of cases away from it.[10] In fact, in a period of constitutional rot and high polarization the correct strategy is to do precisely the opposite: to make the Justices decide more cases, spend less time on each of them and give them less control over what kinds of cases they hear.

The Supreme Court has gained increasing control over its docket because of a series of reforms that began with the 1925 Judges' Bill, so called because the Justices persistently lobbied for it.[11] Most of these reforms occurred in a relatively depolarized environment.[12] They could be justified in terms of the assumptions of a depolarized politics: the Supreme Court needs more time to decide the really important cases, interpret important federal statutes, and decide the basic constitutional rules of the road.[13]

But decreasing the Court's workload and giving it more of a say about which cases it hears has had perverse effects, which multiply as politics becomes more polarized. Allowing the Court to both choose its docket and reduce the number of cases it hears has increased the stakes of each case, thereby contributing to polarization. To be sure, this effect was not an intentional choice by the Justices. Rather, they felt overworked by the increasing number of cases entering the federal system, and they wanted to be able to spend more time on a smaller number of cases. Under the leadership of Chief Justice William Rehnquist, who was widely viewed as an able administrator, the Court's docket shrank almost in half, to the delight of most of the sitting Justices.[14] It is not completely accidental that the Supreme Court's docket decreased during a period of increasing polarization. To be sure, no matter what the Court did, polarization was already happening, but the Court's decisions did not help matters.

Giving the Court control over its docket need not always contribute to polarization. For example, it allows the Justices to dodge difficult or ideologically charged cases. Very often the Court lets certain issues percolate in the lower federal courts, and only intervenes once a decade. But the same ability also gives the Justices incentives to pick a high percentage of cases that become ideological flash points. Perhaps more to the point, it also gives a liberal or a conservative majority much greater ability to structure a course of decisions that will move the Court in a particular ideological direction.[15] Controlling the docket allows the Court to change the practical meaning of the Constitution far more quickly. As a result, giving the Justices the power to control their docket may also increase the percentage of cases that generate—and maintain—polarization.

Hearing fewer cases also gives the Justices incentives to write longer opinions, longer dissents, and multiple concurrences. Equally important, it means that the Justices also have more time to write individual concurrences and dissents that advertise the Justices' views and signal to litigants the kinds of cases that a Justice wants them to bring in the future.

Thus, if we want to lower the stakes of judicial appointments, the best way to do this is to make the Court decide more cases, not less. Increasing the Court's workload and reducing the Justices' control over their docket may limit the Justices' ability to shape litigation campaigns, and it may help the Court seem like less of an ideological and partisan institution. Because the Court will have to take more cases it does not choose, there will probably be more unanimous decisions. There will also be more opinions in which the Justices do not divide according to the standard liberal/conservative, Democratic/ Republican lines. In other words, giving the Justices less power to choose the cases they hear may, at the margins, decrease the salience of ideological divisions, increase collegiality, and counteract the Court's role as a policy vanguard.

4. *Using sunrise provisions that will encourage bipartisan reform.* To further reduce incentives for partisan hardball, Congress could structure some or all of these reforms using sunrise provisions. Whereas *sunset* provisions automatically expire at a specified date in the future, *sunrise* provisions automatically start at a specified date in the future.[16]

The point of using sunrise provisions for reforms to the judiciary is that it will be more difficult to predict which party will benefit the most from them. Because members of Congress do not know who will benefit, they have greater incentives to choose rules that are sensible from a bipartisan perspective and will benefit the country as a whole.

Taken together, the goal of these reforms is to decrease Congressional incentives for constitutional hardball and to create modest incentives for more unanimous opinions and decisions that cross-cut ideological divisions among the Justices. The goal is *not* to produce more "moderate" judicial decisions, whatever that might mean. Rather, it is to restore trust and norms of bipartisan cooperation among politicians by removing incentives for bad behavior, and to promote collegiality among the Justices themselves.

It is important to put these suggestions in their proper perspective. Reforms to the judiciary are far less important in dealing with constitutional rot than reforms to the system of political representation and reforms that reduce economic inequality. Even so, political activists may focus on Supreme Court reform because the Court's work is highly salient, and because they fear that the Supreme Court will block other needed reforms.

In the long run, however, the most effective cure for what ails the federal judiciary is political depolarization, the subject of the next chapter. This will change the political supports for judicial review and once again make it possible to reestablish rough divisions between high and low politics. The reforms offered here can only do so much, but every little bit helps.

PART III
CONCLUSION

12
The Turn of the Cycles

Part I of this book argued that the United States is in the middle of a slow, difficult transition to a new political regime featuring a new dominant party, probably the Democrats. This transition has been made all the more difficult by the fact that we are at a high point in the cycle of political polarization and suffering from years of constitutional rot.

It is possible that Donald Trump will be able to squeeze out a second Electoral College victory. It is also possible that the Republican Party's politicians at the state level will continue to jigger election rules in order to stay in power even without national majority support. High polarization and constitutional rot may help the current dominant party, the Republicans, cling to power for a time. Yet although these strategies may succeed in the short run, the medium- to long-term odds are against them. The Reagan regime is ending.

Part II explained how the cycles of constitutional time affect the federal judiciary. We should not expect that the federal judiciary will be of much help in extricating the country from polarization and constitutional rot. At best the federal judiciary will be impotent; at worst it will exacerbate polarization, increase inequality, legitimate rot, and throw obstacles in the way of reform.

Because of life tenure and strategies of partisan entrenchment, the federal judiciary is a lagging indicator of the cycles of constitutional time. That means that the judiciary will continue to experience the effects of rot and polarization long after electoral politics has turned the corner. This is not a reason to jettison judicial review. Rather, it is a reason not to expect too much from the federal courts or from the Supreme Court during this difficult period.

A traditional justification for judicial review is that courts can protect democracy from politicians who subordinate relatively powerless minorities and attempt to entrench themselves in power. But courts can perform this task only under certain conditions. Among other things, this task assumes that judges appointed by different parties possess a shared reality and can agree about what is actually happening in the country so that they can effectively respond to it. Polarization and rot undermine this assumption. Strong polarization and motivated reasoning among elites will make it hard for the courts to protect democracy in the way that constitutional theory expects them to.

The Cycles of Constitutional Time. Jack M. Balkin, Oxford University Press (2020). © Jack Balkin 2020.
DOI: 10.1093/oso/9780197530993.001.0001

Members of the current dominant party—the Republicans—are attempting to lock in political power and insulate themselves from changing demographics. Judges appointed by Republican politicians—carefully identified and fostered by successful political and legal networks—are likely to share their values and their worldview. As a result, these judges are likely to be unconcerned by—or even sympathetic to—Republican politicians' practices of political entrenchment. Given such judges' understanding of social reality—which they share with political and legal elites of the party that appointed them—they will not understand the party's entrenching tactics as especially antithetical to democracy, but rather as part of the ordinary rough-and-tumble of democratic struggle. In the alternative, they will conclude that they can and should play no role in policing these entrenching tactics.

As a result, in a highly polarized politics with conflict extension and motivated reasoning, we cannot expect the federal judiciary to protect democracy because judges of different parties will have very different views about what democracy is, how to protect it, and indeed, about what is actually happening in the country. Given these obstacles, the most that we can hope for is that the judiciary will not slow down the country's slow climb out of constitutional rot, or actively make things worse.

Because the judiciary is not the most likely source of depolarization or constitutional renewal, the final chapter returns once again to the political process and the party system. My goal is to explain how polarization and rot might eventually give way, and how we might finally emerge from our recent unpleasantness. As physicist Niels Bohr once said, predictions are difficult, especially about the future.[1] But the analysis I've offered in the book offers a structure for analyzing the challenges ahead.

In this final chapter, I offer a few ideas about how things might play out in the years to come. I emphasize the word "might," because I have been given no crystal ball for seeing the future. I will also omit a wide range of important policy issues and considerations—including foreign policy questions—that may roil American law and politics, and may change the trajectory of events in unforeseen ways. Think only of how the first half of twentieth-century American politics was shaped by two world wars. And consider how the current worldwide pandemic—and future public health crises—will upset existing political assumptions.

Instead, in this chapter, I am interested in a very specific set of questions. The first is how our dysfunctional political polarization might eventually recede. The second is how our advanced case of constitutional rot might someday end. On both questions I am guardedly optimistic. But the path to political renewal will not be easy.

The 2016 election and its aftermath give us some good clues about what the structure of the party system is likely to look like in the new regime. That election is the result of fifty years of evolution from the end of the New Deal coalition. In the New Deal arrangement, the two parties faced off over class issues, but each was internally divided over social issues and issues of identity (especially race). Today, the two parties primarily face off over social issues and issues of identity, while each party is internally divided on questions of class and economic policy.

The Democratic Party is likely to be the dominant party in the next regime, and it will continue to be the more economically egalitarian of the two parties for some time to come. Nevertheless, the nature of the Democratic Party has changed so much in the past fifty years that this may limit the kinds of reforms that will benefit working-class and poor people. The root problem is that the Democratic Party is no longer the party of the New Deal coalition united on issues of class: rather, it is a coalition of working-class people with socially liberal college graduates, professionals, and progressive neoliberals. (Despite the way that the media generally describes things, the Democrats still have a large working-class base, but whereas the Republican working-class base is almost all white, the Democratic working-class base is multiracial.)

Working-class and poor people will probably do better in the new regime than in the current Reagan regime because the Democratic Party's brand is more egalitarian than the Republican Party's brand. But the left wing of the party will probably not be running the show, at least in the short run. Instead, the economically liberal wing of the party will be only one element in a larger Democratic coalition. It will have to apply continual political pressure on the more business-friendly neoliberal wing in order to achieve genuine economic reform. Because the Democratic Party is now unified on issues of identity, but not class, the disagreements between the two wings of the party will eventually undermine the coalition. But that, I predict, is many years in the future. Conversely, the Republican Party will experience increasing tensions between its populist wing and its business-friendly, deregulatory wing.

The incoherence and internal divisions within the two emerging party coalitions allow us to see how our current toxic political polarization will end. It shows how new forms of cross-party alliances will become possible, and suggests some of the issues that will drive depolarization. Whoever figures out how to create these cross-party coalitions will drive the direction of reform. Put another way, if the populist/working-class wings of the two parties do not find common ground, the neoliberal wings of the two parties probably will. In the latter case, economic reforms will be far more limited. But dealing with the increasing economic inequality of the past forty years is crucial if the country is to halt and reverse its constitutional rot.

The coming regime is not going to be sunshine, lollipops, and rainbows. Real change that breaks the stranglehold of economic inequality will only come from difficult times that still lay ahead. To paraphrase Bette Davis, fasten your seat belts, we are in for a bumpy ride.

A. How Polarization Leads to Disjunction

In chapter 2 I argued that Trump is likely to be a disjunctive president who closes out the Reagan era. Disjunction normally means that the dominant coalition is breaking down in disagreements. But how is that possible if the two parties are becoming ever more polarized? Indeed, because political polarization is asymmetric, the Republicans are far more united ideologically than the Democrats, who still have many moderates and conservatives in their party.

Before the rise of Donald Trump, the Republican Party was in the midst of a civil war between its conservative establishment and Tea Party insurgents. But Trump managed to unify Republicans: first, by cleverly playing on cultural and racial divisions to get the party's base solidly behind him, and second, by giving both religious and economic conservatives almost everything they wanted—lower taxes for the wealthy, deregulation, and very conservative judges. The most important conservative media organizations, initially wary of Trump, have become his most devoted propagandists. And Trump's divisive and demagogic strategies have bound Republicans ever more tightly together in loyalty to him and in opposition to the Democratic Party. It would seem that the fetid combination of bitter polarization and Trump's demagoguery is keeping Republicans together. How, then, can one say that the party's coalition is breaking down?

Yet asymmetric polarization—whereby the Republican party has moved decisively to the right while the Democrats have moved only slightly to the left—has actually helped cause the breakup of the contemporary Republican Party, not prevented it. The last two coalitional breakdowns—involving the Republican Party in the 1930s and the Democratic Party in the 1980s—occurred in relatively nonpolarized times. Breakdown in an era of strong polarization works a little differently.

Basically, there are two ways for a political collation to lose members. One is that people become disaffected and defect. The other is that the coalition loses the inability to reproduce itself in the next generation—it loses the battle for the hearts and minds of the young people who become voters with each passing year.[2] An example of the first kind of loss is Reagan Democrats leaving the New Deal coalition and signing on to the Reagan coalition. An example of the second kind of loss is young baby boomers and Gen Xers deciding that they liked the Republicans better than Democrats and voting Republican most of their adult lives.

Pronounced asymmetric polarization does not cause messy breakups of the kind that happened within the Democratic Party in the 1970s. Rather, asymmetric polarization makes it increasingly difficult for the coalition to reproduce itself in the next generation. In a depolarized politics, mass defection and failure of reproduction may be equally important problems. But in a highly polarized politics, failure to reproduce becomes the more important phenomenon.

In fact, Republicans have faced both challenges. College educated voters and professionals, who used to be a crucial part of the traditional Republican party in the middle of the twentieth century, have been leaving the party for some time now. They have left gradually and relatively quietly. This makes some sense. When these voters see that the party is ever more ideologically blinkered and impervious to reality, they conclude that it's not even worth fighting for the soul of the party. So they just leave, without much drama. Put another way, increasing polarization may cause defections to be slow and quiet rather than quick and noisy.

Conservative media strategies have not helped. Fox News, conservative talk radio, and the right-wing internet have repeatedly played to conservative insurgents, the Tea Party, and what became Trump's political base. Key conservative media personalities such as Sean Hannity, Rush Limbaugh, Bill O'Reilly, Laura Ingraham, and Tucker Carlson were not particularly interested in giving equal time to the perspectives of educated professionals and moderate Republicans. Seeking high ratings, they appealed to the fears and grievances of working-class whites and repeatedly denounced elite culture. This likely dampened the voices of the people who left the party.

For a long time, this conservative media strategy and the move to conservative identity politics worked just fine. Over the course of the Reagan regime, but especially since the turn of the twenty-first century, the Republican Party has gradually traded in professionals and college graduates for working-class whites. Because there are many more working-class whites than college-educated whites, losing the latter is hardly noticeable. Indeed, if the party is able to attract enough white working-class voters, it may be a very good bargain indeed. That, it seems, has been the point of the Republican Party's increasing embrace of a politics organized around white identity, Christian identity, and perpetual grievance.

In the long run, however, the failure to reproduce the coalition in successive generations may be more important than success in winning over white working-class voters. A party's coalition has to reproduce itself over time in order to stay viable nationally. That means that a successful political party is not only a coalition of interest groups, but also a coalition of generations. There have to be lots of young Republicans constantly joining the party as well as old Republicans (who eventually die off), or the party withers away.

Asymmetric polarization has poisoned this process of generational replacement. As *New York Times* columnist David Brooks recently noted, "the generation gap is even more powerful when it comes to Republicans. To put it bluntly, young adults hate them."[3] A 2018 Pew survey showed that "Democrats enjoy a 27-percentage-point advantage among Millennial voters (59% are Democrats or lean Democratic, 32% are Republican or lean Republican)," a gap that has been growing in recent years.[4] Younger voters are recoiling from the party precisely because it has polarized, especially on cultural and racial issues.[5] So instead of a fight within the party—the familiar scenario of a coalition that breaks apart— young people just don't show up in the first place.

B. A New Regime Without a Social Movement Party

Meanwhile, the Democrats seem slowly to be developing a new governing majority. But they are not yet supported by the kind of transformative social movement that often accompanies a new regime.[6] The nationwide protests in the spring of 2020 against police racism may mark the begining of such a mobilization, but we will not know for sure until after this book is published. In any case, the coming transformation seems different from the transformations of 1860, 1932, or 1980. Moreover, unlike 1932, there is not yet a powerful social movement to represent and defend organized labor. Without a powerful labor movement, the interests of working people will likely be underprotected. This will make it difficult to reverse economic inequality, which is one of the important sources of constitutional rot.

This doesn't mean that there won't be a new dominant party or a new majority coalition. It doesn't mean there won't be reform. It just means that we should not expect the new regime, at least in its initial stages, to have a powerful transformative energy of the kind the country witnessed during Reconstruction or the New Deal. The president will still appoint the federal judiciary, and still control the federal bureaucracy. Constitutional change will continue apace in the federal courts. The bureaucracy will still engage in interstitial lawmaking.

But legislative reforms may occur more slowly. The Democrats may have a growing demographic advantage, but because they are concentrated in cities and the coasts, they have a decided geographical disadvantage.[7] As things stand currently, Democrats continually have to win large majorities of the national popular vote to maintain control of the House, and they will have to overcome the Senate's increasingly worrisome malapportionment to obtain control there as well. Democrats will also have to get rid of the Senate filibuster, because it makes no sense in a polarized politics with parliamentary-style parties.

Taken together, these obstacles are quite serious. The result may be only modest, slow change, which will often be frustrating. Perhaps more important, these obstacles will make it harder to chip away at the causes of constitutional rot.

In chapter 2, I mentioned Stephen Skowronek's "waning of political time" thesis. Skowronek predicts that presidential leadership styles will become more similar to each other. The president's job will increasingly become artful policy management in the face of institutional constraints. Presidents may have only limited options to shake up the system. Politics may offer only opportunities for pragmatic adjustments, compromises, and policy kludges. Of course, if, heaven forbid, we face a serious crisis or emergency, or a war on our own soil, that will change the opportunities for transformative leadership significantly.

Eventually accumulated impediments will fall away, decay, be reformed, or overthrown. Opportunities for reconstructive leadership may someday emerge again. (Once again, crisis and emergency may create these opportunities.) A social movement may yet arise and take over the Democratic Party (for good or for ill). But all that is still in the future.

C. The New Party Configuration

Crucial to the politics of the next several decades is the reconfiguration of the two major political parties. Slow changes in the composition of the Democratic and Republican parties have reshaped (1) their demographics, (2) the issues on which they face off against each other, and (3) the issues that internally divide them. The two parties today are very different from the ones that existed at the close of the New Deal/Civil Rights regime in the late 1970s.

Julia Azari and Marc Hetherington have pointed out that the electoral maps of recent presidential elections look much like the electoral map in 1896, but with the parties reversed.[8] In 1896 Republicans won the Northeast, most of the Great Lakes region, and the coasts, while Democrats controlled the rural areas of the South and Mountain West. By the elections of 2012 and 2016 these allegiances had flipped. Gary Miller and Norman Schofield have also emphasized the analogy to 1896, and they have offered a theory of why the party coalitions have evolved in the way they did.[9] The discussion that follows builds on these scholars' work.

In 1896 the parties were opposed on issues of social identity (race being the most important) and internally divided on questions of class and economic inequality. Ever since Reconstruction, the Democratic and Republican parties had fought about the issues produced by the Civil War, while suppressing growing differences within each party over how to deal with rapid economic, social, and technological change, and the increasing economic inequality that resulted.

Following the 1896 election, these internal fissures became increasingly pronounced, and the parties slowly began to evolve, with many immigrants and urban workers joining rural voters in the Democratic Party. This created the possibility of a new coalition organized around the regulation of business and the protection of labor. By FDR's election in 1932, the parties now faced off on issues of class and economic inequality, while both parties were internally divided on social issues, and—especially for the Democrats—race. Republicans—the party of Lincoln—were still considered the more egalitarian party on racial issues for some time. Democrats, by contrast, had to continually manage the tension between their Southern wing, which was committed to Jim Crow and white supremacy, and their Northern liberal wing, which was friendlier to black civil rights.

This process of party evolution continued throughout the New Deal/Civil Rights Regime. The presidential wing of the Democratic Party favored racial liberalism. Eventually this alienated many Southern whites, as well as many working-class white ethnics in the North and West, the so-called Nixon Democrats and Reagan Democrats. Republicans gladly welcomed these disaffected Democrats into the party. Republican politicians eventually realized that they could simultaneously expand their coalition and destroy the New Deal coalition by emphasizing race and culture war issues that appealed to white working-class voters.

During the Reagan regime, the party successfully neutered organized labor, which had been a key Democratic constituency. Perhaps equally important, the Republican Party adopted a strategy of political polarization to gain majority status. Republican politicians successfully used cultural and racial wedge issues to turn the South Republican and to cater to evangelical Christians and other working-class whites.

But this strategy of cultural polarization had unintended consequences. Many college-educated Republican voters, including Northeastern moderates, suburbanites, and professionals, became increasingly disaffected and became Democrats or Democratic-leaning independents. Meanwhile, national Democratic Party leaders, including Bill Clinton, Barack Obama, and Hillary Clinton, actively sought support from businesses and professionals, especially in the financial and technology sectors. This reshuffling of allegiances slowly transformed the Democratic coalition. The Democrats regained their competitiveness nationally, but the New Deal coalition was not coming back.

The Republican strategy of political polarization and culture wars, and the Democrats' appeal to socially liberal college graduates and professionals, eventually changed the composition of both parties. Before the Reagan regime began, each party was organized around issues of class and economic power. Today, at the close of the Reagan regime, each party is organized around issues of identity and status.[10] Republicans have long accused Democrats of engaging in identity politics—that is, catering to the interests of women, minorities, and LGBTQ people. But the contemporary Republican Party is no less organized around identity—in this case, white and Christian identity.[11] Following the rise of the Tea Party and Donald Trump, party activists have perfected the party's politics of rage and grievance—the Republican version of identity politics.

By the beginning of the twenty-first century, the parties are once again opposed to each other on issues of identity (race, ethnicity, religion, social liberalism) and internally divided on issues of class and economic inequality. This continuous rotation of positions has produced the reverse of the 1896 election that Azari, Hetherington, Miller, and Schofield noted.

As before, the arrangement is not perfectly symmetrical. The Democrats—the party of FDR— continue to favor egalitarian economic and social policies. The Democratic "brand" is economically liberal, and the Republican "brand" is economically conservative. But the Democratic party—including especially the presidential candidates Barack Obama and the Clintons—welcomed socially liberal college-educated professionals and neoliberals into their party. They sought contributions from wealthy corporate donors.

Meanwhile, organized labor, debilitated in the Reagan regime, became a less powerful factor in Democratic politics than it had been in the heyday of the New Deal coalition. Ironically, Republicans helped transform the Democratic Party by doing everything in their power to destroy and defund unions, leading Democrats to look elsewhere for new voters (and campaign contributors). Democrats became increasingly a coalition of educated cosmopolitans, women, minorities, and white working-class voters who still remained in the party. The influx of new voters led the Democrats to a pro-immigration stance. Meanwhile, the Republicans have become a coalition of corporate and business interests, evangelical Christians, and socially conservative working-class whites. Their new voters have led the Republican Party, which was once quite pro-immigration, to become increasingly hostile to immigration.

Although the parties are now squared off on issues of culture and identity, both parties are likely to witness internal fights over economic justice and class issues. The expression of these conflicts about economic justice, however, will be different in both parties for two reasons.

First, class conflicts will play out differently in each party because each party has different ideas about identity and race. As we saw with Obamacare and its Medicaid expansion, Republicans will find it difficult to support economically egalitarian reforms that get coded as benefiting racial minorities. Instead, Republican reformers will be drawn to economic reforms that they can successfully label as "family-friendly" and cannot be racialized by reform opponents.

Second, conflicts over class will play out differently in each party because the two parties' brands are different. The Democrats are far more egalitarian on multiple dimensions and generally support increasing national power, while the Republican brand remains economically conservative, small-government, and oriented toward states.

This new party configuration is important for two reasons. First, it limits the kind and degree of transformative change that is possible in the near future. Second, it plants the seeds of depolarization, which may bear fruit years from now.

D. The Limits of a Cosmopolitan Party

Many progressives and liberals are hoping that a new regime led by the Democratic Party will break through the economic inequality that is undermining American democracy. If my analysis is correct, we should expect limited but not revolutionary change, at least in the regime's early years. Democrats will continue to be united around social issues and issues of identity, but they will be less unified when it comes to issues of class and economic inequality. They will find it difficult to make the significant changes necessary to break down the institutions and policies that have exacerbated economic inequality and helped produce constitutional rot.

To be sure, Democrats will continue to be more far more economically egalitarian than Republicans for some time—that is part of their brand. But it will be hard to get moderate, business-friendly Democrats and corporate donors to support many important changes. In fact, as the regime develops, the Democratic Party will face increasingly serious conflicts over economic justice and class issues. For the time being, Democrats may find it easiest to unite around social liberalism. In today's Democratic Party, an ambitious candidate can be moderately liberal or very liberal on economics. But on social issues one should be firmly on the left.

Republicans face a different, but complementary set of incentives. For the time being, it will be very hard for them to move to the center on social issues. They have spent too much time establishing their position in the culture wars for that. But as the party becomes increasingly identified with white working-class voters, there is space for strategic realignment on certain issues of class and economic equality, as long as these issues are not coded as socially liberal or seen as especially benefiting minority groups. Thus, Republican politicians can move to the center on class issues if they support family-friendly economic policies that are coded as helping white working-class people. (This requirement—that the policies offer no hint of redistribution to minorities—is similar to problems Democrats faced during the New Deal.)[12]

Republicans can also make populist attacks on Big Tech (whose leaders tend to be liberal Democrats). Republicans can even get behind certain kinds of antitrust reforms to the extent that this can be sold as benefiting white working-class voters and not as the federal government attempting to regulate the economy. I expect that ambitious Republicans will attempt variations on these general themes until they find a model that maximizes their potential base of support.[13] What that model will ultimately look like, however, is not foreordained: it will be shaped by many factors, including the views of the party's powerful donors. Previous attempts at moving to the center (much less the left) on class issues have been foiled by the donor base—which appears to care most about deregulation and upward redistribution.

In sum, in the new configuration, the two parties will continue to be opposed on social and identity issues. But both parties are going to have a populist wing and a neoliberal wing.

Although both parties are internally divided on class, they are most definitely not identical on class issues. The Democratic Party, for the foreseeable future, is likely to be far more economically egalitarian than the Republican Party. It is unlikely to abandon its commitments to universal health care, the environment, and other economic issues. But moderate Democrats—and some of the party's wealthiest donors—will be more conservative than much of the party.

We can tell a complementary story about Republicans. As a result of its successful cultural strategy, the Republican Party has absorbed many economic populists, who, among other things, support Medicare and Social Security, and might also advocate programs that support traditional families. But the party's donor base and its activist networks mean that it is not going to get behind very liberal economic programs.

Given this configuration, even if the Democratic Party is the dominant party in the new regime, it will be difficult to achieve real change on economic issues and break down the massive inequality of the Reagan era with only Democratic votes. The Democrats are now a cosmopolitan party, organized around issues of identity and divided on issues of class. They are no longer the party of the New Deal.

As strange as it may sound in today's political climate, economic progressives will need help from the other side of the aisle. If they do not figure out how to do this, the neoliberal wings of the two parties are likely to set the agenda. That suggests that real change awaits the end of party polarization.

E. How Constitutional Rot Ends

In the 2010s the parties were bitterly divided on almost every question. But history suggests that polarization does not continue forever. If the country is to renew itself and move past its current case of constitutional rot, politics will have to depolarize. Let me describe how that might come about.

History suggests two possible paths for getting past constitutional rot and reforming American politics. These correspond, roughly speaking, to the era of the Civil War and Reconstruction and to the Progressive Era.

Under the first path, one of the two major political parties becomes so dominant that it can push through its reform program without much resistance. This might happen because the other party is discredited, so that it falls apart or loses most of its influence. There are two examples in American history. The first is the period of the 1810s, when the Federalist Party collapsed, in part due to the ill-fated Hartford Convention that flirted with secession. Former Federalists who had not already done so left politics or flocked to the Jeffersonian Republican Party. The Jeffersonians became the only effective political party in the country, leading to the Era of Good Feelings. The second example is the period between 1865 and 1873, when the Democratic Party, whose stronghold was in the South, was effectively shut out of governance by the Reconstruction Republicans. Republicans prevented Southern Senators and Representatives from sitting in Congress until Southern States created new state constitutions and ratified the Fourteenth Amendment.

I don't think that this model of reform makes much sense today. The two major political parties are both strongly competitive, and will probably be so for some time. It is possible that Donald Trump will so discredit the Republican Party that it will hemorrhage supporters and become a small regional party. But I don't think that's the most likely scenario. First, in many parts of the country, the two parties are evenly matched and competitive. Second, the party's base of support in the rural United States, the South and Mountain West, will remain, and Republicans look likely to dominate state and local governments there for some time. Third, the Republican Party retains a powerful influence in conservative media. Fourth, as long as the party continues to cater to its donor class of wealthy businesses and individuals, it will retain powerful sources of financial support.

In any case, even if Trump did manage to thoroughly discredit the Republican Party, periods of one-party rule in the United States tend to be fleeting. The Era of Good Feelings was short-lived, and intraparty disagreements soon broke Jefferson's party apart. After the Civil War, Republicans eventually tired of suppressing violent resistance by Southern whites, and the country faced an economic recession. Democrats retook the House in 1874, leading to the end of Republican hegemony and the beginning of an intense period of party competition.

There is a second model of reform that seems more analogous to the present. In this model, constitutional rot so disgusts Americans that reform movements develop in both parties. The party coalitions shift slowly, the most salient issues before the country change, and depolarization begins. Depolarization, in turn, creates the possibility of new policy initiatives that cross-cut the two party coalitions, as well as opportunities for good-government reforms.

The best historical example of this model is the end of the Gilded Age and the beginning of the Progressive Era. Because I believe that we are in our Second Gilded Age, and because I predict that we are slowly moving into our Second Progressive Era, I think this is the most likely scenario.

The 1896 election is generally regarded as the turning point. Since the Civil War, national politics had been organized around responsibility for the Civil War, race, and Reconstruction. By 1896, near the close of the First Gilded Age, huge waves of immigration, the creation of a large urban working class, technological innovation, and the rise of powerful business monopolies led the two major political parties to realign around a new set of controversies and issues. Although a populist insurgency failed, movements for reform sprang up in both political parties. Gradually, the parties depolarized, leading to the Progressive Era and ultimately to the New Deal. In a space of twenty years, a strongly divided United States had transformed into what Mark Graber calls the long state of courts and parties.

The transition was hardly smooth. The first two decades of the twentieth century were a period of deep social unrest, capped by US entry into World War I. The nation's huge inequalities of wealth did not disappear until the Great Depression, which in turn was followed by the Second World War.

The movement from the First Gilded Age to the Progressive Era is the most likely analogy to our present circumstances. We are currently living through a Second Gilded Age. For the past forty years our politics has been organized increasingly around race and the culture wars. Two parties have emerged from that contest. Each party is an unwieldy coalition. Republicans have shed large numbers of educated professionals and suburbanites and are now a coalition of wealthy business interests and the white working class, especially in the Mountain West and South. The Democrats have become a coalition of educated professionals, white women, African Americans, Latinos, Asians, and other minorities, especially on the coasts. Organized labor, once a central component of the old New Deal coalition, remains mostly aligned with the Democrats, but it has been transformed from manufacturing to service and public sector work, and it is only a shell of its former self.

Because the dividing line between the parties is now identity rather than class, each party's coalition cross-cuts class lines. Each party now represents business and professional interests, which we might call its cosmopolitan/neoliberal wing. And each party represents working-class interests, which we might call its populist/working-class wing. Although the media tends to identify the working class with white cultural conservatives, especially in the South and West, much of the Democrats' base is also working-class, consisting of both whites and racial and ethnic minorities.

One might think that given the bitterness of status politics, the propaganda efforts of conservative media, and the relentless demagoguery of the Trump presidency, polarization in the United States will never recede. But ironically, the very forces that led to a politics organized around identity rather than class have produced incoherent party coalitions that will eventually drive the country away from its current zero-sum politics.

The 2016 election—in which Donald Trump incongruously promised to lead a plutocratic party to rescue working-class voters, and Bernie Sanders and Hillary Clinton fought over the soul of the Democratic Party—made it possible to see how the current party system will eventually depolarize. For many years, the two parties will probably continue to disagree vehemently about culture war issues of religion, sexuality, and race. But the populist/working-class wings of both parties have overlapping interests, as do each party's cosmopolitan/neoliberal wings. Just as in the early years of the twentieth century, new issues are likely to displace older ones, diluting the power of identity-based politics.

In particular, issues concerning globalization, the fate of the social safety net, public health, the power of technology companies and monopolies, immigration, and trade may cross-cut party coalitions. Even environmental issues may offer the possibility for cross-party alliances. Although the Republican Party has become the party of climate-change denialism, the actual effects of climate change are real. They will draw the focus of enterprising politicians in both parties, even if Republicans must describe the issues differently.

The Reagan regime reorganized party coalitions around questions of identity—which enabled plutocracy, and led to ever-increasing polarization and corruption. My prediction is that the next regime, in which the Democrats are most likely the dominant party, will expose the incoherent features of both parties' coalitions. Neither party can resist these developments, and activists in both parties will likely contribute to them.

Issues of class, mostly submerged as Democrats and Republicans formed their Reagan-era coalitions, have already begun to resurface, much to the chagrin of the Republican Party's business wing. The only question is which politicians in which parties will be able to take advantage of the incoherence and drive the parties' further evolution. Although it seems as if populist Democrats (variously labeled as social democrats and socialists) will take the lead, they are likely to be hobbled by the party's neoliberal wing. The populists in the Democratic Party may have to form alliances across party lines to make any progress at all. If they do not, the future of American politics will be dominated by the two parties' neoliberal wings. If that happens, reform will be limited.

Despite the darkness of our current politics, history offers the possibility of political renewal. But political renewal is not the same thing as quietude. In fact, it is the opposite. If we are moving out of the Second Gilded Age into a Second Progressive Era, we should not expect a smooth transition. The Progressive Era was a time of social upheaval and racial tensions. The country's profound economic inequality was only remedied by a series of catastrophes: two world wars separated by a Great Depression. These disasters destroyed old fortunes and economic structures and created the opportunity for new arrangements.

We should hope that reform is possible on less drastic terms. But we should also recognize that it took us almost half a century to get into our current mess. The problems of American democracy will not be cured overnight, or even in a decade. Constitutional rot is a stubborn condition; emerging from it will be a painful process. The good news is that the cycles of constitutional time are slowly turning. Politics is re-forming. The elements of renewal are available to us, if we have the courage to use them.

Acknowledgments

The idea for this book began with two lectures on our current political problems. The first was the Addison C. Harris Lecture at the University of Indiana Mauer School of Law in Bloomington, delivered on September 13, 2017. It was eventually published as "The Recent Unpleasantness: Understanding the Cycles of Constitutional Time," 94 *Indiana L. J.* 253 (2019). Chapters 1 through 5 are based on this material. The second talk, "Our Polarized Constitution: Judicial Review in the Cycles of Constitutional Time," was the Constitution Day Lecture at Drake Law School on September 20, 2018. Some of the ideas in that lecture were eventually published as "Why Liberals and Conservatives Flipped on Judicial Restraint: Judicial Review in the Cycles of Constitutional Time," 98 *Tex. L. Rev.* 215 (2019). Chapters 7 and 8 are based on this material.

I would like to thank the Indiana-Mauer and Drake Law Schools for their gracious hospitality.

Following an online symposium on Sandy Levinson's and my book, *Democracy and Dysfunction* (University of Chicago Press 2019), I wrote a series of responses to the contributors which appeared on my blog, Balkinization. The argument of chapter 12 developed out of those responses. The symposium and my responses are available at *Balkinization Symposium on Democracy and Dysfunction—Collected Posts*, Balkinization, June 21, 2019, https://balkin.blogspot.com/2019/06/balkinization-symposium-on-democracy.html [https://perma.cc/768A-ZBX7].

Many friends and colleagues commented on the various lectures and materials that eventually became this book. In particular, I would like to thank Bruce Ackerman, Julia Azari, Steve Calabresi, Steve Griffin, Mark Graber, Dawn Johnsen, Mark Kende, Sanford Levinson, Gerard N. Magliocca, Bill Marshall, Frank Pasquale, Eric Posner, David Pozen, Jed Purdy, Corey Robin, Miguel Schor, Steve Skowronek, and Mark Tushnet. Thanks as well to my editor at OUP, David McBride, who helped speed publication.

And last, but certainly not least, I thank my wife, Margret Wolfe, who makes everything possible.

Notes

Chapter 1

1. These include "the War Between the States" and "the War of Northern Aggression." Elaine Marie Alphin, *An Unspeakable Crime: The Prosecution and Persecution of Leo Frank* 23 (2010) (listing multiple Southern euphemisms for the Civil War).
2. NASA, *Total Solar Eclipse August 21, 2017*, Total Eclipse, https://eclipse2017 .nasa.gov [https://perma.cc/LBP4-EQLW].
3. Ibid.
4. NASA, *How Eclipses Work*, Total Eclipse, https://eclipse2017.nasa.gov/how-eclipses-work [https://perma.cc/8CPW-XGLH].
5. See, e.g., Lawrence B. Solum, *Originalism and Constitutional Construction*, 82 Fordham L. Rev. 453, 459 (2013) ("All of [the] members of the originalist family agree on a core idea—meaning is fixed at the time of origin").
6. See, e.g., Jack M. Balkin, *Living Originalism* 277 (2011) (explaining that living constitutionalism is "the claim that the Constitution adapts—and should adapt—to changing times and conditions, and reflect the evolving values of the American people").
7. See, e.g., Trop v. Dulles, 356 U.S. 86, 100–101 (1958) ("The words of the [Eighth] Amendment are not precise, and . . . their scope is not static. The Amendment must draw its meaning from the evolving standards of decency that mark the progress of a maturing society").
8. W. K. C. Guthrie, *In the Beginning* 63 (1957) ("The Greek mind was especially attracted [to] the idea that as in space, so in time, the cosmic movement was circular. Everything returns to what it was before, and what has been will be again"); Endymion Wilkinson, *Chinese History: A Manual* 513 (rev. and enlarged ed. 2000) (describing the five-phase theory of cycles of Chinese history). The great Chinese Classic of Changes, or I Ching, is structured as a cycle of situations through which time and events flow. See Jack M. Balkin, *The Laws of Change: I Ching and the Philosophy of Life* (2009).
9. 3 *Polybius, The Histories* bk. VI, at 299–315 (W. R. Patton, F. W. Walbank, and Christian Habicht trans., 2011).
10. See generally J. G. A. Pocock, *The Machiavellian Moment: Florentine Political Thought and the Atlantic Republican Tradition* 77, 189, 401, 526, 539, 545, 548 (2d ed. 2003).
11. Henry Adams, *History of the United States During the Administrations of James Madison* 380–81 (1986).
12. Arthur Schlesinger Sr., *Paths to the Present* (1949)(chapter 4, "The Tides of National Politics").
13. Arthur Schlesinger Jr., *The Cycles of American History* (1986).
14. It is not clear that Twain ever actually said this. The closest example comes from 2 Mark Twain and Charles Dudley Warner, *The Gilded Age* 178 (1915 [1873]) ("History never repeats itself, but the kaleidoscopic combinations of the pictured present often seem to be constructed out of the broken fragments of antique legends").

15. The expression "constitutional time" is not original with me, but I use it in a specific way—to describe the interaction of multiple cycles of change that affect the fortunes of a constitutional democracy. For a different usage, see Richard Alexander Izquierdo, *The Architecture of Constitutional Time*, 23 Wm. & Mary Bill Rts. J. 1089, 1091 (2015) (defining "constitutional time" as "the extraordinary historical events that destabilize the regime and open space for new interpretations and constructions to change or supplement constitutional meaning"). Both Izquierdo and I adapt the term from Stephen Skowronek's concept of *political time*, discussed in Part II. Skowronek's political time concerns one of the constituent cycles of constitutional time: the rise and fall of political regimes.
16. Jack M. Balkin, The Last Days of Disco: Why the American Political System is Dysfunctional, 94 B.U. L. Rev. 1159, 1160–61 (2014) (arguing that the United States is in a long and difficult transition between political regimes); cf. Richard Primus, *The Republic in Long-Term Perspective*, 117 Mich. L. Rev. Online 1, 3 (Aug. 2018), http://Michigan lawreview.org/wp-content/uploads/2018/08/117MichLRevOnline1_Primus.pdf [https://perma.cc/3EN7-BZA4] ("The conditions that made the twentieth-century system [of democracy in the United States] possible are gone, and they aren't coming back").
17. *The Liberal Tradition in America: an Interpretation of American Political Thought Since the Revolution* (1955).

Chapter 2

1. Lee Drutman, *American Politics Has Reached Peak Polarization*, Vox (Mar. 24, 2016), https://www.vox.com/polyarchy/2016/3/24/11298808/american-politics-peak-polarization [https://perma.cc/RDL4-XM9B]; see also Jeff Lewis, *Polarization in Congress*, voteview.com (Mar. 11, 2018), https://www.voteview.com/articles/party _polarization [https://perma.cc/5VZB-DUJA] (graph of "Liberal-conservative partisan polarization by chamber"). Focusing on partisan distance between the two major parties in Congress, Lewis notes strong polarization in the 1880s and 1890s followed by a steep decline bottoming out in the 1930s and significant increases following 1984, leading to a new peak, even more severe than the 1890s, in the present.
2. Balkin, *The Last Days of Disco*, Chapter 1, n. 16, at 1159.
3. Ibid.
4. Ibid.
5. See Lewis, *Polarization in Congress*, note 1, (showing that in the late 1970s, polarization was still modest).
6. See Geoffrey C. Layman and Thomas M. Carsey, *Party Polarization and "Conflict Extension" in the American Electorate*, 46 Am. J. Pol. Sci. 786, 789 (2002).
7. See ibid.
8. See Stephen Skowronek, *The Politics Presidents Make: Leadership from John Adams to Bill Clinton* (1997); Stephen Skowronek, *Presidential Leadership in Political Time: Reprise and Reappraisal* 135–36 (2d ed. 2011).
9. See Skowronek, *Presidential Leadership in Political Time*, note 8, at 21 (identifying different regimes in American political history); Andrew J. Polsky, *Partisan Regimes in American Politics*, 44 Polity 51, 52–53 (2012) (describing the regimes of American politics in terms of their dominant political parties); cf. Karen Orren and Stephen Skowronek, *The Search for*

American Political Development 61 (2004) (describing earlier literature based on partisan-realignment theory). I employ Skowronek's model of political regimes in this book. There is a broader "regime politics" literature in political science that argues that the Supreme Court is a majoritarian institution that reflects and/or cooperates with the values and commitments of the dominant national political coalition at any point in time. See Terry Peretti, *In Defense of a Political Court* 248 (1999) (arguing that the Court's work obtains its legitimacy from the judiciary's connection to the dominant forces in American politics); Cornell W. Clayton and J. Mitchell Pickerill, *The Politics of Criminal Justice: How the New Right Regime Shaped the Rehnquist Court's Criminal Justice Jurisprudence*, 94 Geo. L.J. 1385, 1391 (2006) ("Rather than a check on majority power, the federal courts often function as arenas for extending, legitimizing, harmonizing, or protecting the policy agenda of political elites or groups within the dominant governing coalition"); Howard Gillman, *Regime Politics, Jurisprudential Regimes, and Unenumerated Rights*, 9 U. Pa. J. Const. L. 107, 108 (2006) ("The influence of regime politics ensures that federal judges, especially at the top of the judicial hierarchy, will have concerns and preferences that are usually in sync with other national power holders"); Thomas M. Keck, *Party Politics or Judicial Independence? The Regime Politics Literature Hits the Law Schools*, 32 Law & Soc. Inquiry 511, 511 (2007) ("For at least fifty years, prominent political scientists have traced the decisions of the U.S. Supreme Court to the policy and political commitments of governing partisan regimes"). The classic account is Robert A. Dahl, *Decision-Making in a Democracy: The Supreme Court as a National Policy-Maker*, 6 J. Pub. L. 279, 294–95 (1957). In this broader regime politics literature, the relevant "regime" need not correspond to a dominant party. The national political coalition might be bipartisan, as it was throughout much of the twentieth century. In addition, the national political regime does not have to follow the periodization presented in this book.

10. Polsky, *Partisan Regimes in American Politics*, note 9, at 52 ("Newly dominant parties propel bursts of broad political change and then preside over longer interludes of relative stability"); see also Skowronek, *The Politics Presidents Make*, note 8, at 35 (noting that presidents are either allied with the dominant party or form part of the opposition); Jack Balkin, *Obama Hoped to Be a Transformational President. He Failed.*, Vox (Jan. 19, 2017), https:// www.vox.com/the-big-idea/2017/1/19/14323552/obama-legacy-reagan-clinton-conservative -liberal [https://perma.cc/Z2Z2-5MQ8].
11. See Polsky, *Partisan Regimes in American Politics*, note 9, at 56–57, 65. The idea of political regimes emerged from earlier political science models that focused on electoral realignments and critical elections, but scholars have shown that these earlier approaches have serious shortcomings. See, e.g., David R. Mayhew, *Electoral Realignments: A Critique of an American Genre* 165 (2002). As a result, regime theories no longer rest on a particular theory of realigning elections.
12. See Polsky, *Partisan Regimes in American Politics*, note 9, at 57. In the alternative, one can define a regime in terms of how it replaces older government arrangements with new and lasting ones. The New Deal's reconstruction of American governance is a good example. See, e.g., Karen Orren and Stephen Skowronek, *Regimes and Regime Building in American Government: A Review of Literature on the 1940s*, 113 Pol. Sci. Q. 689, 693 (1998–1999) (describing regime building as "a form of elite engineering . . . [that] stabilize[s] . . . governmental operations around a new set of political assumptions").
13. Balkin, *The Last Days of Disco*, Chapter 1, n. 16, at 1170–71.

14. See Orren and Skowronek, *The Search for American Political Development*, note 9, at 61; Polsky, *Partisan Regimes in American Politics*, note 9, at 52. Some scholars treat the realigning election of 1896 as the beginning of a new Republican regime, while others, like Skowronek, do not. See Skowronek, *The Politics Presidents Make*, note 8, at 230–33 (arguing that Theodore Roosevelt was still working within the Republican regime created in 1860).
15. Balkin, *The Last Days of Disco*, Chapter 1, n. 16, at 1170.
16. Ronald Brownstein, *The Hidden History of the American Electorate (II)*, Nat'l J. (Aug. 24, 2012), https://www.yahoo.com/news/hidden-history-american-electorate-ii -175214333. html [https://perma.cc/M5JN-YMCP] (describing Obama's "coalition of the ascendant").
17. Nate Cohn, *How the Obama Coalition Crumbled, Leaving an Opening for Trump*, N.Y. Times (Dec. 23, 2016), https://www.nytimes.com/2016/12/23/upshot/how-the-obama-coalition-crumbled-leaving-an-opening-for-trump.html [https://perma.cc/66ZG-WHPZ].
18. Sean Trende and David Byler, *Republican Party the Strongest It's Been in 80 Years*, Real Clear Pol. (Nov. 17, 2016), https://www.realclearpolitics.com/articles/2016 /11/17/republican_party_the_strongest_its_been_in_80_years.html [https://perma.cc/UZX9-XXPW].
19. Ibid.
20. Eric Boehm, *Democrats Got Wrecked Again in State Legislative Races, and It Matters More than You Might Think*, Reason (Nov. 14, 2016), https://reason.com/blog /2016/11/14/the-2016-election-turned-more-state-legi [https://perma.cc/PGH2-Y9QH].
21. David Frum, *The Great Republican Revolt*, Atlantic (Jan./Feb. 2016), https://www.theatlantic.com/magazine/archive/2016/01/the-great-republican-revolt/419118 [https://perma.cc/D554-WYVT].
22. See, e.g., Jane Mayer, Dark Money: The Hidden History of the Billionaires Behind the Rise of the Radical Right 165–68 (2016) (describing the role of powerful funders who fostered the Tea Party movement); Nicholas Confessore, *Koch Brothers' Budget of $889 Million for 2016 Is on Par with Both Parties' Spending*, N.Y. Times (Jan. 26, 2015), https://www.nytimes.com/2015/01/27/us/politics/kochs-plan-to-spend-900-million -on-2016-campaign.html [https://perma.cc/PC9Y-MJZD].
23. Pew Research Ctr., *Wide Gender Gap, Growing Educational Divide in Voters' Party Identification* 1–2 (Mar. 20, 2018), https://www.courthousenews.com/wp -content/uploads/2018/03/PewPartyID.pdf [https://perma.cc/U94C-6W4Q].
24. Thomas E. Mann and Norman J. Ornstein, *It's Even Worse than It Looks: How the American Constitutional System Collided with the New Politics of Extremism* 44 (2012) (describing consequences of Republican strategies of polarization).
25. *United States Presidential Election Results*, Encyclopedia Britannica, https:// www.britannica.com/topic/United-States-Presidential-Election-Results-1788863 [https://perma.cc/PX7E-ZW9S].
26. Skowronek, *The Politics Presidents Make*, note 8, at 30; Skowronek, *Presidential Leadership in Political Time,* note 8, at 27. Skowronek distinguishes political time from secular time, which describes the evolution of power structures. Skowronek, *The Politics Presidents Make*, note 8, at 30. He argues that as time moves forward, institutions thicken and interests coalesce, making it increasingly difficult for Presidents to displace the existing order and create a new one.
27. Skowronek, *The Politics Presidents Make*, note 8, at 36.

28. Ibid. at 36–39; Skowronek, *Presidential Leadership in Political Time,* note 8, at 92–98.
29. Skowronek, *Presidential Leadership in Political Time,* note 8, at 94.
30. Skowronek, *The Politics Presidents Make,* note 8, at 41–43; Skowronek, *Presidential Leadership in Political Time,* note 8, at 99–104.
31. Skowronek, *The Politics Presidents Make,* note 8, at 14, 88, 350.
32. Skowronek, *Presidential Leadership in Political Time,* note 8, at 99–104.
33. Skowronek, *The Politics Presidents* Make, note 8, at 43–45; Skowronek, *Presidential Leadership in Political Time,* note 8, at 105–13.
34. Skowronek, *Presidential Leadership in Political Time,* note 8, at 105–13.
35. Skowronek, *The Politics Presidents Make,* note 8, at 39–41; Skowronek, *Presidential Leadership in Political Time,* note 8, at 86–92.
36. Skowronek, *The Politics Presidents Make,* note 8, at 39–41.
37. The next seven paragraphs are adapted from Jack M. Balkin, *What Kind of President Will Trump Become?, Part I,* Balkinization (Nov. 13, 2016), https://balkin .blogspot.com/2016/11/what-kind-of-President-will-trump_13.html [https://perma.cc/H8S3 -EN56].
38. Bradford Richardson, *Trump Compares Himself to Reagan,* Hill (Sept. 1, 2015), http://thehill.com/blogs/ballot-box/Presidential-races/252483-trump-compares-himself-to - reagan [https://perma.cc/HCS3-9J74]; Anjali Shastry, *Trump Likens Himself to Reagan as a Truly Conservative Candidate,* Wash. Times (Jan. 24, 2016), https://www.washington times.com/news/2016/jan/24/donald-trump-likens-himself-ronald-reagan-truly-co [https:// perma.cc/G7FD-DLE2]; Karen Tumulty, *How Donald Trump Came Up with "Make America Great Again,"* Wash. Post (Jan. 18, 2017), https://www.washington post.com/politics/how-donald-trump-came-up-with-make-america-great-again/2017/01/17 /fb6acf5e-dbf7-11e6-ad42-f3375f271c9c_story.html [https://perma.cc/8AZL-BMVQ] (explaining that Trump was originally unaware that his slogan was based on Reagan's 1980 slogan "Let's Make America Great Again").
39. Marc A. Thiessen, *Why Conservative Christians Stick with Trump,* Wash. Post (Mar. 23, 2018), https://www.washingtonpost.com/opinions/why-conservative-christians -stick-with-trump/2018/03/23/2766309a-2def-11e8-8688-e053ba58f1e4_story.html?utm _ term=.99af931845cc [https://perma.cc/48MD-ESR7] (describing Trump's support for Christian conservatives); Jeffrey Toobin, *The Conservative Pipeline to the Supreme Court,* New Yorker (Apr. 17, 2017), https://www.newyorker.com/magazine/2017/04/17/the - conservative-pipeline-to-the-supreme-court [https://perma.cc/UZ2T-X5GR] (describing the influence of the Federalist Society on Trump's judicial appointments).
40. See Stephen Skowronek, *Is Donald Trump the Great Disrupter? Probably Not.*, Wash. Post (Apr. 24, 2017), https://www.washingtonpost.com/opinions/is-donald-trump -the-great-disruptor-probably-not/2017/04/24/99c86938-25d9-11e7-bb9d-8cd6118e1409 _story.html?utm_term=.b8ef7a0f0915 [https://perma.cc/6WV6-27MS] (arguing that Trump is not a reconstructive President).
41. John Wagner and Juliet Eilperin, *Once a Populist, Trump Governs Like a Conservative Republican,* Wash. Post (Dec. 6, 2017), https://www.washingtonpost .com/politics/once-a-populist-trump-governs-like-a-conservative-republican/2017/12/05 /e73c6106-d902-11e7-b1a8-62589434a581_story.html?utm_term=.79caf19edeb7 [https:// perma.cc/SK8D-94KG].
42. On Obama's pre-emptive presidency, see Balkin, *Obama Hoped to Be a Transformational President. He Failed,* note 10.

43. Katie Glueck, *Trump Blames George W. Bush for 9/11*, Politico (Feb. 13, 2016), https://www.politico.com/blogs/south-carolina-primary-2016-live-updates-and-results/2016 / 02/gop-debate-2016-trump-911-219260 [https://perma.cc/GVV2-CGEB] (describing Trump's criticisms of George W. Bush during the 2016 campaign); see also Bernie Becker, *Trump's 6 Populist Positions*, Politico (Feb. 13, 2016), https://www.politico.com/story /2016/02/donald-trump-working-class-voters-219231 [https://perma.cc/3HW2-BCWM] (describing Trump's departures from Republican orthodoxy during the 2016 campaign).
44. See Jack M. Balkin, *What Kind of President Will Trump Become?, Part II—Donald Trump and the Politics of Disjunction*, Balkinization (Nov. 14, 2016), https://balkin.blogspot.com/2016/11/what-kind-of-President-will-trump.html [https://perma .cc/K2TS-DXFR].
45. Skowronek, *The Politics that Presidents Make*, note 8, at 40.
46. Balkin, *What Kind of President Will Trump Become?, Part II* note 37.
47. Skowronek, *The Politics that Presidents Make*, note 8, at 40; see also Richard Kreitner, *What Time Is It? Here's What the 2016 Election Tells Us About Obama, Trump, and What Comes Next*, The Nation (Nov. 22, 2016), https://www.thenation.com /article/what-time-is-it-heres-what-the-2016-election-tells-us-about-obama-trump-and-what-comes-next [https://perma.cc/5Y2G-4EML] (interview with Skowronek explaining why Trump is unlikely to be a reconstructive president and may be disjunctive).
48. For other assessments arguing that Trump is a disjunctive President, see Julia Azari, *Trump's Presidency Signals the End of the Reagan Era*, Vox (Dec. 1, 2016), https://www.vox.com/mischiefs-of-faction/2016/12/1/13794680/trump-presidency-reagan-era-end [https://perma.cc/ANM7-Z2A3]; Corey Robin, *The Politics Trump Makes*, n+1 (Jan. 11, 2017), https://nplusonemag.com/online-only/online-only/the-politics-trump-makes [https://perma.cc/PZ5P-PSVE].
49. See Skowronek, *The Politics Presidents Make*, note 8, at 32; Stephen Skowronek, *Twentieth-Century Remedies*, 94 B.U. L. Rev. 795, 801 (2014).
50. Skowronek, *The Politics Presidents Make*, note 8, at 427–28; see also Skowronek, *Presidential Leadership in Political Time*, note 8, at 181–86 (arguing that the age of transformative presidencies is over); Stephen Skowronek, *Twentieth-Century Remedies*, note 49 (2014) (same).
51. See Skowronek, *The Politics Presidents Make*, note 8, at 55–58, 442–44.
52. Ibid. at 407, 442–44.
53. Ibid. at 442–44.
54. Skowronek, *Twentieth-Century Remedies*, note 49, at 803 (arguing that President Obama has correctly perceived the "new reality . . . that, for all intents and purposes, the interdependence of interests has rendered the reconstructive option counterproductive").
55. Balkin, *Living Originalism*, Chapter 1, n. 6, at 35.
56. Balkin, *The Last Days of Disco*, Chapter 1, n. 16, at 1185–87.
57. Gerard N. Magliocca, *The Tragedy of William Jennings Bryan: Constitutional Law and the Politics of Backlash* 2–5 (2014); Polsky, *Partisan Regimes in American Politics*, note 9, at 64–65.
58. See generally R. Hal Williams, *Realigning America: McKinley, Bryan, and the Remarkable Election of 1896* (2010).

Chapter 3

1. See Lewis, *Polarization in Congress*, Chapter 2, n. 1.
2. Richard White, *The Republic for Which It Stands: The United States During Reconstruction and the Gilded Age, 1865–1896*, at 67, 211, 327, 337, 403 (2017) (describing the Republican strategy of "waving the bloody shirt").
3. See Lewis, *Polarization in Congress*, Chapter 2, n. 1.
4. Byron E. Shafer, *The American Political Pattern: Stability and Change, 1932–2016*, at 134 (2016). One could further divide Republicans into Regular Republicans and Northeastern Republicans. Ibid. at 34–35.
5. Ibid. at 53–57.
6. Ibid. at 132–39.
7. Ibid. at 139–40; Richard H. Pildes, *Why the Center Does Not Hold: The Causes of Hyperpolarized Democracy in America*, 99 Calif. L. Rev. 273, 287–97 (2011) (arguing that the Voting Rights Act of 1965, which broke the South's one-party monopoly, is an important cause of polarization).
8. Steven Levitsky and Daniel Ziblatt, *How Democracies Die* 146–51 (2018) (describing Gingrich's strategy of demonizing his political allies); Mann and Ornstein, *It's Even Worse than It Looks*, Chapter 2, n. 24, at 35–39 (same).
9. See Steven M. Teles, *The Rise of the Conservative Legal Movement: The Battle for Control of the Law* 135–80 (2008) (describing how funders helped shape the conservative legal movement); Joseph Fishkin and David E. Pozen, *Asymmetric Constitutional Hardball*, 118 Colum. L. Rev. 915, 951–56 (2018) (describing creation of conservative counterinstitutions).
10. Mann and Ornstein, *It's Even Worse than It Looks*, Chapter 2, n. 24, at 51–58 (describing asymmetric polarization); Michael Barber and Nolan McCarty, *Causes and Consequences of Polarization*, in Am. Political Sci. Ass'n, Negotiating Agreement in Politics 19–26 (Jane Mansbridge and Cathie Jo Martin eds., 2013) (reviewing evidence of asymmetric polarization).
11. Frank Newport, *Conservative Democrats, Liberal Republicans Hard to Find*, Gallup (Sept. 2, 2009), https://news.gallup.com/poll/122672/conservative-democrats-liberal-republicans-hard-to-find.aspx [https://perma.cc/E2SB-78SC].
12. Levitsky and Ziblatt, *How Democracies Die*, note 8, at 145–75 (describing the Republican strategy of obstruction and polarization from the 1990s onward); Mann and Ornstein, *It's Even Worse than It Looks*, Chapter 2, n. 24, at 55, 84–90 (same).
13. Doyle McManus, *Bush's Vow To Unite Encounters a Great Divide*, L.A. Times (Dec. 14, 2000), http://articles.latimes.com/2000/dec/14/news/mn-65530 [https://perma.cc/WM63-B97J].
14. *Karl Rove—The Architect*, PBS: Frontline (Apr. 12, 2015), https://www.pbs.org/wgbh/pages/frontline/shows/architect/rove/2004.html [https://perma.cc/4PL6-ALR8].
15. Lee Drutman, *Yes, the Republican Party Has Become Pathological. But Why?* Vox (Sept. 22, 2017), https://www.vox.com/polyarchy/2017/9/22/16345194/republican-party-pathological [https://perma.cc/5F7B-56L4] (arguing that given the nature of their coalition Republicans had good reason to adopt polarization strategies to ensure electoral success).
16. Ibid.; see also Matt Grossmann and David A. Hopkins, *Asymmetric Politics: Ideological Republicans and Group Interest Democrats* (2016) (arguing that Republican voters reward candidates who value ideological purity and refuse to compromise).

As the country polarized, Republicans also led the way by engaging in more and more constitutional hardball, straining and breaking existing conventions of mutual tolerance and institutional forbearance for partisan advantage. See Fishkin and Pozen, *Asymmetric Constitutional Hardball*, note 9, (describing Republicans' increasing use of constitutional hardball).

17. Balkin, *The Last Days of Disco*, Chapter 1, n. 16, at 1193–94.
18. See Gillian E. Metzger, *Foreword: 1930s Redux: The Administrative State Under Siege*, 131 Harv. L. Rev. 1 (2017).
19. See Stephen Skowronek, *The Conservative Insurgency and Presidential Power: A Developmental Perspective on the Unitary Executive*, 122 Harv. L. Rev. 2070 (2009).
20. See Shafer, *The American Political Pattern*, note 4, at 173–74.
21. Ibid. (arguing that period of gridlock leading to crises followed by omnibus bills characterizes the "Era of Partisan Volatility").
22. See Lee Drutman, *Breaking the Two-Party Doom Loop: The Case for Multiparty Democracy in America* (2020) (arguing for ranked-choice voting and many other reforms to encourage the formation of multiple parties); Sanford Levinson and Jack M. Balkin, *Democracy and Dysfunction* (2019) (arguing for repealing the federal statute that requires single member House districts, ranked-choice voting, and reform of the Electoral College).
23. See Lewis, *Polarization in Congress*, Chapter 2, n. 1. (showing cycle of party polarization in Congress).
24. Nolan McCarty, *Polarization: What Everyone Needs to Know* (2019); Ezra Klein, *Why We're Polarized* (2020).
25. McCarty, *Polarization*, note 24; Nolan McCarty, Keith T. Poole, and Howard Rosenthal, *Polarized America: The Dance of Ideology and Unequal Riches* (2016).
26. Peter H. Lindert and Jeffrey G. Williamson, *American Incomes 1774–1860*, NBER Working Paper No. w18396 (September 15, 2012), https://papers.ssrn.com/sol3/papers.cfm?abstract_id=2147106, at 24.
27. Campbell Gibson and Kay Jung, *Historical Census Statistics On The Foreign-Born Population Of The United States: 1850 to 2000*, Working Paper No. 81, Census.gov, https://www.census.gov/population/www/documentation/twps0081/twps0081.pdf [https://perma.cc/XV35-RJKC].
28. McCarty, Poole, and Rosenthal, *Polarized America*, note 25, at 123–25.
29. Ibid. at 123.
30. Ibid.
31. Ibid. at 123.
32. Ibid. at 123–24.
33. Pollock v. Farmers' Loan & Trust Company, 157 U.S. 429 (1895), aff'd on rehearing, 158 U.S. 601 (1895).
34. Bill Chappell, *U.S. Income Inequality Worsens, Widening To A New Gap*, NPR.org, September 26, 2019, https://www.npr.org/2019/09/26/764654623/u-s-income-inequality-worsens-widening-to-a-new-gap [https://perma.cc/8L27-NWP4]; Taylor Telford, *Income Inequality in the United States Is the Highest It's Been Since Census Bureau Started Tracking It, Data Shows*, Washington Post, September 26, 2019, https://www.washingtonpost.com/business/2019/09/26/income-inequality-america-highest-its-been-since-census-started-tracking-it-data-show/ [https://perma.cc/7QT6-PMND].

35. William H. Frey, *US Foreign-Born Gains Are Smallest in a Decade, Except in Trump States*, Brookings Institute, October 2, 2019, https://www.brookings.edu/blog/the-avenue/2019/10/01/us-foreign-born-gains-are-smallest-in-a-decade-except-in-trump-states/ [https://perma.cc/RZ9Y-XDJR].

Chapter 4

1. See Sanford Levinson and Jack M. Balkin, *Constitutional Crises*, 157 U. Pa. L. Rev. 707 (2009).
2. See, e.g., Jessica Schulberg and Sam Levine, *Trump Inches the U.S. Closer to Constitutional Crisis*, HuffPost (Feb. 4, 2017) http://www.huffingtonpost .com/entry/trump-constitutional-crisis-judge-robart_us_58964292e4b09bd304bba74f [https://perma.cc/U8SU-Q8DV] (quoting Senator Patrick Leahy's statement that President Trump "seems intent on precipitating a constitutional crisis").
3. See, e.g., David Cole, *Trump's Constitutional Crisis*, N.Y. Rev. Books (May 10, 2017), http://www.nybooks.com/daily/2017/05/10/trumps-constitutional-crisis-james-comey/ [https://perma.cc/97RN-87PZ] ("This is a constitutional crisis"); Alexandra Wilts, *Comey Fired: America Is Witnessing a Constitutional Crisis, Says Leading Democrat*, Independent (May 10, 2017), http://www.independent.co.uk/news/world/americas/us -politics/james-comey-fired-donald-trump-constitutional-crisis-fbi-director-russian -investigation-latest-news-a7727341.html [https://perma.cc/4F5G-LD3A] (quoting Representative Keith Ellison's remark that "we are witnessing a constitutional crisis unfold before our very eyes").
4. Jonathan Chait, *The Constitutional Crisis Is Already Underway*, N.Y. Mag.: Daily Intelligencer (June 2, 2018), http://nymag.com/daily/intelligencer/2018/06/the -constitutional-crisis-is-already-underway.html [https://perma.cc/8Q86-2YC2]; Robert Reich, *We're Living a Constitutional Crisis*, Am. Prospect (July 24, 2018), http://prospect.org/article/were-living-constitutional-crisis [https://perma.cc/YAJ4-GPBM]; Eugene Robinson, *The Constitutional Crisis Is Here*, Wash. Post (May 21, 2018), https://www.washingtonpost.com/opinions/the-constitutional-crisis-is-here/2018/05/21 /deaf19b2-5d27-11e8-a4a4-c070ef53f315_story.html?utm_term=.854f7f8a567e [https:// perma.cc/L4FM-37MS].
5. Levinson and Balkin, *Constitutional Crises*, note 1, at 711, 714–15.
6. Ibid. at 714, 721–29 (describing "type one" crises).
7. Ibid. at 714, 729–38 (describing "type two" crises).
8. Ibid. at 729–31 (giving the example of President Abraham Lincoln taking a different view of the power to respond to rebellion than his predecessor, President James Buchanan).
9. Ibid. at 714, 738–46 (describing "type three" crises).
10. Ibid.
11. Keith Whittington's typology distinguishes between crises of operation and crises of fidelity. Crises of operation occur when "important political disputes cannot be resolved within the existing constitutional framework." Crises of operation occur when "important political actors threaten to become no longer willing to abide by existing constitutional arrangements or systematically contradict constitutional proscriptions." Keith E. Whittington, Yet Another Constitutional Crisis?, 43 Wm. & Mary L. Rev. 2093, 2101, 2109–2110 (2002). These formulas overlap with the three types of crises just described. Whether one adopts Whittington's typology or Levinson's and mine, all of us agree that

a constitutional crisis arises when the constitutional system is unable to contain political struggle within its terms.

12. Cf. Jack M. Balkin, *Constitutional Hardball and Constitutional Crises*, 26 Quinnipiac L. Rev. 579, 590 (2008) ("Many so-called 'constitutional crises' are not real crises at all, but rather heated disagreements about the Constitution in which people fear (whether reasonably or unreasonably) that the system will spin out of control").
13. Levinson and Balkin, *Constitutional Crises*, note 1, at 722–23 (noting that American presidents have never asserted prerogative powers to act outside the Constitution; instead they offer controversial interpretations that justify their actions).
14. See, e.g., Schulberg and Levine, *Trump Inches the U.S. Closer to Constitutional Crisis*, note 2.
15. See Trump v. Hawaii, 138 S. Ct. 2392 (2018) (describing the course of the litigation from Trump's first executive order through his third executive order, upheld by the Supreme Court).
16. See, e.g., Daniel Bush, *Trump Firing Mueller Would "Create a Constitutional Crisis," Sen. Warner Says*, PBS: NewsHour (Apr. 19, 2018), https://www.pbs.org /newshour/show/trump-firing-mueller-would-create-a-constitutional-crisis-sen-warner-says [https://perma.cc/MW29-TKAG]; Brandon Carter, *Booker Says Mueller Firing Would Be 'Constitutional Crisis'*, Hill (Jan. 26, 2018), http://thehill.com/homenews /senate/370883-booker-trump-considering-firing-mueller-could-cause-constitutional-crisis [https://perma.cc/C6HV-R595]; Cole, *Trump's Constitutional Crisis*, note 3 (arguing that Comey firing was a crisis); Wilts, *Comey Fired*, note 3 (same).
17. Constitutionality of Legislation Extending the Term of the FBI Director, 35 Op. O.L.C. 1, 3 (June 20, 2011) ("The FBI Director is removable at the will of the President. . . . No statute purports to restrict the President's power to remove the Director"), https://www .justice.gov/sites/default/files/olc/opinions/2011/06/31/fbi-director-term_0.pdf [https:// perma.cc/5PVF-9H4P]; Robert Chesney, *Backgrounder: The Power to Appoint & Remove the FBI Director*, Lawfare (May 10, 2017), https://www.lawfareblog.com /backgrounder-power-appoint-remove-fbi-director [https://perma.cc/2GXD-HBTP] ("Congress at no point has attempted to constrain the President's removal power").
18. 28 C.F.R. § 600.7(d) (2017) ("The Special Counsel may be disciplined or removed from office only by the personal action of the Attorney General. The Attorney General may remove a Special Counsel for misconduct, dereliction of duty, incapacity, conflict of interest, or for other good cause, including violation of Departmental policies"). A related concern was the fear during the Meuller investigation that the president would refuse a subpoena by Special Prosecutor Mueller. This never happened, and so the issue did not arise. See, e.g., Paul Rosenzweig, *What Would Actually Happen if Trump Refused a Subpoena?*, Atlantic (May 26, 2018), https://www.theatlantic.com/politics/archive /2018/05/trump-mueller-russia-subpoena/560981 [https://perma.cc/LC6M-C3VA] ("Many would call the President's refusal to obey a court's lawful order a 'constitutional crisis,' and that's probably accurate").
19. Cf. Levinson and Balkin, *Constitutional Crises*, note 1, at 714 ("Disagreement and conflict are natural features of politics. The goal of constitutions is to manage them within acceptable boundaries").
20. Jack Goldsmith, *Will Donald Trump Destroy the Presidency?*, The Atlantic (Oct. 2017), https://www.theatlantic.com/magazine/archive/2017/10/will-donald-trump-destroy

-the-presidency/537921 [https://perma.cc/E5BB-S5HB] ("Though many worried that Nixon would disobey the Supreme Court in 1974 when it ordered him to turn over his incriminating tapes to a special prosecutor, Nixon famously acquiesced").

21. Levinson and Balkin, *Constitutional Crises*, note 1, at 742 (arguing that failure to comply with an order from the Supreme Court would have precipitated a "type one" crisis).
22. Cf. ibid. at 745 ("People may have regarded Watergate, the 2000 election, and the *Steel Seizure Case* as crises not because they were crises in the sense we describe, but because they feared that they would become that sort of crisis").
23. See, e.g., Garrett Epps, *The Census Case Could Provoke a Constitutional Crisis*, The Atlantic, July 8, 2019, https://www.theatlantic.com/ideas/archive/2019/07/census-case-could-provoke-constitutional-crisis/593425/.

Chapter 5

1. See Jack M. Balkin, *Constitutional Crisis and Constitutional Rot, in* Constitutional Deomocracy in Crisis? 13 (Mark A. Graber, Sanford Levinson and Mark Tushnet, eds., 2018); Jack M. Balkin, *Constitutional Rot*, in Can It Happen Here?: Authoritarianism in America 19 (Cass R. Sunstein ed., 2018).
2. Balkin, *Constitutional Rot*, note 1, at 20. John Finn uses the term "constitutional rot" in a somewhat different sense. While I focus on a decline in the twin values of democracy and republicanism, Finn argues that constitutional rot can occur "even . . . when constitutional institutions appear to be in good repair." John Finn, *Peopling the Constitution* 32 (2014). In Finn's theory, a constitutional system rots when constitutional questions are reduced to purely legal questions, and the public becomes disengaged from the maintenance and defense of constitutional values.
3. Thomas Paine, *Rights of Man: Being an Answer to Mr. Burke's Attack on the French Revolution* (1791), reprinted in *Thomas Paine: Collected Writ*ings 433, 565 (Eric Foner ed., 1995) ("Res-publica, the public affairs, or the public good; or, literally translated, the *public thing* . . . refer[s] to what ought to be the character and business of government").
4. See *Paine, Rights of Man,* in *Paine: Collected Writings*, note 3, at 565; Gordon S. Wood, *The Creation of the American Republic, 1776–1787*, at 55–56 (1969); Jack M. Balkin, *Republicanism and the Constitution of Opportunity*, 94 Tex. L. Rev. 1427, 1433 (2016).
5. Balkin, *Constitutional Rot*, note 1, at 19–20.
6. See, e.g., Pete V. Domenici and Alice M. Rivlin, *Proposal for Improving the Congressional Budget Process*, Brookings (July 17, 2015), https://www.brookings .edu/research/proposal-for-improving-the-congressional-budget-process [https://perma.cc /BWX5-8U7Q] ("In the face of increasing partisan polarization and frequent gridlock, Congress and the executive branch have lurched from one budget crisis to another and kept the government running by means of continuing resolutions and massive omnibus appropriations bills. They have sought to force themselves to make decisions by resorting to special, sometimes bizarre devices, including the super committee, the fiscal cliff, and sequestration").
7. Balkin, *Constitutional Rot*, note 1, at 19–20.
8. Ibid.
9. For an excellent discussion of the importance of these norms in preserving democratic government, see Levitsky and Ziblatt, *How Democracies Die*, Chapter 3, n. 8, at 102–17 (2018).

10. Ibid. at 7–8.
11. Ibid. at 102–17.
12. Balkin, *Constitutional Crisis and Constitutional Rot,* note 1; Levitsky and Ziblatt, *How Democracies Die*, Chapter 3, n. 8 at 102–17.
13. Balkin, *Constitutional Rot*, note 1, at 21.
14. See Nancy Bermeo, *On Democratic Backsliding*, 27 J. Democracy 5, 5 (2016) (explaining democratic backsliding as "the state-led debilitation or elimination of any of the political institutions that sustain an existing democracy"); Aziz Huq and Thomas Ginsburg, *How to Lose a Constitutional Democracy*, 65 UCLA L. Rev. 78 (2018) (describing "democratic retrogression"). On the idea of constitutional hardball, see Mark Tushnet, *Constitutional Hardball*, 37 J. Marshall L. Rev. 523, 523 (2004).
15. Walter Isaacson, *Benjamin Franklin: An American Life* 459 (2003).
16. *The Records of the Federal Convention of 1787*, Volume 2, at 642 (Max Farrand ed., rev. ed. 1966).
17. See Carl J. Richard, *Greeks and Romans Bearing Gifts: How the Ancients Inspired the Founding Fathers* (2009) (describing the influence of Aristotle, Cicero, Polybius, and other classical authors on the Founders).
18. See ibid.; Ganesh Sitaraman, *The Crisis of the Middle-Class Constitution* 11–12 (2017) (describing the process of corruption of republics).
19. Philip Pettit, *Republicanism: A Theory of Freedom and Government* 210–11 (1997) (arguing that the basic problem of republics is to promote resilience and stability in the face of continual sources of temptation and corruption); Wood, *The Creation of the American Republic*, note 4, at 105 ("Precisely because republics required civic virtue and disinterestedness among their citizens, they were very fragile polities, extremely liable to corruption"); Balkin, *Republicanism and the Constitution of Opportunity*, note 4, at 1444 ("Time is the great enemy of republics, because as time goes on and circumstances change, corruption finds ever-new ways of entering the system, weakening the institutions and practices that ensure republican government").
20. See James W. Ceaser, *Presidential Selection: Theory and Development* 61 (1979) ("The possibility of a national demagogue was one of the greatest fears of the Founders and literally frames *The Federalist*, being mentioned in both the first and last numbers"); Zephyr Teachout, *The Anti-Corruption Principle*, 94 Cornell L. Rev. 341, 352 (2009) ("The Constitution was intended to provide structural encouragements to keep the logic and language of society as a whole from becoming corrupt, representing a technical and moral response to what they saw as a technical and moral problem").
21. Sanford Levinson and Jack M. Balkin, *Democracy and Dysfunction* 70–76 (2019)(describing how the Constitution protects against demagogues).
22. See Balkin, *Constitutional Rot*, note 1, at 21–23.
23. Ibid. at 21.
24. Ibid. at 25; Timothy Snyder, *The Road to Unfreedom: Russia, Europe, America* (2018) (arguing that Russia employs propaganda strategies and tactics it had previously used on its own people to disrupt liberal democracies in Europe and the United States); Nicholas Confessore and Daisuke Wakabayashi, *How Russia Harvested American Rage to Reshape U.S. Politics*, N.Y. Times (Oct. 9, 2017), https://www.nytimes.com/2017/10/09/technology/russia-election-facebook-ads-rage.html [https://perma.cc/KMF7-F58K].

25. Balkin, *Constitutional Rot*, note 1, at 21; Kelly Born and Nell Edgington, Hewlett Found., *Analysis of Philanthropic Opportunities to Mitigate the Disinformation/Propaganda Problem* 7–17 (2017), https://hewlett.org/wp-content /uploads/2017/11/Hewlett-Disinformation-Propaganda-Report.pdf [https://perma.cc/UUN7-PJYR]; Robert Faris, Hal Roberts, Bruce Etling, Nikki Bourassa, Ethan Zuckerman, and Yochai Benkler, Berkman Klein Ctr. for Internet & Soc'y, *Partisanship, Propaganda, & Disinformation: Online Media and the 2016 U.S. Presidential Election* 25–31 (2017), https://dash.harvard.edu/bitstream/handle/1 /33759251/2017-08_electionReport_0.pdf?sequence=9&isAllowed=y [https://perma.cc /U9GM-U9SX]; Alice Marwick and Rebecca Lewis, Data & Soc'y Research Inst., *Media Manipulation and Disinformation Online* (2017), https://datasociety.net/pubs/oh / DataAndSociety_MediaManipulationAndDisinformationOnline.pdf [https://perma.cc/P653 -W6AD].
26. Born and Edgington, *Analysis of Philanthropic Opportunities to Mitigate the Disinformation/Propaganda Problem*, note 25, at 4; cf. Jason Stanley, *How Propaganda Works* 93, 108–109, 120 (2015) (explaining that in democracies, propaganda harms shared ideals of public reason and erodes empathy toward others).
27. Balkin, *Constitutional Rot*, note 1, at 26 (arguing that successful propaganda enhances motivated reasoning and tribalism); cf. Stanley, *How Propaganda Works*, note 26, at 120–26 (explaining that propaganda shuts off rational debate about policy and can be used to undermine empathy for minority groups).
28. Balkin, *Constitutional Rot*, note 1, at 25 (propaganda undermines trust between citizens and between citizens and officials necessary for democracy to function); Stanley, *How Propaganda Works*, note 26, at 96, 108–109, 120–24 (describing how propaganda undermines the forms of reasoning necessary to democracy).
29. Balkin, *Constitutional Rot*, note 1, at 22 (describing the Four Horsemen of Constitutional Rot).
30. Stephen M. Griffin, *Broken Trust: Dysfunctional Government and Constitutional Reform* 20 (2015).
31. Balkin, *Constitutional Rot*, note 1, at 22; Griffin, *Broken Trust*, note 30, at 20–21.
32. Balkin, *Constitutional Rot*, note 1, at 22–23.
33. See, e.g., John Voorheis, Nolan McCarty and Boris Shor, *Unequal Incomes, Ideology and Gridlock: How Rising Inequality Increases Political Polarization* (Aug. 21, 2015), https://papers.ssrn.com/sol3/papers.cfm?abstract_id=2649215 [https://perma.cc/J8DD -WPWM].
34. Balkin, *Constitutional Rot*, note 1, at 22.
35. For the most recent version of this argument, which was well known to the Framers, see Sitaraman, *The Crisis of the Middle-Class Constitution*, note 18, at 232–39; Ganesh Sitaraman, *Economic Structure and Constitutional Structure: An Intellectual History*, 94 Tex. L. Rev. 1301, 1320 (2016) ("The founding generation embraced the middle-class-constitutional theory that relative economic equality was necessary for republican government").
36. Sitaraman, *The Crisis of the Middle-Class Constitution*, note 18, at 11–12; Sitaraman, *Economic Structure and Constitutional Structure: An Intellectual History*, note 35, at 1304.
37. Sitaraman, *The Crisis of the Middle-Class Constitution*, note 18, at 5; Sitaraman, *Economic Structure and Constitutional Structure: An Intellectual History*, note 35, at 1302.
38. Balkin, *Republicanism and the Constitution of Opportunity*, note 4, at 1442.

39. Douglass G. Adair, *The Intellectual Origins of Jeffersonian Democracy: Republicanism, the Class Struggle, and the Virtuous Farmer* 50–52 (Mark E. Yellin ed., 2000) (1964).
40. Heather Cox Richardson, *To Make Men Free: A History of the Republican Party* xii, 4, 6–7, 9 (2014); Gordon S. Wood, *Empire of Liberty: A History of the Early Republic, 1789–1815*, at 498 (2009).
41. See Adair, *The Intellectual Origins of Jeffersonian Democracy*, note 39, at 52; Wood, *Empire of Liberty*, note 40, at 151–52; James Madison, *A Candid State of Parties*, Nat'l Gazette, Sept. 22, 1792, at 378 (arguing for a party opposed to monarchism and hereditary privilege, which Madison associated with the Federalist Party).
42. Richardson, *To Make Men Free*, note 40, at 6–7.
43. Ibid. at 13.
44. Ibid. at 6–7; see also Eric Foner, *Free Soil, Free Labor, Free Men: The Ideology of the Republican Party Before the Civil War* 46–50, 59–60, 63–65, 87–91 (1995) (describing Republican and Free Soil critiques of Southern society, which blamed the expansion of slavery for impoverishing whites who did not own slaves, undermining social mobility, and perpetuating aristocracy); Andrew Shankman, *Introduction: Conflict for a Continent: Land, Labor, and the State in the First American Republic*, in *The World of the Revolutionary American Republic: Land, Labor and the Conflict for a Continent* 1, 17 (Andrew Shankman ed., 2014).
45. See generally Jacob S. Hacker, *The Great Risk Shift: The New Economic Insecurity and the Decline of the American Dream* (rev. and expanded ed. 2008) (describing how Republican policies have enriched business interests and wealthy donors by shifting risks of capitalism onto the poor and middle class).
46. See *U.S. Federal Individual Income Tax Rates History, 1862–2013 (Nominal and Inflation-Adjusted Brackets)*, Tax Foundation (October 17, 2013), https://taxfoundation.org /us-federal-individual-income-tax-rates-history-1913-2013-nominal-and-inflation-adjusted -brackets [https://perma.cc/86V6-3USH] (showing that top marginal rate for a married couple filing jointly in 1979 was 70%, compared to 39.6% in 2013).
47. Hacker, *The Great Risk Shift*, note 45, at 118–21.
48. See Martin Gilens, *Affluence and Influence: Economic Inequality and Political Power in America* 77–85 (2014) (arguing that when preferences of low- or middle-income Americans diverge from those of the affluent, there is virtually no relationship between policy outcomes and the desires of less advantaged groups).
49. See Jacob S. Hacker and Paul Pierson, *Winner-Take-All Politics: How Washington Made the Rich Richer—and Turned Its Back on the Middle Class* (2010) (describing how fiscal and regulatory policies over several decades undermined public goods and services to shift income to wealthier Americans).
50. See, e.g., Facundo Alvaredo, Lucas Chancel, Thomas Piketty, Emmanuel Saez, and Gabriel Zucman, *Inequality Is Not Inevitable— but the US 'Experiment' Is a Recipe for Divergence*, Guardian (Dec. 14, 2017), https://www.theguardian.com /inequality/ 2017/dec/14/inequality-is-not-inevitable-but-the-us-experiment-is-a-recipe-for-divergence?CMP=share_btn_tw [https://perma.cc/83FR-5CQT] ("The tax bill . . . will turbocharge inequality in America. Presented as a tax cut for workers and job-creating entrepreneurs, it is instead a giant cut for those with capital and inherited wealth. It's a bill that rewards the past, not the future"); John Cassidy, *The Final G.O.P. Tax Bill Is a Recipe for Even More Inequality*, New Yorker (Dec. 14, 2017), https://www.newyorker .com/news/ our-columnists/the-final-gop-tax-bill-is-a-recipe-for-even-more-inequality [https://

perma.cc/TGF8-FTEC] ("As virtually every independent study has shown, the G.O.P. plan showers most of its goodies (tax cuts) on the richest people in the country while doing little for poor and middle-income households").

51. Michael Signer lists four characteristic features of demagogues: (1) they fashion themselves as a man or woman of the common people, as opposed to the elites; (2) their politics depends on a powerful, visceral connection with the people that dramatically transcends ordinary political popularity; (3) they manipulate this connection, and the raging popularity it affords, for their own benefit and ambition; and (4) they threaten or outright break established rules of conduct, institutions, and even the law. Michael Signer, *Demagogue: The Fight to Save Democracy from its Worst Enemies* 35 (2009).
52. Ceaser, *Presidential Selection*, note 20, at 320 (describing "soft" demagogues as those who flatter the public); Jeffrey K. Tulis, *The Rhetorical Presidency* 28 (1987) (same); see also Aristotle, *Politics* bk. V, at 463 [1313b] (Harris Rackam, trans. Loeb Classical Library ed. 1932) ("The demagogue is the flatterer of the people"); James Fenimore Cooper, *The American Democrat* 120–28 (Liberty Classics 1981) (1838) (explaining that demagogues flatter the people in order to lead them); and 121 ("The peculiar office of a demagogue is to advance his own interests, by affecting a deep devotion to the interests of the people").
53. See Ceaser, *Presidential Selection*, note 20, at 57, 194 (noting that "hard demagogues" emphasize emotional appeals and divisive rhetoric); Cooper, *The American Democrat*, note 52, at 122–23 ("The demagogue is . . . a detractor of others . . . [who] appeals to passions and prejudices rather than to reason, and is in all respects, a man of intrigue and deception, of sly cunning and management"); cf. Aristotle, *Politics*, note 52, at 439 [1310b] ("For almost the greatest number of tyrants have risen, it may be said, from being demagogues, having won the people's confidence by slandering the notables").
54. Tulis, *The Rhetorical Presidency*, note 52, at 29 ("The hard demagogue attempts to create or encourage divisions among the people in order to build and maintain his constituency. Typically, this sort of appeal employs extremist rhetoric that ministers to fear").
55. Signer, *Demagogue*, note 51, at 35.
56. See, e.g., *The Federalist* No. 1 (Alexander Hamilton) ("Of those men who have overturned the liberty of republics, the greatest number have begun their career by paying an obsequious court to the people, commencing demagogues and ending tyrants"); Stan van Hooft, *Hope (The Art of Living)* 96 (2014) ("Promising to save their people from oppression and exploitation, to bring an end to their humiliation and defeats, to restore the dignity and power of their race . . . has always been the modus operandi of fascist demagogues and populist rabble-rousers").
57. See, e.g., Jim Ruth, *I Hate Donald Trump. But He Might Get My Vote*, Wash. Post (June 28, 2016), https://www.washingtonpost.com/opinions/i-hate-donald-trump-but-he -might-get-my-vote/2016/06/28/ddeee5f8-398d-11e6-9ccd-d6005beac8b3_story.html?utm_term=.ae4080e3d8eb [https://perma.cc/YE35-KT6M].
58. See Molly Ball, *Donald Trump and the Politics of Fear*, Atlantic (Sept. 2, 2016), https://www.theatlantic.com/politics/archive/2016/09/donald-trump-and-the-politics-of -fear/498116 [https://perma.cc/2429-XEMT] (explaining how Trump generates fear of immigrants, crime, and loss of social order); Jonathan Tilove, *The Rhetorical Brilliance of Donald Trump, Demagogue for President*, Statesman: First Reading (Nov. 23, 2016), http://politics.blog.mystatesman.com/2016/11/23/the-rhetorical-genius-of-donald-trump-demagogue-for-President [https://perma.cc/GC4G-5H9U] (describing Trump's rhetorical techniques).

59. Trevor Hughes, *Trump Calls to 'Drain the Swamp' of Washington*, USA Today (Oct. 18, 2016), https://www.usatoday.com/story/news/politics/elections/2016/2016/10/18/donald-trump-rally-colorado-springs-ethics-lobbying-limitations/92377656 [https://perma.cc/ZE64-K85L].
60. Kate Brannen, *Trump Family's Endless Conflicts of Interest: Chapter and Verse*, Newsweek (July 3, 2017), http://www.newsweek.com/trump-familys-endless-conflicts-interest-chapter-and-verse-631216 [https://perma.cc/6T3S-M4CG] (offering a list of a examples "of the vast number of issues that require oversight and scrutiny during this presidency"); Joy Crane and Nick Tabor, *501 Days in Swampland*, N.Y. Mag.: Daily intelligencer (Apr. 2, 2018), http://nymag.com/daily/intelligencer/2018/04/trump-and-co-are-stealing-america-blind-timeline.html [https://perma.cc/JAH5-5VVU] ("More than at any time in history, the President of the United States is actively using the power and prestige of his office to line his own pockets . . . there has proved to be no public policy too big, and no private opportunity too crass, to exploit for personal profit"); *How Donald Trump Is Monetising His Presidency*, Economist (July 20, 2017), https://www.economist .com/news/business/21725303-six-months-mr-trumps-conflicts-interest-look-even-worse-how-donald-trump-monetising [https://perma.cc/6D5T-EKJC] ("Mr. Trump already appears to be monetising the presidency"); Jeremy Venook, *Trump's Interests vs. America's, Dubai Edition*, Atlantic (Aug. 9, 2017), https://www.theatlantic.com/business/archive/2017/08 / donald-trump-conflicts-of-interests/508382 [https://perma.cc/22JB-4JD3] (offering "an attempt to catalogue the more clear-cut examples of conflicts of interest that have emerged so far").
61. See, e.g., Alexandra Berzon, *Donald Trump's Business Plan Left a Trail of Unpaid Bills*, Wall St. J. (June 9, 2016), https://www.wsj.com/articles/donald-trumps-business-plan-left-a-trail-of-unpaid-bills-1465504454 [https://perma.cc/ZP6W-E6D6].
62. See, e.g., Jordan Fabian, *Leaks Continue to Plague Trump White House Despite Crackdown*, Hill (June 9, 2018), http://thehill.com/homenews/administration /391430-leaks-plague-trump-white-house-with-no-end-in-sight [https://perma.cc/VVA8 -9KPB]; Mark Hay, *Trump's Failure to Hire People Is Doing Serious Damage*, Vice (June 7, 2018), https://www.vice.com/en_us/article/d3kwww/trump-administration-understaffing-crisis [https://perma.cc/8TVQ-S6RY]; Matthew Yglesias, *Trump's Administration Can't Clean House Because Its Leader Is Too Soaked in Scandal*, Vox (July 11, 2018), https://www.vox.com/policy-and-politics/2018/7/11/17546970/trump-pruitt-shine [https://perma.cc/MK5P-G3RT].
63. Stephanie Sugars, *From Fake News to Enemy of the People: An Anatomy of Trump's Tweets*, CPJ.org, January 30, 2019, https://cpj.org/blog/2019/01/trump-twitter-press-fake-news-enemy-people.php [https://perma.cc/5EXP-A2GR].
64. Adam Liptak, *Clash Between Trump and House Democrats Poses Threat to Constitutional Order*, New York Times, May 7, 2019, https://www.nytimes.com/2019/05/07/us/politics/trump-democrats.html [https://perma.cc/9TYQ-FR9S]; Jonathan Shaub, *The Prophylactic Executive Privilege, Lawfare*, June 14, 2019, https://www.lawfareblog.com/prophylactic-executive-privilege [https://perma.cc/3TEA-EJNA].
65. Shane Harris, Josh Dawsey, and Carol D. Leonnig, *Former White House Officials Say They Feared Putin Influenced the President's Views on Ukraine and 2016 Campaign*, Washington Post, December 19, 2019, https://www.washingtonpost.com/national-security/former-white-house-officials-say-they-feared-putin-influenced-the-presidents-views-on-

ukraine-and-2016-campaign/2019/12/19/af0fdbf6-20e9-11ea-bed5-880264cc91a9_story.html [https://perma.cc/E3D8-V97U].

66. Special Counsel Robert S. Mueller, III, *Report on the Investigation Into Russian Interference in the 2016 Presidential Election, Volume I* (US Department of Justice, March 2019), at 5.
67. Mueller, *Report On The Investigation Into Russian Interference In The 2016 Presidential Election, Volume I*, at 3–6, 157–58; Mark Mazzetti, Maggie Haberman, Nicholas Fandos, and Michael S. Schmidt, *Intimidation, Pressure and Humiliation: Inside Trump's Two-Year War on the Investigations Encircling Him*, New York Times, February 19, 2019, https://www.nytimes.com/2019/02/19/us/politics/trump-investigations.html [https://perma.cc/3FV3-5S6A].
68. Philip Bump, *How Trump's Conversations with Putin Overlapped with His Emerging Ukraine Conspiracy Theories*, Washington Post, Dec. 20, 2019, https://www.washingtonpost.com/politics/2019/12/20/how-trumps-conversations-with-putin-overlapped-with-his-emerging-ukraine-conspiracy-theories/ [https://perma.cc/UA3A-HSJE]; Harris, Dawsey, and Leonnig, *Former White House Officials Say They Feared Putin Influenced the President's Views on Ukraine and 2016 Campaign*, note 65.
69. The evidence is summarized in the House Judiciary Committee's Impeachment report, *Impeachment of Donald Trump, President of the United States, Report of the Committee on the Judiciary, House of Representatives*, https://assets.documentcloud.org/documents/6579566/House-Judiciary-Committee-Impeachment-Report.pdf.
70. Mike DeBonis, *McConnell's Vow of "Total Coordination" with White House on Senate Impeachment Trial Angers Democrats*, Washington Post, Dec. 13, 2019, https://www.washingtonpost.com/politics/mcconnells-vow-of-total-coordination-with-white-house-on-senate-impeachment-trial-angers-democrats/2019/12/13/9cb5a258-1dc7-11ea-b4c1-fd0d91b60d9e_story.html [https://perma.cc/86VP-DZR5] ("In a late Thursday interview with Fox News host Sean Hannity, McConnell (R-Ky.) all but guaranteed a Trump acquittal, saying there was 'zero chance' the president would be removed from office, and promised 'total coordination' with the White House and Trump's defense team"); Mckay Coppins, How Mitt Romney Decided Trump Is Guilty, The Atlantic, February 5, 2020, https://www.theatlantic.com/politics/archive/2020/02/romney-impeach-trump/606127/ [perma.cc/8Q34-3MPM] ("The president's acquittal has been all but certain for weeks, as Republicans have circled the wagons to protect Trump."); Mark Leibovich, Romney, Defying the Party He Once Personified, Votes to Convict Trump, New York Times, February 5, 2020, https://www.nytimes.com/2020/02/05/us/politics/romney-trump-impeachment.html [perma.cc/X4PZ-WW7D] ("[Romney's] vote cast into relief the rapid evolution of the Republican Party into an entity that has wholly succumbed to the vise grip of Mr. Trump").
71. See sources cited in note 60, supra; *Trump's 2,000 Conflicts Of Interest (And Counting), Citizens for Ethics*,https://www.citizensforethics.org/2000-trump-conflicts-of-interest-counting/ [https://perma.cc/2SZ9-ESKX]; David Leonhardt and Ian Prasad Philbrick, *Trump's Corruption: The Definitive List*, New York Times, Oct. 28, 2018, https://www.nytimes.com/2018/10/28/opinion/trump-administration-corruption-conflicts.html [https://perma.cc/C4RT-WPA4]; *Presidential Profiteering: Trump's Conflicts Got Worse In Year Two, Citizens for Responsibility and Ethics in Washington (CREW)*, https://www.citizensforethics.org/presidential-profiteering-trumps-conflicts-got-worse/ [https://perma.cc/25ZT-8G8A.
72. Brian Naylor, *Government Watchdog: Trump's Trips To Florida Costing Taxpayers Millions*, NPR.org, February 5, 2019, https://www.npr.org/2019/02/05/691684859/

government-watchdog-trumps-trips-to-florida-costing-taxpayers-millions [https://perma.cc/RA79-HPHZ]; Chuck Jones, *Trump's Golf Trips Could Cost Taxpayers Over $340 Million*, Forbes.com, July 10, 2019, https://www.forbes.com/sites/chuckjones/2019/07/10/trumps-golf-trips-could-cost-taxpayers-over-340-million/#248e528728aa [https://perma.cc/L6E7-5G8W]; Liz Johnstone, *Tracking President Trump's Visits to Trump Properties*, NBC News, Dec. 29, 2017, https://www.nbcnews.com/politics/donald-trump/how-much-time-trump-spending-trump-properties-n753366 [https://perma.cc/Z9E4-7CDF].

73. Eric Lipton, Steve Eder, and Ben Protess, *Those Foreign Business Ties? The Trump Sons Have Plenty Too*, New York Times, Oct. 11, 2019, https://www.nytimes.com/2019/10/11/us/politics/donald-trump-jr-eric-trump-business.html [https://perma.cc/7QM4-RPBA]; Bill McCarthy, *Eric Trump's False Claim that the Trump Family "Got Out of All International Business,"* Polifact, October 18, 2019, https://www.politifact.com/truth-o-meter/statements/2019/oct/18/eric-trump/eric-trumps-false-claim-trump-family-got-out-all-i/ [https://perma.cc/Z9E4-7CDF].
74. *Presidential Profiteering*, note 71; *Trump's 2,000 Conflicts Of Interest (And Counting)*, note 71; David A. Fahrenthold, Josh Dawsey, Jonathan O'Connell, and Michelle Ye Hee Lee, *When Trump Visits His Clubs, Government Agencies and Republicans Pay to Be Where He Is*, Washington Post, June 20, 2019, https://www.washingtonpost.com/politics/when-trump-visits-his-clubs-government-agencies-and-republicans-pay-to-be-where-he-is/2019/06/20/a4c13c36-8ed0-11e9-adf3-f70f78c156e8_story.html [https://perma.cc/XH62-JDXY].
75. The Foreign Emoluments Clause (Article I, Section 9, Clause 8) prohibits any person "holding any Office of Profit or Trust under" the United States from accepting "any present, Emolument, Office, or Title, of any kind whatever, from any King, Prince, or foreign State" without Congress' consent. The Domestic Emoluments Clause (Article II, Section 1, Clause 7) prohibits the president from receiving "any other Emolument [beyond a fixed compensation] from the United States, or any of them." Note that while Congress has the power to permit presidents to receive emoluments (for example gifts) from foreign governments, this does not apply to the Domestic Emoluments Clause. On the definition of "emolument," see John Mikhail, *The 2018 Seegers Lecture: Emoluments and President Trump*, 53 Val. U. L. Rev. 631, 666 (2019).
76. Zachary Basu, *Trump*: "*You People with This Phony Emoluments Clause,*" Axios, October 21, 2019, https://www.axios.com/donald-trump-phony-emoluments-clause-g7-summit-44369ec1-d0ad-42a3-89f8-df6067ee48b8.html [https://perma.cc/K2LN-SFMF]; Abbey Marshall, *Trump Claims He's the Victim of "Phony Emoluments Clause,"* Politico, October 21, 2019, https://www.politico.com/news/2019/10/21/trump-emoluments-clause-053289 [https://perma.cc/WM6B-ML7M].
77. Jonathan Martin and Maggie Haberman, *Fear and Loyalty: How Donald Trump Took Over the Republican Party*, New York Times, December 21, 2019, https://www.nytimes.com/2019/12/21/us/politics/trump-impeachment-republicans.html [https://perma.cc/99E6-WUDT].
78. Marty Lederman, *The Problem Isn't GOP Senators' Lack of "Impartiality"—It's That They're All Insisting the President Did Nothing Wrong*, Balkinization, December 19, 2019, https://balkin.blogspot.com/2019/12/the-problem-isnt-gop-senators-lack-of.html [https://perma.cc/LDX5-7JRS]; Marty Lederman and Benjamin Wittes, *Even Getting Caught Red-Handed Isn't Enough*, The Atlantic, September 30, 2019, https://www.theatlantic.com/

ideas/archive/2019/09/condemn-trump-before-his-misconduct-becomes-norm/599155/ [https://perma.cc/GN9E-NMVL].

79. Robert Costa and Karoun Demirjian, *GOP Embraces a Debunked Ukraine Conspiracy to Defend Trump from Impeachment*, Washington Post, Dec. 3, 2019, https://www.washingtonpost.com/politics/gop-embraces-a-debunked-ukraine-conspiracy-to-defend-trump-from-impeachment/2019/12/03/af3aa372-15ea-11ea-8406-df3c54b3253e_story.html [https://perma.cc/9KZN-MTMV].
80. Steven Levitsky and Daniel Ziblatt, *How Democracies Die*, Chapter 3, n. 8, at 146–51; Mann and Ornstein, *It's Even Worse than It Looks*, Chapter 2, n. 24, at 35–39; Yochai Benkler, Robert Faris, and Hal Roberts, *Network Propaganda: Manipulation, Disinformation and Radicalization in American Politics* (2018); Jane Mayer, *The Making of the Fox News White House*, The New Yorker, March 4, 2019, https://www.newyorker.com/magazine/2019/03/11/the-making-of-the-fox-news-white-house [https://perma.cc/S2XM-772U]; McKay Coppins, *The Man Who Broke Politics*, The Atlantic, October 17, 2018, https://www.theatlantic.com/magazine/archive/2018/11/newt-gingrich-says-youre-welcome/570832/ [https://perma.cc/WG2Y-Y6BA].
81. Philip Bump, *Yet Again, Trump Falsely Blames Illegal Voting for Getting Walloped in California*, Washington Post, July 23, 2019, https://www.washingtonpost.com/politics/2019/07/23/yet-again-trump-falsely-blames-illegal-voting-getting-walloped-california/ [https://perma.cc/FE5U-KLC4]; *Trump Pledges "Major Investigation Into Voter Fraud,"* BBC News, January 25, 2017, https://www.bbc.com/news/world-us-canada-38746559 [https://perma.cc/3XSS-8AKY]; *Studies Contradict Trump Claim That Voter Fraud Is "Very, Very Common,"* The Associated Press, October 18, 2016, https://fortune.com/2016/10/18/studies-contradict-trump-claim-that-voter-fraud-is-very-very-common/ [https://perma.cc/U5AL-ZRPK].
82. Brian Rosenwald, *Talk Radio's America: How an Industry Took Over a Political Party That Took Over the United States* (2019); Benkler, Faris, and Roberts, *Network Propaganda*, note 80; Mayer, *The Making of the Fox News White House*, note 80.
83. For a standard history of the Gilded Age, see White, *The Republic For Which It Stands*, Chapter 3, n. 2.
84. Ibid. at 3 (describing "a country transformed by immigration, urbanization, environmental crisis, political stalemate, new technologies, the creation of powerful corporations, income inequality, failures of governance, mounting class conflict, and increasing social, cultural, and religious diversity").
85. Ibid. at 2.
86. A famous Joseph Keppler cartoon from 1889 shows the trusts portrayed as huge bags of money looming over tiny senators ready to do their bidding. See *The Bosses of the Senate*, United States Senate, https://www.senate.gov/artandhistory/art/artifact/Ga _Cartoon/Ga_cartoon_38_00392.htm [https://perma.cc/DD4U-38U2].
87. White, *The Republic For Which It Stands*, Chapter 3, n. 2, at 3–5.
88. Ibid.
89. 163 U.S. 537 (1896) (upholding separate but equal facilities on railway carriages).
90. 189 U.S. 475 (1903) (refusing to intervene in Alabama's scheme for disenfranchisement of African Americans).
91. Glenn Wallach, "*A Depraved Taste for Publicity*": *The Press and Private Life in the Gilded Age*, 39 American Studies 1 (Spring 1998), 31–57.

92. See Randall S. Sumpter, *Think Journalism's a Tough Field Today? Try Being a Reporter in the Gilded Age*, The Conversation, October 4, 2018, at http://theconversation.com/think-journalisms-a-tough-field-today-try-being-a-reporter-in-the-gilded-age-103420 [https://perma.cc/5HJQ-NABC] ("Fakes became so common that an article in an 1892 issue of The Journalist estimated that the majority of stories supplied to newspapers by local news bureaus and press associations were fiction"); see generally Randall S. Sumpter, *Before Journalism Schools: How Gilded Age Reporters Learned the Rules* (2018) (describing technological changes that undermined newspaper profits and led to cut-throat competition and sensationalism).
93. Ted Curtis Smythe, *The Gilded Age Press, 1865–1900* (2003); David R. Spencer, *The Yellow Journalism: The Press and America's Emergency as a World Power* (2007).
94. For a brief introduction to the Progressive Era, see Maureen A. Flanagan, *Progressives and Progressivism in an Era of Reform*, Oxford Research Encyclopedia of American History (2016), http://americanhistory.oxfordre.com/view/10.1093/acrefore/9780199329175.001.0001/acrefore-9780199329175-e-84 [https://perma.cc/JNP6-4VWH].

Chapter 6

1. Kermit L. Hall (ed.), *The Oxford Companion to the Supreme Court of the United States* (2d ed. 2005) at 976–78 (Stevens); 88–90 (Blackmun); 102–105 (Brennan); 1067–71 (Warren); 725–26 (Peckham); 1086–87 (White); 371072 (Fuller); 629–630 (McReynolds).
2. Mark A. Graber, *Kahn and the Glorious Long State of Courts and Parties*, 4 Constitutional Studies 1, 2, 21 (2019); Ron Kahn, *Social Constructions, Supreme Court Reversals, and American Political Development: Lochner, Plessy, Bowers, but Not Roe*, in *The Supreme Court and American Political Development*, edited by Ronald Kahn and Ken I. Kersch, 67–116, 102–103 (2006).
3. See Paul Brest, Sanford Levinson, Jack M. Balkin, Akhil Reed Amar, and Reva B. Siegel, *Processes of Constitutional Decisionmaking* 1747–48 (7th ed. 2018) (table of Justices).
4. Michael J. Graetz and Linda Greenhouse, *The Burger Court and the Rise of the Judicial Right* (2016).
5. See Alan I. Abramowitz, *The Disappearing Center: Engaged Citizens, Polarization, and American Democracy* 139–42 (2010) (comparing polarization between 95th and 108th Congresses); Thomas E. Mann and Norman J. Ornstein, *It's Even Worse than It Looks: How the American Constitutional System Collided With the New Politics of Extremism* 51–58 (2012) (describing relatively sharp movement of Republicans to the right since the late 1970s); Michael Barber and Nolan McCarty, *Causes and Consequences of Polarization*, in Am. Political Sci. Ass'n, Negotiating Agreement in Politics 19, 21 (Jane Mansbridge and Cathie Jo Martin eds., 2013) ("In the past 40 years, the most discernable trend has been the marked movement of the Republican Party to the right"); see also Nolan McCarty et al., *Polarization Is Real (and Asymmetric)*, Wash. Post: Monkey Cage (May 15, 2012), http://themonkeycage.org/2012/05/15/polarization-is-real-and-asymmetric/ http://perma.cc/36M5-VWDR] ("The data are clear that [contemporary political polarization] is a Republican-led phenomenon where very conservative Republicans have replaced moderate Republicans and Southern Democrats"); Nolan McCarty, *What We Know and Don't Know About Our Polarized*

Politics, Wash. Post: Monkey Cage (Jan. 8, 2014), http://wapo.st/1ifmRzK [http://perma.cc/3N3B-JKB2] ("The evidence points to a major partisan asymmetry in polarization. Despite the widespread belief that both parties have moved to the extremes, the movement of the Republican Party to the right accounts for most of the divergence between the two parties [since the 1970s]").

6. Jeffrey Toobin, *After Stevens*, The New Yorker (Mar. 22, 2010), http://www.newyorker.com/reporting/2010/03/22/100322fa_fact_toobin. [https://perma.cc/Q9GS-CQQG] ("For many decades, there have been moderate Republicans on the Court—John M. Harlan II and Potter Stewart (appointed by Eisenhower), Lewis F. Powell and Harry Blackmun (Nixon), David H. Souter (Bush I). Stevens is the last of them, and his departure will mark a cultural milestone").
7. Neal Devins and Lawrence Baum, *The Company They Keep: How Partisan Divisions Came to the Supreme Court* 4 (2019).
8. Keith E. Whittington, *"Interpose Your Friendly Hand": Political Supports for the Exercise of Judicial Review by the United States Supreme Court*, 99 American Political Science Review 4 (2005): 583–96 (arguing that politicians support judicial review to overcome political and institutional obstructions to achieving their policy goals); Keith Whittington, *Political Foundations of Judicial Supremacy: The President, the Supreme Court, and Constitutional Leadership in U.S. History* 105–60 (2007)(listing a series of reasons why politicians support judicial review); Mark A. Graber, *The Nonmajoritarian Difficulty: Legislative Deference to the Judiciary*, 7 Stud. Am. Pol. Dev. 35, 37 (1993) ("Elected officials in the United States encourage or tacitly support judicial policymaking both as a means of avoiding political responsibility for making tough decisions and as a means of pursuing controversial policy goals that they cannot publicly advance through open legislative and electoral politics").
9. Mark A. Graber, *Constructing Judicial Review*, 8 Ann. Rev. Pol. Sci. 425, 427–28, 446 (2005).
10. See Justin Crowe, *Building the Judiciary: Law, Courts, and the Politics of Institutional Development* (2012)(describing the history of Congress's construction of a powerful federal judiciary).
11. Whittington, *Political Foundations of Judicial Supremacy*, note 8, at 230–84.
12. Jack M. Balkin and Sanford Levinson, *The Processes Of Constitutional Change: From Partisan Entrenchment To The National Surveillance State*, 75 Fordham L. Rev. 489 (2006)(discussing purposes of partisan entrenchment); Howard Gillman, *How Political Parties Can Use the Courts to Advance Their Agendas: Federal Courts in the United States, 1875–1891*, 96 Am. Pol. Sci. Rev. 511, 515–17 (2002) (showing how late nineteenth-century Republicans expanded federal court jurisdiction to promote their policy goals and entrench their party); Jack M. Balkin and Sanford Levinson, *Understanding The Constitutional Revolution*, 87 Va. L. Rev. 1045 (2001)(explaining theory of partisan entrenchment); cf. Ran Hirschl, Towards Juristocracy 39 (2004) (noting how politicians in many different countries profit "from an expansion of judicial power").
13. 5 U.S. (1 Cranch) 137 (1803).
14. 531 U.S. 98 (2000).
15. Mark A. Graber, *The Nonmajoritarian Difficulty*, note 8, at 36 ("prominent elected officials consciously invite the judiciary to resolve those political controversies that they cannot or would rather not address").
16. 410 U.S. 113 (1973).

17. Robert A. Dahl, *Decision-Making in a Democracy: The Supreme Court as a National Policy-Maker*, Journal of Public Law 6 (1957): 279, 293, 295.
18. Balkin and Levinson, *The Processes Of Constitutional Change*, note 12, at 534
19. Whittington, *Political Foundations of Judicial Supremacy*, note 8, at 154–55; Dahl, *The Supreme Court as a National Policy-Maker*, note 17, at 294; Charles L. Black Jr., *The People and the Court* 52 (1960).
20. Along these lines, Martin Shapiro, Alec Stone Sweet, and Gordon Silverstein have compared judicial review to using a junkyard dog to protect your property. If the dog is mean enough and unwilling to take orders from anyone, it will scare off trespassers. However, it may occasionally bite the hand that feeds it. See Gordon Silverstein, *Sequencing the DNA of Comparative Constitutionalism: A Thought Experiment*, 65 Md. L. Rev. 49, 50 (2006) (citing Martin Shapiro and Alec Stone Sweet, *On Law, Politics, And Judicialization* 163–64 (2002)).
21. Mark A. Graber, *The Countermajoritarian Difficulty: From Courts to Congress to Constitutional Order*, 4 Ann. Rev. L. Soc. Sci. 361, 367 (2008); Whittington, *Political Foundations of Judicial Supremacy*, note 8, 166–67 ("In a hostile political environment, the law and the judiciary may be the best defense that a president has").
22. Whittington, *Political Foundations of Judicial Supremacy*, note 8, at 105; see also sources cited in Chapter 9, n. 26.
23. Whittington, *Interpose Your Friendly Hand*, note 8.
24. See *Confirmation Hearing on the Nomination of John G. Roberts Jr. to Be Chief Justice of the United States Before the S. Comm. on the Judiciary*, 109th Cong. 55–56 (2005) ("Judges are like umpires. Umpires don't make the rules, they apply them. The role of an umpire and a judge is critical. They make sure everybody plays by the rules, but it is a limited role. Nobody ever went to a ball game to see the umpire").
25. Frederick Schauer, *The Supreme Court, 2005 Term: Foreword: The Court's Agenda—And The Nation's*, 120 Harv. L. Rev. 4, 8 (2006) ("neither constitutional decisionmaking nor Supreme Court adjudication occupies a substantial portion of the nation's policy agenda or the public's interest").
26. Jack M. Balkin and Sanford Levinson, *The Processes Of Constitutional Change: From Partisan Entrenchment To The National Surveillance State*, 75 Fordham L. Rev. 489 (2006); Howard Gillman, *How Political Parties Can Use the Courts*, note 12; Jack M. Balkin and Sanford Levinson, *Understanding The Constitutional Revolution*, 87 Va. L. Rev. 1045 (2001).
27. Kevin J. McMahon, *Reconsidering Roosevelt on Race: How the Presidency Paved the Road to Brown* (2003).
28. Balkin and Levinson, *Understanding the Constitutional Revolution*, note 12, at 1067–68.
29. See Brest et al., *Processes of Constitutional Decisionmaking*, note 3, at 1750–53 (table of Justices).
30. Balkin and Levinson, *Understanding the Constitutional Revolution*, note 12, at 1068–69; Balkin and Levinson, *The Processes of Constitutional Change*, note 12, at 496.
31. See Barry J. McMillion, *The Blue Slip Process for U.S. Circuit and District Court Nominations: Frequently Asked Questions*, Congressional Research Service, October 2, 2017, https://fas.org/sgp/crs/misc/R44975.pdf (describing the history and practice of the blue slip system by which home state senators could object to judicial nominations).
32. Balkin and Levinson, *The Processes of Constitutional Change*, note 12, at 496.
33. Balkin and Levinson, *Understanding the Constitutional Revolution*, note 12, at 1073; Balkin and Levinson, *The Processes of Constitutional Change*, note 12, at 496–97.

34. Balkin and Levinson, *The Processes of Constitutional Change*, note 12, at 497.
35. Kevin J. McMahon, *Nixon's Court: His Challenge to Judicial Liberalism and Its Political Consequences* 6 (2011) (arguing that Nixon only cared about a handful of key issues when making his Supreme Court appointments, and that "that politics far more than ideology drove all six of his choices for the Court"); see also 172, 177–79 (noting that Nixon did not regard abortion as an important constitutional issue).
36. 410 U.S. 113 (1973).
37. Balkin and Levinson, *Understanding the Constitutional Revolution*, note 12, at 1065–66; Gillman, *How Political Parties Can Use the Courts*, note 12, at 512–13; Balkin and Levinson, *The Processes of Constitutional Change*, note 12, at 490–91, 534–35.
38. Balkin and Levinson, *Understanding the Constitutional Revolution*, note 12, at 1065–66; Balkin and Levinson, *The Processes of Constitutional Change*, note 12, at 490–91.
39. On the role of the median Justice, see Lee Epstein and Tonja Jacobi, *Super Medians*, 61 Stan. L. Rev. 37 (2008); Andrew D. Martin, Kevin M. Quinn, and Lee Epstein, *A Multidisciplinary Exploration: The Median Justice On The United States Supreme Court*, 83 N.C.L. Rev. 1275 (2005).
40. There is now a large literature on how the Justices create their own agendas for decision. Vanessa Baird, *Answering the Call of the Court: How Justices and Litigants Set the Supreme Court Agenda* (2007); Richard L. Pacelle Jr., *The Transformation of the Supreme Court's Agenda: From the New Deal to the Reagan Administration* (1991); Sanford Levinson, *Strategy, Jurisprudence, and Certiorari*, 79 Va. L. Rev. 717 (1993) (reviewing H. W. Perry Jr., *Deciding to Decide: Agenda Setting in the United States Supreme Court* (1991)); H.W. Perry Jr., *Deciding to Decide: Agenda Setting in the United States Supreme Court* (1991); Lee Epstein, Jeffrey A. Segal, and Jennifer Nicoll Victor, *Dynamic Agenda-Setting on the United States Supreme Court: An Empirical Assessment*, 39 Harv. J. on Legis. 395 (2002); Robert L. Boucher Jr. and Jeffrey A. Segal, *Supreme Court Justices as Strategic Decision Makers: Aggressive Grants and Defensive Denials on the Vinson Court*, 57 J. Pol. 824 (1995); Gregory A. Caldeira and John R. Wright, *The Discuss List: Agenda Building in the Supreme Court*, 24 Law & Soc'y Rev. 807 (1990); Joseph Tanenhaus et al., *The Supreme Court's Certiorari Jurisdiction: Cue Theory, in Judicial Decision-Making* 111 (Glendon Schubert ed., 1963).
41. Balkin and Levinson, *Understanding the Constitutional Revolution*, note 12, at 1074–75; Balkin and Levinson, *The Processes of Constitutional Change*, note 12, at 503–505.
42. Jack M. Balkin, *Constitutional Redemption: Political Faith in an Unjust World* 179–82, 201–203 (2011); Jack M. Balkin, *Living Originalism* 306–307 (2011).
43. Balkin and Levinson, *Understanding the Constitutional Revolution*, note 12, at 1062–63; See Sanford Levinson, *Return of Legal Realism*, The Nation, Jan. 8, 2001, at 8. Justice Stephen Breyer has articulated the distinction this way:

> Politics in our decision-making process does not exist. By politics, I mean . . . will it help certain individuals be elected? . . . Personal ideology or philosophy is a different matter. . . . Judges have had different life experiences and different kinds of training, and they come from different backgrounds. Judges appointed by different presidents of different political parties may have different views about the interpretation of the law and its relation to the world.

Stephen G. Breyer, *The Work of the Supreme Court*, Am. Acad. of Arts and Sci., Sept.-Oct. 1998, at 47, quoted in Howard Gillman, *What's Law Got to Do with It? Judicial*

Behavioralists Test the "Legal Model" of Judicial Decision Making, 26 Law & Soc. Inquiry 465, 490 n.26 (2001).

Chapter 7

1. See Barry Friedman, *The Cycles of Constitutional Theory*, 67 Law & Contemp. Probs., Summer 2004, at 149, 157–64 (2004) (detailing the shifts).
2. Davison M. Douglas, *The Rhetorical Uses of* Marbury v. Madison: *The Emergence of a "Great Case,"* 38 Wake Forest L. Rev. 375, 386–402 (2003) (explaining how turn-of-the-century conservatives looked to strong judicial review to resist popular demands for economic regulation); Friedman, *The Cycles of Constitutional Theory*, note 1, at 157 ("From 1890 until 1937 . . . progressives were troubled by [judicial review]; conservatives admired its preservationist and anti-democratic character").
3. Friedman, *The Cycles of Constitutional Theory*, note 1, at 157–58; J. Patrick White, *The Warren Court Under Attack: The Role of the Judiciary in a Democratic Society*, 19 Md. L. Rev. 181, 196 (1959) ("One is struck by the irony that liberals and conservatives have today adopted views completely the reverse of those each held in the constitutional crisis of the 1930's").
4. In his 2004 article on cycles of constitutional theory, Barry Friedman did not purport to offer a general explanation for the cycles, but suggested that conservatives or liberals supported judicial review or judicial restraint depending on whether the political branches or the courts were more progressive or conservative in a particular period. See Friedman, *The Cycles of Constitutional Theory*, note 1, at 157–58, 164–65. This was not intended to be a complete account because the president and Congress might be held by different parties, the federal and state governments might have a different political valence, and so too might different state and local governments. In addition, political control of legislatures can change from year to year, while views about judicial review tend to be more durable. By contrast, this book tries to offer a more general structural explanation of the cycles based on the nature of the American party system.
5. See *generally* Reva B. Siegel, The Supreme Court 2012 Term—Foreword: Equality Divided, 127 Harv. L. Rev. 1 (2013) (describing long-term shifts in the Supreme Court's docket from cases vindicating the equality claims by minority litigants to cases vindicating equality claims by white litigants).
6. See, e.g., Wisconsin v. Yoder, 406 U.S. 205, 207 (1972) (holding for Old Order Amish plaintiff); Sherbert v. Verner, 374 U.S. 398, 399, 402 (1963) (holding for Seventh-Day Adventist plaintiff).
7. See, e.g., Masterpiece Cakeshop, Ltd. v. Colorado Civil Rights Comm'n, 138 S. Ct. 1719 (2018) (reversing, on grounds of religious discrimination, decision against religious objector to same-sex marriage); Trinity Lutheran Church of Columbia, Inc. v. Comer, 137 S. Ct. 2012 (2017) (upholding right of church-run religious school to participate in state-funded playground resurfacing program); Burwell v. Hobby Lobby, 134 S. Ct. 2751 (2014) (upholding a Religious Freedom Restoration Act (RFRA) challenge to employer contraceptive mandate by conservative Christian corporate owner who objected to subsidizing use of certain contraceptives by employees); Good News Club v. Milford Cent. Sch., 533 U.S. 98, 102–103 (2001) (upholding right of Christian group to use public school after hours for religious meetings).

8. This feature, too, has changed over time, especially since the Judiciary Act of 1925, Pub. L. No. 68–415, 43 Stat. 936. See *generally* Margaret Meriwether Cordray and Richard Cordray, *The Philosophy of Certiorari: Jurisprudential Considerations in Supreme Court Case Selection*, 82 Wash. U. L.Q. 389, 391–94 (2004).
9. If we go back to 1969, the numbers are fourteen and four. However, the Republican party was not a movement party until the 1980s, and so several of the older Republican appointments turned out to be moderate or liberal. Since 1980, all but one Republican appointees have been conservative, and since 1991, all have been movement conservatives who are unlikely to become moderates, much less liberals.
10. See Martin Shapiro, *Fathers and Sons: The Court, The Commentators, and the Search for Values*, in Vince Blasi ed., *The Burger Court: The Counter-Revolution that Wasn't*, 220–22 (1983)(arguing that criticisms of the Warren Court by an older generation that lived through the constitutional struggle over the New Deal gave way to support for Warren Court decisions in the next generation, which had lived through *Brown v. Board of Education* and the civil rights revolution).
11. Whittington, *Political Foundations of Judicial Supremacy*, Chapter 6, n. 8. at 232 ("institutional and coalitional pressures that push political actors to turn to the Court for constitutional leadership have become more pervasive over the course of American history").
12. Pollock v. Farmers' Loan & Trust Company, 157 U.S. 429, modified on reh'g, 158 U.S. 601, 637 (1895) (striking down the 1894 Federal Income Tax).
13. United States v. E. C. Knight Co., 156 U.S. 1 (1895) (limiting the federal government's power to enforce the Sherman Act).
14. 198 U.S. 45 (1905) (striking down state maximum hours law for bakers).
15. Keith E. Whittington, *Judicial Review of Congress Before the Civil War*, 97 Geo. L.J. 1257, 1267 (2009)("Judicial review did not occupy the same place in the constitutional system of the early nineteenth century as it does now, but the Court was busy laying the foundations for that practice and establishing its role as a forum for testing the limits of congressional powers"); Mark A. Graber, *Naked Land Transfers and American Constitutional Development*, 53 Vand. L. Rev. 73 (2000)(explaining how the Supreme Court ban on naked land transfers helped establish judicial review in the antebellum era).
16. See Howard Gillman, *How Political Parties Can Use the Courts to Advance Their Agendas*, Chapter 6, n. 12, at 515–21 (describing institutional changes designed to promote economic nationalism).
17. Alexander M. Bickel, *The Least Dangerous Branch: The Supreme Court At The Bar Of Politics* 16–17 (1962).
18. Learned Hand, *The Bill of Rights* 73 (1958) ("For myself it would be most irksome to be ruled by a bevy of Platonic Guardians, even if I knew how to choose them").
19. Whittington, Political Foundations of Judicial Supremacy, Chapter 6, n. 8, at 23, 30–31, 52–53.
20. Ibid. at 73 (noting that when a reconstructive presidency begins, the Supreme Court usually defends the constitutional values of the previous constitutional order).
21. A.L.A. Schechter Poultry Corp. v. United States, 295 U.S. 495 (1935) (striking down provisions of the National Industrial Recovery Act of 1933).
22. Lucas A. Powe Jr., *The Supreme Court and the American Elite, 1789–2008* 179 (2009)("Wilson mistakenly thought that McReynolds' position on trusts was a proxy for progressive beliefs generally. McReynolds instead was a reactionary, whose votes would affect almost a quarter-century of constitutional doctrine"); see also 194 (describing Clarke's

exit from the Court as a "shocker," which occurred "because he couldn't stand McReynolds and wanted to work for U.S. entry into the League of Nations").

23. Jeff Shesol, *Supreme Power: Franklin Roosevelt versus the Supreme Court* 40–41 (2010).
24. Stewart retired in 1981, likely waiting long enough for a Republican president to replace him.
25. See Office of Legal Policy, U.S. Dep't of Justice, Report to the Attorney General, The Constitution in the Year 2000: Choices Ahead in Constitutional Interpretation (1988); Office Of Legal Policy, U.S. Dep't Of Justice, Guidelines On Constitutional Litigation (1988).
26. 410 U.S. 113 (1973).
27. 347 U.S. 483 (1954).
28. Whittington, *Political Foundations of Judicial Supremacy*, Chapter 6, n. 8, at 117–20.
29. Elmo Richardson, *The Presidency of Dwight D. Eisenhower* 108 (1991); see Stephen J. Wermiel, *The Nomination of Justice Brennan: Eisenhower's Mistake? A Look at the Historical Record*, 11 Constitutional Commentary 515, 534–36 (1994–1995) (noting that although Eisenhower may never have "spoken these precise words," the quote is "right in substance, if not in fact").
30. Brennan was a Catholic Democrat: his appointment signaled that Eisenhower was moderate and nonpartisan, and, Eisenhower hoped, would also attract Catholic Democrats to the Republican Party. Sheldon Goldman, *Picking Federal Judges: Lower Court Selection from Roosevelt Through Reagan* 116 (1997) (explaining that Eisenhower wanted to woo Catholic Democrats to the Republican Party); David Yalof, *The Pursuit of Justices: Presidential Politics and the Selection of Supreme Court Nominees* 55, 60–61 (2001). Warren was a popular reform governor of California (nominated by both parties in 1950!) who had been instrumental in getting Eisenhower the Republican nomination in 1952. Eisenhower admired him and viewed him as a statesman of great integrity. *Yalof, The Pursuit of Justices* at 45–46.
31. Yalof, *The Pursuit of Justices*, note 30, at 41–42.
32. 505 U.S. 833 (1992).
33. 517 U.S. 620 (1996).
34. 539 U.S. 538 (2003).
35. Thomas M. Keck, The Most Activist Supreme Court in History: The Road to Modern Judicial Conservatism 201–203 (Chicago: University of Chicago Press, 2004).
36. See Board of Trustees of University of Alabama v Garrett, 531 U.S. 356, 372–74 (2001) (holding the Americans with Disabilities Act to the extent that it allowed suits for money damages against the states.); United States v Morrison, 529 U.S. 598, 602 (2000) (striking down the civil rights remedy in the Violence Against Women Act that allowed women to sue their attackers in federal court); Kimel v Florida Board of Regents, 528 U.S. 62, 67 (2000) (holding the Age Discrimination in Employment Act invalid to the extent that it allowed suits for money damages against the states); Alden v Maine, 527 U.S. 706, 712 (1999) (holding that states could not be sued in state court to enforce the Fair Labor Standards Act); College Savings Bank v Florida Prepaid Postsecondary Education Expense Board, 527 U.S. 666, 691 (1999) (holding the Trademark Remedy Clarification Act invalid to the extent that it allowed suits for money damages against the states);Florida Prepaid Postsecondary Education Expense Board v College Savings Bank, 527 U.S. 627, 630 (1999) (invalidating the Patent and Plant Variety Protection Remedy Clarification Act to the

extent that it allowed suits for money damages against the states); Printz v United States, 521 U.S. 898, 935 (1997) (invalidating provisions of the Brady Act that required state and local government officials to enforce a federal regulatory program); City of Boerne v Flores, 521 U.S. 507, 536 (1997) (holding the Religious Freedom Restoration Act (RFRA) unconstitutional as applied to state governments because it was beyond Congress's powers to enforce the Fourteenth Amendment); Seminole Tribe of Florida v Florida, 517 U.S. 44, 47 (1996) (invalidating a provision of the Indian Gaming Regulatory Act that eliminated the states' Eleventh Amendment immunity from suit in federal court); United States v Lopez, 514 U.S. 549, 551 (1995) (invalidating the Gun Free School Zones Act as beyond Congress's commerce powers); New York v United States, 505 U.S. 144, 149 (1992) (invalidating "take-title" provision of Low-Level Radioactive Waste Policy Act on grounds that Congress may not commandeer state legislatures to pass regulations).

37. 554 U.S. 570 (2008) (holding that the Second Amendment protects an individual right to use firearms in the home for purposes of self-defense).
38. 561 U.S. 742 (2010) (applying the Second Amendment right of self-defense to the states).
39. Parents Involved in Community Schools v. Seattle School District No. 1, 551 U.S. 701 (2007).
40. Shelby County v. Holder, 570 U.S. 529 (2013).
41. 558 U.S. 310 (2010).
42. See, e.g., Janus v. Am. Fed'n of State, Cty. & Mun. Emps., Council 31, 138 S. Ct. 2448, 2478 (2018) (holding that requiring nonmembers of public sector unions to pay fees toward collective bargaining violates the First Amendment); Nat'l Inst. of Family & Life Advocates v. Becerra, 138 S. Ct. 2361, 2378 (2018) (enjoining enforcement of California law requiring pro-life pregnancy centers to provide certain factual information to patients); Harris v. Quinn, 134 S. Ct. 2618, 2644 (2014) (striking down agency-fee provision of Illinois's Public Labor Relations Act); McCutcheon v. FEC, 572 U.S. 185, 227 (2014) (striking down aggregate limits on federal campaign contributions); Ariz. Free Enter. Club's Freedom Club PAC v. Bennett, 564 U.S. 721, 754, 755 (2011) (striking down Arizona law providing "matching funds" to publicly funded state candidates when privately funded opponents spend over a certain amount); Sorrell v. IMS Health Inc., 564 U.S. 552, 580 (2011) (striking down a Vermont law restricting the sale and disclosure of physicians' prescription records); Citizens United v. FEC, 558 U.S. 310, 372 (2010) (striking down statutory limits on corporate electioneering).
43. Cf. Thomas M. Keck, *Policy Party or Duty, Party, Policy, or Duty: Why Does the Supreme Court Invalidate Federal Statutes*?, 101 American Political Science Review 2 May 2007, at 321–38, 328 ("the judicial appointment process makes it particularly likely that the justices will side with the presidential wing of their own partisan coalition").
44. Whittington, *Political Foundations of Judicial Supremacy*, Chapter 6, n. 8, at 105–107
45. See Clark M. Neily III, *Terms Of Engagement: How Our Courts Should Enforce The Constitution's Promise Of Limited Government* 129–30 (2013); Ilya Shapiro, *Against Judicial Restraint*, National Affairs (Fall 2016), https://www.nationalaffairs.com/publications/detail/against-judicial-restraint [https://perma.cc/LCE3-YQ3E]; Clark Neily, Judicial Engagement Means No More Make-Believe Judging, 19 Geo. Mason L. Rev. 1053 (2012); Supreme Court at a Crossroads: Judicial Engagement vs. Judicial Restraint: What Should Conservatives Prefer?, Institute For Justice, http://ij.org/event/supreme-court-crossroads-judicial-engagement-vs-judicial-restraint-conservatives-prefer/ [https://perma.cc/F6VX-QPGQ].

46. Keith E. Whittington, *The Least Activist Supreme Court in History? The Roberts Court and the Exercise of Judicial Review*, 89 Notre Dame L. Rev. 2219, 2221 (2014)("Conservative politicians continue to rail against judicial activists, as evidenced by everything from bills introduced in Congress to party platforms to congressional hearings") (footnotes omitted).
47. Ibid. at 2221, 2224.
48. See Shapiro, *Against Judicial Restraint*, note 45 (arguing that "judicial review is constitutional and appropriate . . . if we want a government that stays within its limited powers" and "we should be concerned only that the Court 'get it right,' regardless of whether that correct interpretation leads to the challenged law being upheld or overturned"); George F. Will, *The Limits of Majority Rule*, National Affairs 160, 169–72, Summer 2016, https://www.nationalaffairs.com/publications/detail/the-limits-of-majority-rule [https://perma.cc/C5AF-9TC7] (asserting that judicial review is necessary to ensure fidelity to "those who framed and ratified" the Constitution); George F. Will, *The False Promise of "Judicial Restraint" in America*, Washington Post (Oct. 21, 2015), https://www.washingtonpost.com/opinions/the-false-promise-of-judicial-restraint/2015/10/21/a0267b36-7760-11e5-a958-d889faf561dc_story.html?noredirect=on&utm_term=.196ad814a556 [https://perma.cc/P29G-L2BJ] ("Reflexive praise of 'judicial restraint' serves the progressives' Hobbesian project of building an ever-larger Leviathan").
49. See Shapiro, *Fathers and Sons*, note 10.
50. Sanford, Levinson, *The Warren Court Has Left the Building: Some Comments on Contemporary Discussions of Equality*, 2002 University of Chicago Legal Forum 119, http://chicagounbound.uchicago.edu/uclf/vol2002/iss1/7. Reviewing Ronald Dworkin's defense of strong judicial review in 1996, Cass Sunstein put it more bluntly: "Earl Warren Is Dead." Cass R. Sunstein, *Earl Warren Is Dead*, The New Republic, May 16, 1996 (reviewing Ronald Dworkin, *Freedom's Law: The Moral Reading of the Constitution* (1996)), https://newrepublic.com/article/62143/earl-warren-dead [https://perma.cc/D65C-45N8].
51. Shesol, *Supreme Power*, note 23.
52. See generally Mark A. Graber, *The Jacksonian Origins of Chase Court Activism*, 25 J. Sup. Ct. Hist. 17, 26–27 (2000) ("Jacksonian sympathizers on the Taney Court almost never voted to declare federal laws unconstitutional because Jacksonians in the executive and legislative branches of the national government almost always successfully prevented constitutionally controversial exercises of national power from becoming national law").
53. 576 U.S. 644 (2015).

Chapter 8

1. Friedman, *The Cycles of Constitutional Theory*, Chapter 7, n. 1, at 149–74. See also Keith E. Whittington, *The New Originalism*, 2 Geo. J.L. & Pub. Pol'y 599, 604 n. 27 (2004) ("Constitutional theory regarding judicial activism and restraint, and relative authority of the various branches of government, is linked to long partisan cycles of reconstruction and affiliation with dominant constitutional norms and institutions").
2. 531 U.S. 98 (2000).
3. Friedman, *The Cycles of Constitutional Theory*, Chapter 7, n. 1, at 162–64.
4. Ibid. at 149.
5. See Shapiro, *Fathers and Sons*, Chapter 7, n. 10, at 218–19.

6. Friedman, *The Cycles of Constitutional Theory*, Chapter 7, n. 1, at 149 ("Theorizing about judicial review necessarily occurs in response to Supreme Court decisions. Those decisions themselves are a function of the composition of the bench, the issues that come before the Court, and the Court's position vis-à-vis the other branches of government"); Jack M. Balkin, *Agreements with Hell and Other Objects of Our Faith*, 65 Fordham L. Rev. 1703, 1719 (1997)("Our theories of the Constitution are makeshift attempts, reflecting the concerns of our era, but dressed up as timeless claims about interpretation").
7. Sanford Levinson, *On Positivism and Potted Plants: "Inferior" Judges and the Task of Constitutional Interpretation*, 25 Conn. L. Rev. 843 (1993); Seth F. Kreimer, *Exploring the Dark Matter of Judicial Review: A Constitutional Census of the 1990s*, 5 Wm. & Mary Bill of Rts. J. 427, 430–31 (1997) ("although accounts of the Supreme Court's legislative confrontations are legion, few commentators survey the landscape outside of the 'high practice' of constitutional confrontation between legislature and judiciary at the Supreme Court level, and law review literature is virtually devoid of informed discussion of the realities of the ways in which the Constitution is used by trial courts"). For exceptions, see Kreimer, *Exploring the Dark Matter of Judicial Review*, Neil S. Siegel, *Reciprocal Legitimation in the Federal Courts System*, 70 Vand. L. Rev. 1183 (2017), and Barry Friedman, *The Politics of Judicial Review*, 84 Tex. L. Rev. 257 (2005).
8. For example, Shelby County v. Holder, 570 U.S. 529 (2013), which struck down section 4 of the Voting Rights Act, was decided on June 25, 2013. The next day, June 26, 2013, the Court struck down section 3 of the Defense of Marriage Act in United States v. Windsor, 570 U.S. 744 (2013). Compare Windsor, 570 U.S. at 778 (Scalia, J., dissenting) (Accusing the majority of "aggrandiz[ing] the Court's power and 'diminishing' the power of our people to govern themselves," arguing that "we have no power under the Constitution to invalidate this democratically adopted legislation") with Shelby County, 570 U.S. at 587 (Ginsburg, J., dissenting) ("the Court's opinion can hardly be described as an exemplar of restrained and moderate decisionmaking. Quite the opposite. Hubris is a fit word for today's demolition of the VRA").
9. Thomas M. Keck, *Judicial Politics in Polarized Times* 256–57 (2014)
10. Howard Gillman, *The Collapse of Constitutional Originalism and the Rise of the Notion of the "Living Constitution" in the Course of American State-Building*, 11 Studies in American Political Development, Fall 1997, 191–247.
11. Gilman, *Living Constitution*, note 10, at 218–24; Morton J. Horwitz, *The Supreme Court 1992 Term—Foreword: The Constitution of Change Legal Fundamentality without Fundamentalism*, 107 Harv. L. Rev. 30, 51–56 (1993).
12. See, e.g., Brad Snyder, *Frankfurter and Popular Constitutionalism*, 47 U.C. Davis 343, 360–65 (2013)(describing Frankfurter's frustration with the courts in the 1910s, 1920s, and 1930s and his embrace of judicial restraint and deference to majorities).
13. See David E. Bernstein, From *Progressivism to Modern Liberalism: Louis* D. Brandeis as a Transitional Figure in Constitutional Law, 89 Notre Dame L. Rev. 2029, 2029–31 (2014)(describing progressive hostility toward judicial review); Thomas B. Colby and Peter J. Smith, *The Return of Lochner*, 100 Cornell L. Rev. 527, 543 (2015)(connecting judicial restraint to the emergence of legal realism); Gilman, *Living Constitution*, note 10, at 220 (connecting judicial restraint to pragmatism).
14. See Horwitz, *Constitution of Change*, note 11, at 77 ("Progressive politicians such as Theodore Roosevelt and progressive historians such as Charles and Mary Beard launched

what would become for an entire generation of American thinkers the dominant interpretation of *Lochner*: a shocking example of the Court's capitulation to big business"); see also 78–79 (explaining that various progressives "maintained that the Supreme Court Justices had, under cover of natural law, written their own political or economic views into the Constitution" or had a "commitment to a mechanical jurisprudence that left the Justices out of touch with the changing social reality").

15. See, e.g., Felix Frankfurter, *The Present Approach to Constitutional Decisions on the Bill of Rights*, 28 Harv. L. Rev. 790, 791–93 (1915); Felix Frankfurter, *Hours of Labor and Realism in Constitutional Law*, 29 Harv. L. Rev. 353, 371–72 (1916) (describing decisions like *Lochner* as "impair[ing] that public confidence upon which the healthy exercise of judicial power must rest," and urging deference to legislatures on social and economic issues).
16. 4 Franklin D. Roosevelt, *The Two Hundredth and Ninth Press Conference. May 31, 1935, in 4 The Public Papers and Addresses of Franklin D. Roosevelt* 221 (1938) ("We have been relegated to the horse-and-buggy definition of interstate commerce").
17. 7 Franklin D. Roosevelt, 6 *The Public Papers and Addresses of Franklin D. Roosevelt* 122, 129 (1941) (A "Fireside Chat" Discussing the Plan for Reorganization of the Judiciary. Washington, DC, March 9, 1937).
18. 304 U.S. 144 (1938).
19. Ibid. at 152 n. 4
20. 319 U.S. 624 (1943).
21. 310 U.S. 586 (1940).
22. *Barnette*, 319 U.S. at 638.
23. Ibid. at 666 (Frankfurter, J., dissenting) ("As appeal from legislation to adjudication becomes more frequent, and its consequences more far-reaching, judicial self-restraint becomes more and not less important, lest we unwarrantably enter social and political domains wholly outside our concern").
24. Brown v. Board of Education of Topeka, Kansas, 347 U.S. 483 (1954).
25. Ibid. at 492.
26. Ibid. at 492–93. At the first oral argument in *Brown*, Justice Burton invoked a similar idea: "But the Constitution is a living document that must be interpreted in relation to the facts of the time in which it is interpreted. Did we not go through with that in connection with the child labor cases, and so forth?" Richard Kluger, *Simple Justice: The History of Brown v. Board of Education and Black America's Struggle For Equality* 575 (1975). Note how Burton equates the earlier focus on government power (child labor) to the new concern with civil rights and civil liberties and equality (school desegregation).
27. Charles A. Reich, Mr. *Justice Black and the Living Constitution*, 76 Harv. L. Rev. 673, 729 (1963) ("Today virtually nothing in the Constitution effectively limits the massive advance of government power except the Bill of Rights. It is the final barrier, all others having been overwhelmed"). See also Howard Gillman, *Preferred Freedoms: The Progressive Expansion of State Power and the Rise of Modern Civil Liberties Jurisprudence*, Political Research Quarterly, Vol. 47, No. 3 (Sep., 1994), 623–53, at 625 ("the removal of traditional restrictions on legislative power not only allowed powerholders to take control of a tumultuous economy and mitigate the social costs of industrialization, but also to extend power into areas that these reformers considered inviolate").
28. Reich, *Mr. Justice Black and the Living Constitution*, note 27, at 733–34.
29. 383 U.S. 663 (1966).

30. Ibid. at 665–66.
31. Ibid. at 669.
32. Ibid. at 675–78 (Black, J., dissenting) (pointing out that the Court was adding new rights to the text).
33. 381 U.S. 479, 485–86 (1965).
34. Ibid. at 507 (Black, J., dissenting).
35. Herbert Wechsler, *Toward Neutral Principles of Constitutional Law*, 73 Harv. L. Rev. 1, 15–16 (1959).
36. Alexander M. Bickel, *The Supreme Court 1960 Term—Foreword: The Passive Virtues*, 75 Harv. L. Rev. 40 (1961).
37. Alexander M. Bickel, *The Supreme Court and the Idea of Progress* (1970).
38. Ibid. at 173 (arguing that the Court's desegregation, apportionment, and school prayer cases "are heading toward obsolescence, and in large measure abandonment. . . . it must be read as a lesson").
39. John Hart Ely, *Democracy and Distrust: A Theory of Judicial Review* (1980).
40. John Hart Ely, *The Wages of Crying Wolf: A Comment on Roe v. Wade*, 82 Yale L.J. 920 (1973).
41. Ronald Dworkin, *Taking Rights Seriously* (1978); Laurence Tribe, *American Constitutional Law* (1978); Paul Brest, *The Supreme Court 1975 Term—Foreword: In Defense of the Antidiscrimination Principle*, 90 Harvard Law Review 1 (1976); Owen M. Fiss, *The Supreme Court 1978 Term—Foreword: The Forms of Justice*, 93 Harv. L. Rev. 1 (1979).
42. Johnathan G. O'Neill, *Raoul Berger and the Restoration Of Originalism*, 96 Nw. U.L. Rev. 253, 255 (2001)("Considered in the history of twentieth-century American jurisprudence, Berger's originalism elaborated the legal positivist majoritarianism of Progressive and process jurisprudence"). See also Johnathan O'Neil, *Originalism in American Law and Politics: A Constitutional History* (2005)122–23, 165–66, 187–88 (arguing that both Burger and Bork were influenced by midcentury "process restraint" jurisprudence, but both believed that even this gave judges too much discretion).
43. Griswold v. Connecticut, 381 U.S. 479, 507, 514, 522 (1965) (Black, J., dissenting) (comparing the Court's decision to *Lochner v. New York*).
44. Whittington, *The New Originalism*, note 1, at 601.
45. 6 Franklin D. Roosevelt, *The Public Papers and Addresses of Franklin D. Roosevelt* 124 (1941) (A "Fireside Chat" Discussing the Plan for Reorganization of the Judiciary. Washington, DC, March 9, 1937); see also 359, 362–63 ("The Constitution of the United States Was a Layman's Document, Not a Lawyer's Contract." Address on Constitution Day, Washington, DC, September 17, 1937).
46. See Frank B. Cross, *The Failed Promise of Originalism* 92–96 (2013) (describing the use of adoption history in the Warren Court school prayer, reapportionment, and criminal procedure opinions); see also 136–43 (collecting statistics on the Warren Court's use of originalist rhetoric). Cross notes, for example, that the Warren Court used *The Federalist* "more than any previous Court [in] American history," although usage increased even further in the Burger and Rehnquist Courts' years (at 136). The regular and frequent use of adoption history in Supreme Court opinions began with the Warren Court, not the conservative courts that succeeded it (at 96).
47. Alfred H. Kelly, *Clio and the Court: An Illicit Love Affair*, 1965 Sup. Ct. Rev. 119, 125–26; see also 131 ("In search of some adequate guiding principle upon which to support their

libertarian interventionism in the social order, the reformist activists on the Court initiated a new era of historically oriented adjudication"). The Justices flirted with the idea of using an appeal to the framers of the Fourteenth Amendment to justify overruling *Plessy v. Ferguson*, 163 U.S. 537 (1896). Finding the historical record inconclusive, they eventually settled on social science as the precedent-breaking device. Kelly, *Clio and the Court*, at 142.

48. Jack M. Balkin, *The New Originalism and the Uses Of History*, 82 Fordham L. Rev. 641, 674–75 (2013); Jack M. Balkin, *Why Are Americans Originalist? in Law, Society and Community: Socio-Legal Essays*, in Honour Of Roger Cotterrell, Richard Nobles, and David Schiff, eds. (2014), 309–26. See also Akhil Reed Amar, *America's Unwritten Constitution: The Precedents and Principles We Live By* 198 (2012) (explaining that the reason why the Warren Court overturned so many precedents is that it was returning to "the deepest ideals of the written Constitution").

    Justice Hugo Black, the most famous liberal originalist, exemplified liberals' turn to history both before and during the Warren Court era; indeed, in Bruce Ackerman's words, he is "the original originalist on the modern Supreme Court." Bruce Ackerman, *The Living Constitution*, 120 Harv. L. Rev. 1737, 1799 (2007); see *also* Philip C. Bobbitt, Constitutional Fate: Theory of the Constitution 56 (New York: Oxford University Press, 1982) (explaining that Justice Hugo Black's turn to text and history allowed him "to restore to judicial review the popular perception of legitimacy which the New Deal crisis had jeopardized"); Akhil Reed Amar, *Hugo Black and the Hall of Fame*, 53 Ala. L. Rev. 1221, 1242 (2002) (arguing that Justice Black was the true intellectual leader of the Warren Court).

49. Whittington, *The New Originalism*, note 1, at 601.
50. Ibid.
51. Ibid. at 602 ("The primary commitment within this critical posture was to judicial restraint. Originalist methods of constitutional interpretation were understood as a means to that end.... originalism was thought to limit the discretion of the judge").
52. Ibid. at 601 ("Strikingly, a core theme of originalist criticisms of the Court was the essential continuity between *Lochner v. New York* and *Griswold v. Connecticut*. It is an intriguing feature of conservative critiques of the Court during this era that they mirror the central critique of the Lochner Court favored by the New Dealers in the 1930s: that the justices were essentially making it up and 'legislating from the bench'").
53. See William H. Rehnquist, *The Notion of a Living Constitution*, 54 Tex. L. Rev. 693, 695 (1976)(complaining that "nonelected members of the federal judiciary may address themselves to a social problem" even though they are "responsible to no constituency").
54. Robert H. Bork, The Tempting of America: The Political Seduction of the Law 99 (1990) ("*Griswold*, as an assumption of judicial power unrelated to the Constitution is, however, indistinguishable from *Lochner*"); Robert H. Bork, *Neutral Principles and Some First Amendment Problems*, 47 Ind. L.J. 1, 9–11 (1971)(comparing *Griswold* to *Lochner*.).
55. Whittington, *The New Originalism*, note 1, at 602 ("The originalist Constitution, as [early originalists] imagined it, was primarily concerned with empowering popular majorities").
56. Attorney General Edwin Meese, who championed the development of originalism in the Reagan Justice Department, explained that "like the Warren Court decades later, the Court in the *Lochner* era ignored the limitations of the Constitution and blatantly usurped legislative authority." Edwin Meese III, *A Return to Constitutional Interpretation from Judicial Law-Making*, 40 N.Y.L. Sch. L. Rev. 925, 927 (1996).

57. Bork, *Neutral Principles and Some First Amendment Problems*, note 54, at 6–7; Antonin Scalia, *Originalism: The Lesser Evil*, 57 U. Cin. L. Rev. 849, 854, 863–64 (1989).
58. See Edwin Meese III, Address before the American Bar Association, in *The Great Debate: Interpreting Our Written Constitution* 9 (Paul G. Cassel ed., 1986); Edwin Meese III, U.S. Att'y Gen., Address before the D.C. Chapter of the Federalist Society Lawyers Division (Nov. 15, 1985), in *Office of Legal Policy, U.S. Dept. of Justice, Original Meaning Jurisprudence: A Sourcebook* 91, 95, 96, 98 (1987) (arguing for a "jurisprudence of original intention"); Edwin Meese III, *Construing the Constitution*, 19 U.C. Davis L. Rev. 22, 25–26 (1985) (same). Meese sometimes used the terms "original intention" and "original meaning" interchangeably. See, e.g., Edwin Meese III, *The Supreme Court of the United States: Bulwark of a Limited Constitution*, 27 S. Tex. L. Rev. 455, 465–66 (1986) ("It has been and will continue to be the policy of this administration to press for a jurisprudence of original intention").
59. See Office Of Legal Policy, U.S. Dep't Of Justice, Guidelines On Constitutional Litigation 3–10 (1988) (describing originalist interpretive principles for Reagan Administration lawyers and listing "Decisions Inconsistent with These Principles of Interpretation"); Office of Legal Policy, U.S. Dep't of Justice, Report to the Attorney General, The Constitution in the Year 2000: Choices Ahead in Constitutional Interpretation 185 (1988) (discussing areas for proposed changes in constitutional law); Steven M. Teles, *The Rise of the Conservative Legal Movement: The Battle for Control of the Law* (2008); Steven M. Teles, *Transformative Bureaucracy: Reagan's Lawyers and the Dynamics of Political Investment*, Studies in American Political Development 23 (2009): 61, (describing how the Meese Justice Department sought to promote and legitimize originalism as a method of constitutional interpretation); Dawn E. Johnsen, *Ronald Reagan and the Rehnquist Court on Congressional Power: Presidential Influences on Constitutional Change*, 78 Ind. L.J. 363, 396–99 (2003) (discussing the Reagan Justice Department's Constitution in the Year 2000 project and the Reagan Administration's strategy of judicial appointments to change the direction of constitutional doctrine).
60. See Keck, *The Most Activist Supreme Court in History*, Chapter 7, n. 35, at 281 ("None of the five conservatives, it is worth reiterating, have adopted a posture of pure judicial deference in the Frankfurter mold . . . by the time they came to the bench, the very mission of an independent Supreme Court had come to be identified—in the minds of ordinary citizens and of the justices themselves—with the enforcement of rights-based limits on political action. For the justices to abandon this role would be to call into question the very justification for their office").
61. Jefferson Decker, *The Other Rights Revolution: Conservative Lawyers and the Remaking of American Government* (2016); Amanda Hollis-Brusky, *Ideas with Consequences: The Federalist Society and the Conservative Counterrevolution* (2015); Ann Southworth, *Lawyers and the Conservative Counterrevolution*, 43 Law & Social Inquiry 1698 (2018)(reviewing Decker and Hollis-Brusky); Ann Southworth, *Lawyers of the Right: Professionalizing the Conservative Coalition* (2008); Teles, *The Rise of The Conservative Legal Movement*, note 59; See also Steven M. Teles, *Transformative Bureaucracy: Reagan's Lawyers and the Dynamics of Political Investment*, note 59.
62. Teles, *The Rise of the Conservative Legal Movement*, note 59, at 232 (explaining that, like liberals before them, conservative public litigators were driven to "strip executive institutions of discretion and force them to operate in accordance with clear national rules

or professional standards"); see also 264 (noting that conservative public-interest firms took advantage of "a structural bias in the American legal system orienting public-interest law to challenging governmental discretion and power rather than (as many traditional conservatives preferred) defending it").

63. Ibid. at 231–32, 264, 324 n.29.
64. Ibid. at 324 n.29 (citing Stephen Brown, *Trumping Religion: The New Christian Right, The First Amendment, and The Courts* (2002)).
65. See Keck, *The Most Activist Supreme Court in History*, Chapter 7, n. 35, at 267 ("the conservative justices' chief motivation has been their hostility toward modern liberalism rather than a particular vision of judicial power").
66. Keck, *The Most Activist Supreme Court in History*, Chapter 7, n. 35, at 282.
67. Whittington, *The New Originalism*, note 1, at 604 ("As conservatives found themselves in the majority, conservative constitutional theory—and perhaps originalism—needed to develop a governing philosophy appropriate to guide majority opinions, not just to fill dissents").
68. As the Institute for Justice, a conservative public interest law firm, explained, "Today, we have far more government than the Constitution permits and far less freedom than the Constitution guarantees. We need a cutting-edge approach to judging in order to restore long-lost liberty and keep government in check in the years to come. That approach is judicial engagement." *What Is Judicial Engagement?*, Institute for Justice, http://ij.org/center-for-judicial-engagement/programs/what-is-judicial-engagement [https://perma.cc/L3BL-NYL8].
69. Clint Bolick, *The Proper Role of "Judicial Activism,"* 42 Harvard Journal of Law and Public Policy 1, (2018) ("I define judicial activism as any instance in which the courts strike down a law that violates individual rights or transgresses the constitutional boundaries of the other branches of government. In that regard, the problem with judicial activism is not that there is far too much, but that there has been far too little").
70. Clark M. Neily, III, *Terms of Engagement: How Our Courts Should Enforce the Constitution's Promise of Limited Government* 10 (2013).
71. Edward Whelan, *The Presumption Of Constitutionality*, 42 Harvard Journal of Law and Public Policy 17, 20 (2019) (defining "judicial passivism" as "a court's wrongful failure to enforce constitutional rights and limits on governmental power . . . Judicial restraint is the sound mean between the two extremes of judicial activism and judicial passivism. Judicial restraint means that judges do not wrongly decline to apply democratic enactments").
72. Randy Barnett, *Constraint vs. Deference: Two Possible Meanings of "Judicial Restraint," Volokh Conspiracy*, Washington Post, June 29, 2015, https://www.washingtonpost.com/news/volokh-conspiracy/wp/2015/06/29/constraint-vs-deference-two-possible-meanings-of-judicial-restraint/?utm_term=.c2778e521eca; *What Is Judicial Engagement?*, Institute for Justice, http://ij.org/center-for-judicial-engagement/programs/what-is-judicial-engagement [https://perma.cc/L3BL-NYL8]
73. Raoul Berger, *Government by Judiciary: The Transformation of the Fourteenth Amendment* 154–156 (1977) (arguing that the framers of the Fourteenth Amendment did not intend to incorporate the Bill of Rights); Raoul Berger, *Incorporation of the Bill of Rights: A Nine-Lived Cat*, 42 Ohio St. L.J. 435 (1981)(same); Lino A. Graglia, *"Interpreting" the Constitution: Posner on Bork*, 44 Stan. L. Rev. 1019, 1033–34 (1992) ("There is very little basis for the implausible proposition that the states that ratified the Fourteenth Amendment

understood that it would 'incorporate' the Bill of Rights"); Meese, *The Supreme Court*, note 58, at 463–64 ("Nowhere else has the principle of Federalism been dealt such a politically violent and constitutionally suspect blow as by the theory of incorporation").

74. The turning point in scholarly opinion was the work of Michael Kent Curtis, *No State Shall Abridge: The Fourteenth Amendment and the Bill of Rights* (1986) (showing that the Republican drafters of the Fourteenth Amendment sought to enforce the Bill of Rights against the states).
75. Whittington, *The New Originalism*, note 1, at 601.
76. Antonin Scalia, *Originalism: The Lesser Evil*, note 57.
77. Ibid. at 862–64.
78. Ann Southworth, *Lawyers of the Right: Professionalizing the Conservative Coalition* (2008); Teles, *The Rise of The Conservative Legal Movement*, note 59.
79. See, e.g., See, e.g., Obergefell v. Hodges, 135 S. Ct. 2584, 2626, 2629 (2015) (Scalia, J., dissenting) (calling the Court's decision a "threat to American democracy" and a "judicial Putsch"); United States v. Windsor, 570 U.S. 744, 778 (2013) (Scalia, J., dissenting) ("We have no power to decide this case. And even if we did, we have no power under the Constitution to invalidate this democratically adopted legislation"); Lawrence v. Texas, 539 U.S. 558, 603–604 (2003) (Scalia, J., dissenting) ("Judgments [about legal protection for same-sex relations] are to be made by the people, and not imposed by a governing caste that knows best"); Romer v. Evans, 517 U.S. 620, 652–53 (1996) (Scalia, J., dissenting) (criticizing the Court for imposing its elite values on the citizens of Colorado, who seek "to prevent piecemeal deterioration of the sexual morality favored by a majority"); Planned Parenthood v. Casey, 505 U.S. 833, 1002 (1992) (Scalia, J., concurring in the judgment in part and dissenting in part) ("By foreclosing all democratic outlet for the deep passions this issue arouses. . . . The Court merely prolongs and intensifies the anguish").
80. United States v. Lopez, 514 U.S. 549, 584, 585 (1995) (Thomas, J., concurring) (arguing for reconsidering the substantial effects test in Commerce Clause doctrine).
81. Richard A. Epstein, *Takings: Private Property and the Power of Eminent Domain* 30–31 (1985); Bernard H. Siegan, *Economic Liberties and the Constitution* (1980).
82. See, e.g., Bork, *The Tempting of America*, note 54, at 225 ("If we reject *Lochner* and *Adkins*, then we cannot have *Griswold* and *Roe*"); Robert H. Bork, *The Constitution, Original Intent, and Economic Rights*, 23 San Diego L. Rev. 823, 829–31 (1986); see also Colby and Smith, *The Return of Lochner*, note 13, at 565–69 (noting broad rejection among conservative originalists of Siegan's and Epstein's early attempts to revive constitutional protection of economic liberties).
83. See, e.g., Randy E. Barnett, *Our Republican Constitution: Securing the Liberty and Sovereignty of We the People* 17 (2016) ("Conservatives had inherited their commitment to judicial restraint from the progressive supporters of the New Deal, who had opposed the Supreme Court holding Congress to its enumerated powers"); Randy E. Barnett, *After All These Years, Lochner Was Not Crazy—It Was Good*, 16 Geo. J.L. & Pub. Pol'y 437, 437 (2018) (arguing that *Lochner* was a "reasonable and good decision"); Colby and Smith, The Return of *Lochner*, note 13, at 569–71 ("In the last decade, however, a new wave of libertarian scholars—operating closer to the mainstream of conservative legal thought—has argued anew for a revival of *Lochner*'s aggressive scrutiny for regulations that interfere with economic liberty"); Jack M. Balkin, *"Wrong the Day It Was Decided": Lochner and*

Constitutional Historicism, 85 B.U. L. Rev. 677 (2005)(noting that it is no longer obvious for many legal thinkers that *Lochner* was incorrectly decided).

84. Sixth Annual Rosenkranz Debate—RESOLVED: Courts Are Too Deferential to the Legislature—Event Audio/Video, Federalist Society (Nov. 16, 2013), https://fedsoc.org/commentary/videos/sixth-annual-rosenkranz-debate-resolved-courts-are-too-deferential-to-the-legislature-event-audio-video [https://perma.cc/VEE8-Q9LL].
85. In Brzonkala v. Va. Polytechnic Inst. & State Univ., 169 F.3d 820, 889 (4th Cir. 1999) (Wilkinson, C.J., concurring), aff'd, United States v. Morrison, 529 U.S. 598 (2000), Wilkinson recognized that the Rehnquist Court's federalism revolution was a contemporary form of judicial activism. Ibid. at 893. But he argued that it was a more defensible form of judicial activism than that of the *Lochner* Court or the Warren Court, because "the outcomes of the current era have not consistently favored a particular constituency" (ibid. at 893); because "courts are not motivated by a desire that a *particular* substantive meaning be given to a constitutional term such as commerce, but instead by the duty to find that *some* meaning must exist" (ibid. at 894); and because "our role in this modern era is not as substantive adjudicators, but as structural referees. . . . Instead of aggressively pursuing substantive preferences, this court validates a structural principle found throughout the Constitution" (ibid. at 895). Wilkinson argued that whether courts should incorporate the Bill of Rights was a structural question, not a substantive question (ibid. at 896).
86. *Brzonkala*, 169 F.3d at 895.
87. Ibid. at 896.
88. Ibid.
89. J. Harvie Wilkinson, III, *Cosmic Constitutional Theory: Why Americans Are Losing Their Inalienable Right to Self-Governance* (2012).
90. Ibid. at 57–58 (arguing that *Heller* and *McDonald* are originalist activism); ibid. at 68 (arguing that *Heller* and *McDonald* were an "originalist parallel" to *Roe*, and "showed originalism to be susceptible to the temptation of imposing judicial value judgments based on thin and shaky grounds").
91. Brian Beutler, *The Rehabilitationists*, The New Republic, August 30, 2015, https://newrepublic.com/article/122645/rehabilitationists-libertarian-movement-undo-new-deal [https://perma.cc/M2G2-VXVC] ("'One of the leaders of the Federalist Society—one of the senior staff—said clearly I had the room,' Barnett told me. 'It wasn't that I beat J. Harvie Wilkinson in a debate—who knows?—it's just that the room was with me. The room would not have been with me ten years ago'");Josh Blackman, *The New Republic on "The Rehabilitationists,"* Josh Blackman's Blog, Aug 30, 2015, http://joshblackman.com/blog/2015/08/30/the-new-republic-on-the-rehabilitationists/ [https://perma.cc/Q7UC-6PSD] (describing the event and noting "the shifting tides in the Federalist Society crowd towards the perspective of judicial engagement. It is my distinct sense that people of my generation are much closer to the Volokh-conspiracy wing than the Bork wing").
92. Randy E. Barnett, *Commandeering the People: Why the Individual Health Insurance Mandate is Unconstitutional*, 5 N.Y.U. J.L. & Liberty 581 (2010); Hollis-Brusky, *Ideas with Consequences*, note 61, at 134.
93. Randy Barnett, *Our Republican Constitution*, note 83, at 14–18; Randy E. Barnett, *The Wages Of Crying Judicial Restraint*, 36 Harvard Journal of Law & Public Policy 925, 931–32 (2013).
94. Barnett, *After All These Years*, note 83, at 437.

95. David E. Bernstein, *Rehabilitating Lochner: Defending Individual Rights Against Progressive Reform* (2011).
96. Obergefell v. Hodges, 135 S.Ct. at 2584, 2611–12, 2616–19, 2621–2622 (Roberts, C. J., dissenting) (comparing the majority's decision to *Lochner*).
97. Chevron U.S.A, Inc., v. NDRC, 467 U.S. 837 (1984).
98. Antonin Scalia, *Judicial Deference to Administrative Interpretations of Law*, 1989 Duke L. J. 511.
99. See, e.g., Charles J. Cooper, *Confronting the Administrative State*, 25 Nat'l. Affairs (2015), Fall 2015, at 96, 102–104 () http://www.nationalaffairs.com/publications/detail/confronting-the-administrative-state [https://perma.cc/XH7A-C6TE](arguing "our constitutional order has been subverted" by *Chevron* and other modern administrative law doctrines); John Yoo, *A Thousand Little Tyrants—Obama's Problems Are a Chance to Rein in the Bureaucracy*, Nat'l. Rev., Sept. 16, 2013, at 16, 18 [https://perma.cc/Y7NR-LNG9] (criticizing *Chevron* and the growth of the administrative state under President Obama); Michael S. Greve, *Yoo to Conservatives: Reverse Course*, Law & Liberty (Sept. 9, 2013), http://www.libertylawsite.org/2013/09/09/yoo-to-conservatives-reverse-course/ [https://perma.cc/7LUA-XDPF] (endorsing Yoo's call to "ditch judicial deference").
100. See, e.g., Ruth Colker and James J. Brudney, *Dissing Congress*, 100 Mich. L. Rev. 80, 83 (2001) ("In acting repeatedly to invalidate federal legislation, the Court is using its authority to diminish the proper role of Congress"); Friedman, *The Cycles of Constitutional Theory*, Chapter 7, n. 1, at 161–64; Larry D. Kramer, *The Supreme Court 2000 Term—Foreword: We the Court*, 115 Harv. L. Rev. 4, 14 (2001) ("This Court sees no need to accommodate the political branches at all").
101. Friedman, *The Cycles of Constitutional Theory*, Chapter 7, n. 1, at 162 (emphasis in original).
102. Skowronek, *The Politics Presidents Make*, Chapter 1, n. 8, at 56.
103. See Keck, *The Most Activist Supreme Court*, Chapter 7, n. 35, at 199–201 (arguing that neither liberals nor conservatives are likely to return to Frankfurterian judicial restraint because both have interests in rights-based claims).
104. Mark Tushnet, *Taking The Constitution Away From The Courts* (1999).
105. Larry D. Kramer, *The People Themselves: Popular Constitutionalism and Judicial Review* (2004); Kramer, *We the Court*, note 100.
106. Robert C. Post and Reva B. Siegel, *Equal Protection by Law: Federal Antidiscrimination Legislation After Morrison and Kimel*, 110 Yale L.J. 441, 525–26 (2000); Robert C. Post and Reva B. Siegel, *Protecting the Constitution from the People: Juricentric Restrictions on Section Five Power*, 78 Ind. L.J. 1, 2 (2003); Robert Post and Reva Siegel, *Roe Rage: Democratic Constitutionalism and Backlash*, 42 Harv. C.R.-C.L. L. Rev. 373, 374 (2007).
107. Cass R. Sunstein, *One Case At A Time: Judicial Minimalism On The Supreme Court* (1999).
108. Bruce Ackerman, *We the People Volume 1: Foundations* (1991); Bruce Ackerman, *We the People Volume 2: Transformations* (1998); Bruce Ackerman, *We the People, Volume 3: The Civil Rights Revolution* (2014).
109. David A. Strauss, *The Living Constitution* (2010).
110. Akhil Reed Amar, *America's Constitution: A Biography* (2005); Balkin, *Living Originalism*, Chapter 6, n. 42.
111. See, e.g., Frank Cross, *The Failed Promise of Originalism* 15 (2013) (arguing that originalism is easily manipulated and that judges may "claim to rely on originalist materials

to legitimize their results, even though originalism had little to do with producing those results"); Eric J. Segall, *Originalism as Faith* 12 (2018) (arguing that originalism is based on a mistaken faith that "the original meaning of the text drives Supreme Court decisions"); Mitchell N. Berman, *Originalism is Bunk*, 84 N.Y.U. L. Rev. 1 (2009) (arguing that the theoretical justifications for originalism are unsuccessful); Thomas B. Colby and Peter J. Smith, *Living Originalism*, 59 Duke L.J. 239 (2009) (arguing that originalism has many versions, that originalist theory has been constantly changing, and that originalists tend to adopt whichever version is most likely to produce results they personally favor); Robert C. Post and Reva B. Siegel, *Originalism as a Political Practice: The Right's Living Constitution*, 75 Fordham L. Rev. 545 (2006) (arguing that originalism makes less sense as a coherent methodology of interpretation than as a political practice of mobilized groups who seek political change and vindication of their political values).

112. Cass R. Sunstein, *Radicals in Robes: Why Extreme Right Wing Courts are Wrong for America* (2006).
113. Berman, *Originalism is Bunk*, note 111.
114. Segall, *Originalism as Faith*, note 111.
115. See Eric J. Segall, *Supreme Myths: Why the Supreme Court Is Not a Court and Its Justices Are Not Judges* (2012) (asserting that the Supreme Court's work is inherently political and arguing for judicial restraint); Segall, *Originalism as Faith*, note 111 (same); see also Jeremy K. Kessler, *The Early Years of First Amendment Lochnerism*, 116 Colum. L. Rev. 1915, 1922 (2016) (arguing that "economically libertarian tendencies . . . may be intrinsic to judicial enforcement of civil liberties, regardless of the politics of individual judges" and that "the creation of a truly non-Lochnerian First Amendment would require a fundamental break" with the twentieth century "civil libertarian status quo dating back to the 1940s"); Brad Snyder, *The Former Clerks Who Nearly Killed Judicial Restraint*, 89 Notre Dame L. Rev. 2129, 2153 (2014) (arguing for more research into theories of judicial restraint); Samuel Moyn, *Resisting the Juristocracy*, Boston Review, October 8, 2019, http://bostonreview.net/law-justice/samuel-moyn-resisting-juristocracy [https://perma.cc/2Q3G-TZXF] ("A legal culture less oriented to the judiciary and more to public service in obtaining and using democratic power in legislatures at all levels is the sole path to progress now"); Samuel Moyn, *Stop Worrying About Kavanaugh, Liberals. Start Winning the Political Argument*, Washington Post, September 8, 2019, https://www.washingtonpost.com/news/posteverything/wp/2018/08/08/stop-worrying-about-kavanaugh-liberals-start-winning-the-political-argument/?noredirect=on&utm_term=.eec33aca45f2 [https://perma.cc/6NDV-KUTG] ("Democracy requires judges on both sides of our political divide to be relegated to the margins of national life, rather than have their selection remain the biggest reason elections matter").
116. Levinson, *The Warren Court Has Left the Building*, Chapter 7, n. 50.

Chapter 9

1. 304 U.S. 144 (1938).
2. Ibid. at 152.
3. Ibid. at 152 n. 4.
4. Ibid.

5. Ibid.
6. Ibid.
7. Mark Graber, *Judicial Supremacy and the Structure of Partisan Conflict*, 50 Indiana L. Rev. 141, 161 (2016); Graber, *Kahn and the Glorious Long State of Courts and Parties*, Chapter 6, n. 2, at 2.
8. Mark A. Graber, *Belling the Partisan Cats: Preliminary Thoughts on Identifying and Mending a Dysfunctional Constitutional Order*, 94 B.U. L. Rev. 611, 636–37 (2014).
9. Graber, *Judicial Supremacy and the Structure of Partisan Conflict*, note 7, at 144–45.
10. Ibid. The term "state of courts and parties," is taken from Stephen Skowronek, *Building A New American State: The Expansion Of National Administrative Capacities* 1877–1920, at 24, 29, 31, 39 (1982).
11. See Barry Friedman, *The Birth of an Academic Obsession: The History of the Countermajoritarian Difficulty, Part Five*, 112 Yale L.J. 153, 222–23 (2002); Gary Peller, *Neutral Principles in the 1950s*, 21 U. Mich. J.L. Reform 561, 567 (1988)("The central jurisprudential project of the fifties thinkers was to incorporate legal realist intellectual sophistication into the mainstream of American legal discourse while avoiding the most corrosive aspect of the realist message—that there was no analytically defensible way to distinguish law from politics").
12. Henry Hart and Albert. Sacks, *The Legal Process: Basic Problems in the Making and Application of Law* 4 (tent. ed. 1958).
13. Herbert Wechsler, *Toward Neutral Principles of Constitutional Law*, 73 Harv. L. Rev. 1 (1959).
14. Ibid. at 33; see Peller, *Neutral Principles in the 1950s*, note 11, at 609–11 (arguing that the neutral principles approach failed because for legal process scholars like Wechsler, inquiries into whether power relations between groups were oppressive and subordinating, and whether legislative action built on those relations was legitimate or illegitimate, would turn out to be contested questions of value that required judicial deference to the political branches).
15. Ronald Dworkin, *The Forum of Principle*, 56 N.Y.U. L. Rev. 469 (1981).
16. Ronald Dworkin, *Freedom's Law: The Moral Reading of the Constitution* 17 (1996).
17. John Hart Ely, *Democracy and Distrust: A Theory of Judicial Review* (1980).
18. Ibid. at 75–77.
19. See *Confirmation Hearing on the Nomination of John G. Roberts, Jr.*, Chapter 6, n. 24, at 55–56.
20. Ibid.
21. See, e.g., Neil S. Siegel, *Umpires At Bat: On Integration And Legitimation*, 24 Const. Comm. 701 (2007); Edward Lazarus, *Overall, The Miers Nomination Is Troubling—But It Does Have One Virtue*, Findlaw, Oct. 13, 2005, https://supreme.findlaw.com/legal-commentary/overall-the-miers-nomination-is-troubling-but-it-does-have-one-virtue.html [https://perma.cc/KQ8Q-HUX2].
22. Soon-to-be Justice Brett Kavanaugh, however, embraced the metaphor in a 2015 speech at Catholic University, interpreting it as a call for judicial humility, honesty, and integrity. Brett Kavanaugh, *The Judge as Umpire: Ten Principles* 65 Catholic University Law Review 683 (2016).
23. Dahl, *The Supreme Court as a National Policy-Maker*, Chapter 6, n. 19, at 291.
24. Robert G. Mccloskey, *The American Supreme Court* 261 (Sanford Levinson ed., 5th ed. 2010).

25. See, e.g., Balkin, *Living Originalism*, Chapter 1, n. 6; Jack M. Balkin, *What Brown Teaches Us About Constitutional Theory*, 90 Va L. Rev. 1537, 1538 (2004).
26. This idea that the Supreme Court brings local outliers into line with national values is a familiar descriptive claim about the Supreme Court's practice of judicial review. See, e.g., Michael J. Klarman, *From Jim Crow to Civil Rights* 453 (2004); Whittington, *Political Foundations of Judicial Supremacy*, Chapter 6, n. 8 at 105. Sometimes theorists also invoke the phenomenon as a normative justification of judicial review against the charge of being antidemocratic. See, e.g., Amar, *America's Unwritten Constitution*, Chapter 8, n. 48, at 112; William N. Eskridge Jr, *Some Effects of Identity-Based Social Movements on Constitutional Law in the Twentieth Century*, 100 Mich L Rev 2062, 2373 (2002); Jeffrey Rosen, *The Most Democratic Branch: How the Courts Serve America* 4, 89, 124, 203 (2006). For a critique of the idea of outliers as a *normative* justification for judicial review, see Justin Driver, *Constitutional Outliers*, 81 U. Chi. L. Rev. 929 (2014).
27. Graber, *The Nonmajoritarian Difficulty*, Chapter 6, n. 8, at 36.
28. Neal Devins and Lawrence Baum, *The Company They Keep: How Partisan Divisions Came to the Supreme Court*, 24–25, 40–46 (2019).
29. 163 U.S. 537 (1896); see Michael J. Klarman, *From Jim Crow to Civil Rights: The Supreme Court and the Struggle for Racial Equality* 22–23 (2004)(noting elite consensus).
30. 347 U.S. 483 (1954).
31. See Gene Burns, *The Moral Veto: Framing Contraception, Abortion, and Cultural Pluralism in the United States* 168 (2005)(arguing that abortion reform before Roe was promoted by "an elite movement of physicians, clergy, and legislators"); Mark A. Graber, *The Coming Constitutional Yo-Yo? Elite Opinion, Polarization, and the Direction of Judicial Decision Making*, 56 How. L.J. 661, at 687–88 (2013)(arguing that elites supported abortion and gender equality); see also 688 ("Elite status trumped ideology and partisanship. Affluent, highly educated Republicans on many civil rights and liberties issues had more opinions in common with affluent, highly educated Democrats, than either shared with less fortunate fellow partisans").
32. 408 U.S. 238 (1972).
33. Dahl, *The Supreme Court as a National Policy-Maker*, Chapter 6, n. 19, at 285 ("the chances are about one out of five that a president will make one appointment to the Court in less than a year, better than one out of two that he will make one within two years, and three out of four that he will make one within three years").
34. Ibid. at 285–86.
35. Hall ed., *The Oxford Companion to the Supreme Court of the United States*, Chapter 6, n. 1, at 133 (Byrnes), 181–82 (Clarke), 395–96 (Goldberg).
36. See Devins and Baum, *The Company They Keep*, note 28, at 40 ("Since the appointments of Lewis Powell and William Rehnquist in 1971, the only appointee who was not serving on an appellate court was Elena Kagan (appointed in 2010)"); Steven G. Calabresi and James Lindgren, *Term Limits For The Supreme Court: Life Tenure Reconsidered*, 29 Harv. J.L. & Pub. Pol'y 770–71 (2006)("Although the average tenure of a Supreme Court Justice from 1789 through 1970 was 14.9 years, for those Justices who have retired since 1970, the average tenure has jumped to 26.1 years").
37. Graber, *The Coming Constitutional Yo-Yo*, note 31, at 696–97 (2013); Devins and Baum, *The Company They Keep*, note 28, at 112–15.
38. Devins and Baum, *The Company They Keep*, note 28, at 115–16.

39. Ibid. at 104–18.
40. Devins and Baum, *The Company They Keep*, note 28.
41. Lawrence Baum, *Judges and Their Audiences: A Perspective on Judicial Behavior* 43–49 (2006).
42. Devins and Baum, *The Company They Keep*, note 28, at 24–25, 40–46.
43. Ibid. at 10–11.
44. Ibid.
45. Ibid. at 120–21, 130–40; Graber, *The Coming Constitutional Yo-Yo*, note 31, at 701–703.
46. See Geoffrey C. Layman et al., *Activists and Conflict Extension in American Party Politics*, 104 American Political Science Review 2 May 2010, 324–46 (arguing that party activists play a leading role in driving political polarization and conflict extension in American politics).
47. Devins and Baum, *The Company They Keep*, note 28, at 116–18, 132–36.
48. Ibid.; Hollis-Brusky, *Ideas with Consequences*, Chapter 8, n. 61, at 155–64.
49. Teles, *The Rise of the Conservative Legal Movement*, Chapter 8, n. 61, at 167–73.
50. Ibid.; Hollis-Brusky, *Ideas with Consequences*, Chapter 8, n. 61, at 154–55.
51. Teles, *The Rise of the Conservative Legal Movement*, Chapter 8, n. 61, at 167–73; Hollis-Brusky, *Ideas with Consequences*, Chapter 8, n. 61, at 154–55; Southworth, *Lawyers and the Conservative Counterrevolution*, Chapter 8, n. 61, at 1703.
52. Southworth, *Lawyers and the Conservative Counterrevolution*, Chapter 8, n. 61, at 1704–1705.
53. Ibid.
54. Ibid. at 1705; Hollis-Brusky, *Ideas with Consequences*, Chapter 8, n. 61, at 20–21, 155–64.
55. Devins and Baum, *The Company They Keep*, note 28, at 151, 155–57; Hollis-Brusky, *Ideas with Consequences*, Chapter 8, n. 61, at 4, 20–21, 155–64.
56. Hollis-Brusky, *Ideas with Consequences*, Chapter 8, n. 61, at 169.
57. Devins and Baum, *The Company They Keep*, note 28, at 3, 155.
58. Ibid. at 3–8.
59. Hollis-Brusky, *Ideas with Consequences*, Chapter 8, n. 61, at 26, 45–47, 50, 54–55, 78, 84–85, 135–39 (showing how amicus briefs signed by Federalist Society members signaled the views of conservatives and offered legal arguments and materials for judges to use).
60. See Benjamin Pomerance, *Chief Justice John Roberts and the Coming Struggle for a Respected Supreme Court*, 82 Alb. L. Rev. 449, 451 (2018)("Kennedy remained a politically conservative voter on an increasingly politically conservative Court . . . No one could rationally cast a jurist with such a record as a political liberal, or even a left-leaning centrist"); Jack Goldsmith, *The Shape of the Post-Kennedy Court*, Weekly Standard (July 2, 2018), https://www.weeklystandard.com/jack-goldsmith/the-post-kennedy-supreme-court-isnt-likely-to-be-as-conservative-as-liberals-fear [https://perma.cc/XT26-4GXW] ("Kennedy's progressive votes on social issues and the death penalty, and his rejection of constitutional originalism, camouflaged the reality that he usually voted with the right side of the Court").
61. Graber, *The Coming Constitutional Yo-Yo*, note 31, at 665–66.
62. Ibid.
63. Graber, *Judicial Supremacy and the Structure of Partisan Conflict*, note 7, at 161; Graber, *Kahn and the Glorious Long State of Courts and Parties*, Chapter 6, n. 2, at 2.
64. H. W. Perry Jr. and L. A. Powe Jr., *The Political Battle For The Constitution*, 21 Const. Commentary 641 (2004)("Over the past two generations, the Democratic Party and

Republican Party have come to fundamentally different conceptions of the United States Constitution").

65. Balkin and Levinson, *Understanding the Constitutional Revolution*, Chapter 6, n. 12, at 1062–63.
66. Ibid.
67. Ibid.
68. See Danny Hakim and Michael Wines, *"They Don't Really Want Us to Vote": How Republicans Made It Harder*, New York Times, Nov. 3, 2018, https://www.nytimes.com/2018/11/03/us/politics/voting-suppression-elections.html [https://perma.cc/GMZ6-WUVC] ("Restrictions on voting, virtually all imposed by Republicans, reflect rising partisanship, societal shifts producing a more diverse America, and the weakening of the Voting Rights Act by the Supreme Court in 2013"); (quoting Stanford Law Professor Nate Persilly for the proposition that "We've reached a situation in which the fight over the rules and who gets to vote is seen as a legitimate part of electoral competition").
69. Shelby County v. Holder, 570 U.S. 529 (2013).
70. Rucho v. Common Cause, 139 S. Ct. 2484 (2019).
71. Janus v. Am. Fed'n of State, Cty. & Mun. Emps., Council 31, 138 S. Ct. 2448 (2018).
72. David A. Strauss, *The Modernizing Mission of Judicial Review*, 76 U. Chi. L. Rev. 859 (2009); David A. Strauss, *Modernization and Representation Reinforcement: An Essay in Memory of John Hart Ely*, 57 Stan. L. Rev. 761 (2004).
73. Strauss, *Modernization and Representation Reinforcement*, note 72, at 762; Strauss, *Modernizing Mission*, note 72, at 862.
74. In Kennedy v. Louisiana, 554 US 407 (2008), The Supreme Court held that Louisiana's law imposing the death penalty for raping children was an outlier in a general trend toward elimination of the death penalty for similar crimes. In dissent, Justice Alito responded that the characterization was arbitrary, because six states had recently passed similar laws. Id. at 461 (Alito dissenting). He argued that it was possible that they could be the beginning of a national trend.
75. See Driver, *Constitutional Outliers*, note 26, at 951–56 (arguing that trends are susceptible to multiple interpretations).
76. Graber, *The Nonmajoritarian Difficulty*, Chapter 6, n. 8.
77. See Jack M. Balkin, *The Last Days of Disco: Why the American Political System is Dysfunctional*, 94 B.U. L. Rev. 1159, 1193–95 (2014)(describing the effects of gridlock in empowering the president and increasing polarization and dysfunction).
78. Schauer, *The Supreme Court's Agenda*, Chapter 6, n. 25.
79. See Graber, *Judicial Supremacy and the Structure of Partisan Conflict*, note 7, at 170 (arguing that in time of strong polarization and gridlock, "conservatives and liberals launch litigation campaigns to obtain favorable judicial rulings, knowing that the victorious faction in Court will control at least one veto point outside the judiciary that can be used to prevent the elected branches from interfering with their litigation success").
80. See McCutcheon v. FEC, 134 S. Ct. 1434 (2014) (striking down McCain-Feingold Act's ceilings on total individual contributions to candidates); Citizens United v. FEC, 558 U.S. 310 (2010) (striking down McCain-Feingold Act's restrictions on corporate expenditures near the time of a general or primary election); Davis v. FEC, 554 U.S. 724, 729 (2008) (striking down McCain-Feingold Act's "Millionaire's Amendment, which relaxed relaxed contribution limits for candidates whose opponents contributed large amounts of their own money); FEC v. Wisconsin Right to Life, Inc., 551 U.S. 449 (2007) (upholding

as-applied challenge to McCain-Feingold's restrictions on corporate expenditures); see also Arizona Free Enterprise Club's Freedom Club PAC v. Bennett, 564 U.S. 721 (2011) (invalidating state public financing scheme for attempting to equalize resources between candidates).

81. Shelby County v. Holder, 570 U.S. 529 (2013) (striking down pre-clearance formula in section 4 of the Voting Rights Act and effectively making the preclearance provisions in section 5 unenforceable).
82. See Lamps Plus, Inc. v. Varela, 139 S.Ct. 1407 (2019) (holding that the Federal Arbitration Act bars an order requiring class arbitration when an employer-employee agreement is ambiguous about whether class arbitration is available); Epic Systems Corp. v. Lewis, 138 S. Ct. 1612 (2018) (holding that employees could not use the National Labor Relations Act or the Federal Arbitration Act to escape contract clauses that required individual arbitration and instead pursue claims through class or collective action); DIRECTV, Inc. v. Imburgia, 136 S. Ct. 463 (2015) (rejecting state contract interpretation that would have revived the consumer protection rule pre-empted in *Concepcion*); Am. Express Co. v. Italian Colors Rest., 133 S. Ct. 2304 (2013) (upholding arbitration agreement prohibiting class arbitration, even if costs of individual arbitration would be greater the potential amount of recovery); AT&T Mobility LLC v. Concepcion, 563 U.S. 333 (2011) (pre-empting California rule that deemed unconscionable contractual waivers of the right to class-action arbitration); Rent-A-Center, W., Inc. v. Jackson, 561 U.S. 63 (2010) (holding that arbitrators, not courts, decide whether an arbitration agreement is unconscionable); Buckeye Check Cashing, Inc. v. Cardegna, 546 U.S. 440 (2006) (holding that challenges to arbitration contracts should be decided by arbitrators, not by courts); for criticisms of the Roberts Court's jurisprudence, see Judith Resnik, *Diffusing Disputes: The Public in the Private of Arbitration, the Private in Courts, and the Erasure of Rights*, 124 Yale L.J. 2804 (2015); Christopher R. Leslie, *The Arbitration Bootstrap*, 94 Tex. L. Rev. 265 (2015).
83. See, e.g., Epic Systems Corp. v. Lewis, (limiting collective arbitration); Wal-Mart Stores, Inc. v. Dukes, 564 U.S. 338, 357 (2011) (limiting federal class actions); AT&T Mobility LLC v. Concepcion, (limiting class action arbitration).
84. See Janus v. Am. Fed'n of State, Cty. & Mun. Emps., Council 31, 138 S. Ct. 2448 (2018) (holding that compulsory contributions to public sector unions violated the First Amendment).
85. Keith E. Whittington, *Repugnant Laws: Judicial Review of Acts of Congress from the Founding to the Present* 220–21 (2019)(noting that the Court worked together with the national political branches during this period, and that "the Warren Court was an extension of Congress, not an antagonist of it").
86. See ibid. at 221 (noting that the Warren Court "focused on monitoring the states"); and 237 (chart showing that state invalidations peaked during the 1960s and 1970s while the number of invalidations of federal statutes remained at a fairly low level).
87. See ibid. at 220–21.
88. See Devins and Baum, *The Company They Keep*, note 28, at 122–28 (describing Republican strategies for judicial appointments since Reagan).
89. Ibid. at 128–29; Mark Tushnet, *In the Balance: Law and Politics on the Roberts Court* 74 (2013).
90. Devins and Baum, *The Company They Keep*, note 28, at 128–29. On the differences between the two parties, see Matt Grossman and David A. Hopkins, *Asymmetric Politics: Ideological*

Republicans and Group Interest Democrats (2016); Matt Grossman and David A. Hopkins, *Ideological Republicans and Group Interest Democrats: The Asymmetry of American Party Politics*, Perspectives on Politics 13 (March 2015): 119–39.

91. Devins and Baum, *The Company They Keep*, note 28, at 130.
92. Chief Justice Roberts, for example, has been criticized for his decisions in Sebelius v. NFIB, 567 U.S. 519 (2012) and King v. Burwell, 135 S. Ct. 2480 (2015), each of which saved Obamacare. See, e.g., Josh Gerstein, *Conservatives Steamed at Chief Justice Roberts' Betrayal*, Politico, June 25, 2015, https://www.politico.com/story/2015/06/gop-conservatives-angry-supreme-court-chief-john-roberts-obamacare-119431 [https://perma.cc/7MAZ-CEUL]; Igor Bobic, *Conservatives Brand John Roberts a Traitor for Saving Obamacare*, Huffington Post, June 25, 2015, https://www.huffpost.com/entry/john-roberts-traitor-obamacare_n_7664680 [https://perma.cc/DBT2-TMCY].
93. 3 Charles Warren, *The Supreme Court In United States History 1856–1918* 102, 143–45, 223 (1926); Barry Friedman, *The History of the Countermajoritarian Difficulty, Part II: Reconstruction's Political Court*, 91 Geo. L.J. 1, 38–39 (2002). The Judicial Circuits Act of 1866 did not remove any of the ten sitting Justices. Instead, it provided that "no vacancy in the office of associate justice of the supreme court shall be filled by appointment until the number of associate justices shall be reduced to six." Justices Catron and Wayne died while the Act was in force, reducing the Court to eight members. The Judiciary Act of 1869 then increased the Court's seats to nine.
94. Barry Friedman, *The History of the Countermajoritarian Difficulty, Part II,* note 93, at 40.
95. Shesol, *Supreme Power*, Chapter 7, n. 23, at 355–77 (describing opposition of Democratic Senators, who found themselves making common cause with foes of the New Deal).
96. Sheldon Goldman, *Judicial Confirmation Wars: Ideology And The Battle For The Federal Courts*, 39 U. Rich. L. Rev. 871, 892 (2005).
97. Devins and Baum, *The Company They Keep*, note 28, at 108.
98. Jeremy W. Peters, *In Landmark Vote, Senate Limits Use of the Filibuster*, Nov. 21, 2013, https://www.nytimes.com/2013/11/22/us/politics/reid-sets-in-motion-steps-to-limit-use-of-filibuster.html [https://perma.cc/EE6R-FMV7].
99. Matt Flegenheimer, *Senate Republicans Deploy "Nuclear Option" to Clear Path for Gorsuch*, New York Times, April 6, 2017, https://www.nytimes.com/2017/04/06/us/politics/neil-gorsuch-supreme-court-senate.html [https://perma.cc/GZA7-NXL9].
100. Devins and Baum, *The Company They Keep*, note 28, at xii–xv.
101. *Brett Kavanaugh's Opening Statement: Full Transcript*, New York Times, Sept. 26, 2018, https://www.nytimes.com/2018/09/26/us/politics/read-brett-kavanaughs-complete-opening-statement.html [https://perma.cc/9E8Q-FLEB].
102. Joan Biskupic, *Democrats Look at Packing the Supreme Court to Pack the Vote*, CNN, May 31, 2019, https://www.cnn.com/2019/05/31/politics/democrats-supreme-court-packing-politics/index.html [https://perma.cc/HM7L-F68V].
103. Burgess Everett And Elana Schor, *McConnell's Laser Focus on Transforming the Judiciary*, Politico, October 17, 2018, https://www.politico.com/story/2018/10/17/senate-gop-judges-911935 [https://perma.cc/EJX4-6HN7].
104. Priyanka Boghani, *How McConnell and the Senate Helped Trump Set Records in Appointing Judges*, PBS.org, May 21, 2019, https://www.pbs.org/wgbh/frontline/article/how-mcconnell-and-the-senate-helped-trump-set-records-in-appointing-judges/ [https://

perma.cc/ZSN4-XM9B]; Kelsey Snell, *Senate Rewrites Rules To Speed Confirmations For Some Trump Nominees*, NPR.org, April 3, 2019, https://www.npr.org/2019/04/03/709489797/senate-rewrites-rules-to-speed-confirmations-for-some-trump-nominees [https://perma.cc/B55W-DD7C].

Chapter 10

1. Theodore Roosevelt, *Address of President Roosevelt on the Occasion of the Laying of the Corner Stone of the Pilgrim Memorial Monument, Provincetown, MA* (Aug. 20, 1907), in Washington, DC, Government Printing Office, 1907, at 47.
2. Dred Scott v. Sandford, 60 U.S. (19 How.) 393 (1857) (striking down the Missouri Compromise and holding that blacks could never be citizens).
3. Pollock v. Farmers' Loan & Trust Company, 157 U.S. 429, modified on rehearing, 158 U.S. 601 (1895) (striking down the 1894 Federal Income Tax).
4. The Civil Rights Cases, 109 U.S. 3 (1883) (striking down the public accommodations provisions of the Civil Rights Act of 1875).
5. United States v. Harris, 106 US 629 (1883) (striking down the criminal law provisions of the Ku Klux Klan Act).
6. Plessy v. Ferguson, 163 U.S. 537 (1896) (creating separate but equal doctrine).
7. Berea College v. Kentucky, 211 U.S. 45 (1908) (holding that states could prohibit schools chartered as corporations from admitting both black and white students).
8. Giles v. Harris, 189 U.S. 475 (1903) (refusing to intervene in Alabama's voter disenfranchisement scheme).
9. United States v. E. C. Knight Co., 156 U.S. 1 (1895). By contrast, the lower federal courts used the new antitrust laws primarily to prosecute labor unions. See Herbert Hovenkamp, Enterprise and American Law, 1836–1937 at 228–29 (2009).
10. Adair v. United States, 208 U.S. 161 (1908); see also Coppage v. Kansas, 236 U.S. 1 (1915) (holding that bans on "yellow dog" contracts were unconstitutional.); Loewe v. Lawlor, 208 U.S. 274 (1908) (*Danbury Hatters*) (applying the Sherman antitrust act to labor unions).
11. See Levitsky and Ziblatt, *How Democracies Die*, Chapter 3, n. 8, at 102–17 (2018).
12. Trump v. Hawaii, 138 S. Ct. 2392 (2018).
13. Rucho v. Common Cause, 139 S. Ct. 2484 (2019).
14. Shelby County v. Holder, 570 U.S. 529 (2013).
15. Janus v. Am. Fed'n of State, Cty. & Mun. Emps., Council 31, 138 S. Ct. 2448 (2018).
16. Schauer, *The Supreme Court's Agenda*, Chapter 6, n. 25.
17. See Levitsky and Ziblatt, *How Democracies Die*, Chapter 3, n. 8, at 145 (arguing that the Republican hardball over Merrick Garland's nomination had "trampled on a basic democratic norm . . . and gotten away with it").
18. Kevin J. McMahon, *Will the Supreme Court Still "Seldom Stray Very Far"?: Regime Politics in a Polarized America*, 93 Chi.-Kent L. Rev. 343 (2018)(citing McCloskey, *The American Supreme Court*, Chapter 9, n. 24, at 225).
19. Kevin J. McMahon, *Will the Supreme Court Still "Seldom Stray Very Far"?*, note 18, at 343–44. McMahon's point was about Justice Gorsuch, but the same point applies to Justice Kavanaugh, whose confirmation was also very close.
20. Ibid. at 344.

21. Cf. Eric A. Posner and Adrian Vermeule, *Inside or Outside the System?*, 80 U Chi L Rev 1743, 1765 (2013)(arguing that parties that control the appointments process may "filter out judges who would challenge majority prejudices and filter in judges who share them").
22. Schuette v. Coalition to Defend Affirmative Action, 572 U.S. 291 (2014).
23. Ibid. at 325 (Scalia, J., dissenting).
24. Ibid. at 327 (Scalia, J., dissenting).
25. I use the term "reserve-*Carolene Products*" to refer to courts causing or exacerbating or defects in the political process, and/or making it more difficult for minority groups to protect themselves in the political process. The Justices in the majority in *Shelby County* probably did not believe that they were undermining democracy, although, in my view, that is precisely what they were doing.

    David Bernstein uses the expression "reverse-*Carolene Products*" to refer to the use of judicial review to help a minority group "use their political muscle as other interest groups do, thereby to some degree balancing out their remaining disadvantages in the political system." See David E. Bernstein, "Reverse Carolene Products," the End of the Second Reconstruction, and Other Thoughts on *Schuette v. Coalition to Defend Affirmative Action*, 2013–14 Cato Sup. Ct. Rev. 261. He argues that this may have been the underlying justification of the political process doctrine of Hunter v. Erickson, 393 U.S. 385 (1969), which prevents majority groups from altering the rules of politics to prevent minorities from gaining antidiscrimination protections (ibid. at 277). By contrast, I do not see courts helping minority groups compete in the political process as the *reverse* of the theory of *Carolene Products*, but rather as an *application* of the theory. The point of the political process doctrine is that if majorities are able to change the rules of the game as soon as minorities demonstrate that they are able to protect their interests in the democratic process, this is a defect in democratic politics, and under theory of *Carolene Products*, courts should step in to prevent it.
26. See Nicholas Stephanopoulos, *The Anti-Carolene Court*, 2019 Supreme Court Rev.__(forthcoming 2020), available at https://papers.ssrn.com/sol3/papers.cfm?abstract_id=3483321 (November 21, 2019) (arguing that the Roberts Court has behaved as if it sought to undermine the democratic process, with predictable gains to the Republican Party). Stephanopoulos calls the first problem—staying out when democracy is threatened—"reverse-*Carolene* decisions," and the second problem—using judicial review to prevent reforms that would protect democracy—"perverse-*Carolene* decisions." Draft at 52–53.
27. *Rucho*, 139 S.Ct. at 2506.
28. 139 S.Ct. 2551 (2019).
29. See ibid. at 2587–89 (Breyer, J., concurring in part and dissenting in part).
30. Michael Wines, *Inside the Trump Administration's Fight to Add a Citizenship Question to the Census*, New York Times, Nov. 4, 2018, https://www.nytimes.com/2018/11/04/us/wilbur-ross-commerce-secretary.html [https://perma.cc/BY5L-N94Y] ("Because immigrants and minorities disproportionately vote Democratic, a depressed head count could also expand Republican Party control when new political boundaries are drawn in 2021").
31. Id; Testimony of Secretary Wilbur Ross, Hearing: FY19 Budget - Department of Commerce (EventID=108027) (March 20, 2018), https://www.youtube.com/watch?v=NDWiAiSWgNU&feature=youtu.be&t=36m25s; Hansi Lo Wang, *"I Will Call The AG": Trump Officials Pushed For Census Citizenship Question*, NPR.org, July 30, 2018, https://www.npr.org/

2018/07/30/632847876/i-will-call-the-ag-trump-officials-pushed-for-census-citizenship-question [https://perma.cc/7KFE-2JZ4].

32. Wang, *"I Will Call The AG"*, note 31; Department of Commerce v. New York, 139 S.Ct. at 2574–75.
33. Joan Biskupic, *How John Roberts Killed the Census Citizenship Question*, CNN, September 12, 2019, https://www.cnn.com/2019/09/12/politics/john-roberts-census-citizenship-supreme-court/index.html [https://perma.cc/BE5J-UKLE]("After the justices heard arguments in late April, Roberts was ready to rule for Ross and the administration").
34. Tara Bahrampour, *GOP Strategist and Census Official Discussed Citizenship Question, New Documents Filed by Lawyers Suggest*, Washington Post, June 16, 2019, https://www.washingtonpost.com/dc-md-va/2019/06/15/new-documents-suggest-direct-connection-between-republican-redistricting-strategist-census-bureau-official-over-citizenship-question/ [https://perma.cc/6GNG-462U]; Michael Wines, *Deceased G.O.P. Strategist's Hard Drives Reveal New Details on the Census Citizenship Question*, New York Times, May 30, 2019, https://www.nytimes.com/2019/05/30/us/census-citizenship-question-hofeller.html [https://perma.cc/D7HM-UBF9]
35. Department of Commerce v. New York, 139 S.Ct. at 2575.
36. Ibid. at 2583 (Thomas, J., concurring in part and dissenting in part) ("Where there are equally plausible views of the evidence, one of which involves attributing bad faith to an officer of a coordinate branch of Government, the presumption [of regularity] compels giving the benefit of the doubt to that officer"); ibid. at 2597–98 (Alito, J., concurring in part and dissenting in part) ("To put the point bluntly, the Federal Judiciary has no authority to stick its nose into the question whether it is good policy to include a citizenship question on the census or whether the reasons given by Secretary Ross for that decision were his only reasons or his real reasons").
37. Ibid. at 2582 (Thomas, J., concurring in part and dissenting in part) ("I do not deny that a judge predisposed to distrust the Secretary or the administration could arrange those facts on a corkboard and—with a jar of pins and a spool of string—create an eye-catching conspiracy web"). See also ibid. at 2597 (Alito, J. concurring in part and dissenting in part) (expressing concern that the decision will allow individual judges to question the motives of executive branch officials).
38. Youngstown Sheet & Tube Co. v. Sawyer, 343 U.S. 579 (1952).
39. United States v. Nixon, 418 U.S. 683 (1974).
40. See Michael Klarman, *From Jim Crow to Civil Rights: The Supreme Court and the Struggle for Racial Equality* (2004).
41. Trump v. Mazars USA, LLP (No. 19-715); Trump v. Vance (No. 19-635); Trump v. Deutsche Bank AG (No. 19-760).
42. See Trump v. Vance, 941 F. 3d 631, 641 (2d Cir. 2019), *cert. granted*, 2019 WL 6797730 (December 13, 2019) ("The President has not persuasively explained why, if executive privilege did not preclude enforcement of the subpoena issued in [*United States v.*] *Nixon*, the Mazars subpoena must be enjoined despite seeking no privileged information and bearing no relation to the President's performance of his official functions"); Watkins v. United States, 354 U.S. 178 (1957) (holding that Congress has broad powers to investigate potential corruption, inefficiency, waste, or any issues related to potential legislation).

Chapter 11

1. For an early appraisal of this scenario, see James McGregor Burns, *Packing the Court: The Rise of Judicial Power and the Coming Crisis of the Supreme Court* (2009). Burns's proposed remedy was quite drastic: he argued that the president should simply refuse to obey the Court's edicts. This proposal seems unrealistic, especially after two centuries of politicians constructing judicial review to serve their ends.
2. See, e.g., David E. Bernstein, *Lawless: The Obama Administration's Unprecedented Assault on the Constitution and the Rule of Law* (2015).
3. Many different versions of this idea have been proposed. My arguments here draw on (and slightly modify) the proposal of Roger Cramton and Paul Carrington. Paul D. Carrington and Roger C. Cramton, *The Supreme Court Renewal Act: A Return to Basic Principles*, in Roger C. Cramton and Paul D. Carrington, eds., *Reforming The Court: Term Limits For Supreme Court Justices* 467 (2006); Paul D. Carrington and Roger C. Cramton, *The Supreme Court Renewal Act: A Return to Basic Principles* (July 5, 2005), https://zfacts.com/metaPage/lib/2005-SUPREME-COURT.pdf [https://perma.cc/4V3W-F3BL].

   In 2009, I showed how the Cramton-Carrington proposal would work in practice, starting with the 1951 Supreme Court. Jack M. Balkin, *The Rotation of the Justices: A Thought Experiment*, Balkinization, May 20, 2009, https://balkin.blogspot.com/2009/05/rotation-of-justices-thought-experiment.html [https://perma.cc/FB59-VNRZ]. The Cramton-Carrington proposal is also the basis of the campaign by Fix the Court; see *Leading Constitutional Scholars Propose Resolution to the Supreme Court Confirmation Madness*, Fix the Court, June 29, 2017, https://fixthecourt.com/2017/06/tlproposalrelease/ [https://perma.cc/9NXD-XD9H]. In addition to Cramton and Carrington's proposal, See Steven G. Calabresi and James Lindgren, *Term Limits For The Supreme Court: Life Tenure Reconsidered*, Chapter 9, n. 36 (arguing for a constitutional amendment); Philip D. Oliver., *Systematic Justice: A Proposed Constitutional Amendment to Establish Fixed, Staggered Terms for Members of the United States Supreme Court*, 47 Ohio St. L.J. 799 (1986)(same); see L. A. Powe Jr., *Go Geezers Go: Leaving the Bench*, 25 Law & Soc. Inquiry 1227, 1235 (2000); L. A. Powe Jr., *Old People and Good Behavior*, 12 Const. Comment. 195, 196–97 (1995) (arguing that "life tenure is the Framers' greatest lasting mistake"); see also L. A. Powe Jr., *Marble Palace, We've Got a Problem—With You, in Reforming The Court: Term Limits For Supreme Court Justices*, at 99, 107; Sanford Levinson, *Contempt of Court: The Most Important "Contemporary Challenge" to Judging*, 49 Wash. & Lee L. Rev. 339, 341–42 (1992); Sanford Levinson, *Life Tenure and the Supreme Court: What Is To Be Done?*, in *Reforming The Court: Term Limits For Supreme Court Justices*, at 375, 376; Judith Resnik, *Judicial Selection and Democratic Theory: Demand, Supply, and Life Tenure*, 26 Cardozo L. Rev. 579, 641 (2005)("Article III could similarly be reinterpreted to require guaranteed terms yet also to permit a mandatory, statutorily-fixed retirement age"); Akhil Reed Amar and Steven G. Calabresi, *Term Limits for the High Court*, Washington Post, August 9, 2002, https://www.washingtonpost.com/archive/opinions/2002/08/09/term-limits-for-the-high-court/646134cd-8e13-4166-9474-5f53be633d7c/?utm_term=.b335e294188c [https://perma.cc/9V59-P2QR] (suggesting multiple methods for achieving term limits); see also Ryan C. Black and Amanda C. Bryan, *The Policy Consequences of Term Limits on the U.S. Supreme Court*, 42 Ohio N.U.L. Rev. 821 (2016)(discussing various proposals); Vicki C. Jackson, *Packages of Judicial Independence: The Selection and Tenure of Article*

III Judges, 95 Geo. L.J. 965, 997, 1000–1006 (2007) (summarizing the debates); Michael J. Mazza, *A New Look at an Old Debate: Life Tenure and the Article III Judge*, 39 Gonz. L. Rev. 131, 133, 143–47, 155–62 (2003) (describing the history of term-limit proposals in the late nineteenth and twentieth centuries).

4. Akhil Reed Amar and Ian Ayres, *A Spare Justice or Two?*, Los Angeles Times, May 7, 2009, https://www.latimes.com/archives/la-xpm-2009-may-07-oe-ayres7-story.html [https://perma.cc/W49S-LVPD] (arguing for the advantages of presidents nominating multiple Justices at a time).
5. See R. Sam Garrett and Denis Steven Rutkus, Cong. Research Service, RL 33118, *Speed of Presidential and Senate Actions on Supreme Court Nominations, 1900–2010* 1 (Aug. 6, 2010) ("The data indicate that the entire nomination-and-confirmation process (from when the President first learned of a vacancy to final Senate action) has generally taken almost twice as long for nominees after 1980 than for nominees in the previous 80 years").
6. See 28 U.S.C. § 1 (2006) ("The Supreme Court of the United States shall consist of a Chief Justice of the United States and eight associate justices, any six of whom shall constitute a quorum"); Jonathan Remy Nash, *The Majority That Wasn't: Stare Decisis, Majority Rule, And The Mischief Of Quorum Requirements*, 58 Emory L.J. 831, 842–44 (2009)(noting that although the Constitution specifies quorum requirements for the House and Senate in Article I, section 5, "with respect to the federal judiciary, in contrast, the Constitution is silent . . . Congress has established quorum requirements for the federal courts").
7. See Paul Brest, Sanford Levinson, Jack M. Balkin, Akhil Reed Amar, and Reva B. Siegel, *Processes of Constitutional Decisionmaking*, Chapter 6, n. 3, at 1750–53 (table of Justices).
8. U.S. Const. art. I, § 8, cl. 9; U.S. Const. art. III, § 1.
9. Ibid.; See 28 U.S.C. § 1 (2006) (setting number of justices and quorum); Marin K. Levy, *Visiting Judges*, 107 Calif. L. Rev. 68, 71–72 (2019)(noting that Congress has allowed lower federal court judges to sit by designation in other courts since 1814, and that Supreme Court Justices have served as circuit judges since the country's founding).

   Calabresi and Lindgren argue that the Cramton-Carrington proposal violates the Appointments Clause of Article III, which states that the president "shall nominate, and by and with the Advice and Consent of the Senate, shall appoint Ambassadors, other public ministers and Consuls, Judges of the supreme Court, and all other Officers of the United States, whose Appointments are not herein otherwise provided for, and which shall be established by Law." U.S. Const. art. III, § 2, as well as the Good Behaviour Clause, which provides that "the Judges, both of the supreme and inferior Courts, shall hold their Offices during good Behaviour." U.S. Const. art. III, § 1. See Steven G. Calabresi and James Lindgren, *Term Limits For The Supreme Court: Life Tenure Reconsidered*, Chapter 9, n. 36, at 859–68. They argue that because "the Appointments Clause plainly contemplates a separate office of judge of the Supreme Court, it is hard to see how that office could constitutionally be filled for only eighteen years and not for life." Ibid. at 859. The text, however, does not tell us what the office of a "Judge[] of the supreme Court" entails. Congress has the powers to decide the number and quorum of Justices, require Justices to ride circuit as lower court judges, and, under Article I, section 8, clause 9, to organize the lower federal courts. These powers would seem to give Congress considerable leeway in defining the duties of the office of a Supreme Court Justice, even if the Justice enjoys his or her commission for life during good behavior.

10. Tara Leigh Grove, *The Structural Safeguards Of Federal Jurisdiction*, 124 Harv. L. Rev. 869, 888–916 (2011)(describing history of jurisdiction stripping attempts by Congress).
11. Judiciary Act of 1925, Pub. L. No. 68–415, 43 Stat. 936. The Court's discretionary jurisdiction actually began with the 1891 act that created the intermediate courts of appeals, and a 1916 act that gave it power to decline to hear some state court appeals. But neither change was considered very extensive or very important at the time. See Edward A. Hartnett, *Questioning Certiorari: Some Reflections Seventy-Five Years After the Judges' Bill*, 100 Colum. L. Rev. 1643, 1649–51, 1657–60 (2000). By contrast, the Justices, and especially Chief Justice Taft, lobbied hard for the 1925 Act, which gave them considerable control over the cases they heard. Ibid. at 1660–1704.
12. See generally Margaret Meriwether Cordray and Richard Cordray, *The Philosophy Of Certiorari: Jurisprudential Considerations In Supreme Court Case Selection*, 82 Wash. U. L. Q. 389, 391–94 (2004)(offering a brief history of the Justices' increasing control over their own docket.).
13. As Robert Post explains, "by ceding to the Court significant authority to shape its own docket, the Act essentially recognized the Court as the supervisor of the system of federal law." Robert Post, *The Supreme Court Opinion as Institutional Practice: Dissent, Legal Scholarship, and Decisionmaking in the Taft Court*, 85 Minn. L. Rev. 1267, 1273 (2001). Chief Justice Taft's justification for the Court's new discretionary jurisdiction is consistent with the role of courts in a depolarized politics: "The Supreme Court's function is for the purpose of expounding and stabilizing principles of law for the benefit of the people of the country, passing upon constitutional questions and other important questions of law for the public benefit." Hartnett, *Questioning Certiorari*, note 11, at 1664–65 (quoting Jurisdiction of Circuit Courts of Appeals and United States Supreme Court: Hearing Before the House Comm. on the Judiciary, 67th Cong. 2 (1922)).
14. See Arthur D. Hellman, *The Shrunken Docket Of The Rehnquist Court*, 1996 Sup. Ct. Rev. 403 (1996)(noting that "From 1971 through 1988, the United States Supreme Court was hearing and deciding an average of 147 cases each Term" but that "the 1995 Term, which came to an end in July 1996, yielded only 77 plenary decisions—half the number that the Court was handing down a decade earlier").
15. See Vanessa A. Baird, *Answering the Call of the Court: How Justices and Litigants Set the Supreme Court Agenda* (2007)(explaining how the Justices signal the kinds of cases that they want litigants to bring, thus increasing the policymaking power of the Supreme Court).
16. Daniel E. Herz-Roiphe and David Singh Grewal, *Make Me Democratic, But Not Yet: Sunrise Lawmaking And Democratic Constitutionalism*, 90 N.Y.U.L. Rev. 1975 (2015); Sofia Ranchordas, *Constitutional Sunsets and Experimental Legislation* (2014).

Chapter 12

1. Fred R. Shapiro and Joseph Epstein, eds., *The Yale Book of Quotations* 92 (2006). This has been attributed to many others, including Yogi Berra, Mark Twain, and Samuel Goldwyn.
2. Several important discussions of generational shifts in party affiliation have been offered in the context of theories of party realignment. But the idea that later generations like a party less than previous generations is distinct from the claim that there are realigning

elections. For examples of these arguments, see James L. Sundquist, *Dynamics of the Party System: Alignment and Realignment of Political Parties in the United States* 45–47, 304–308 (1983); Paul Allen Beck, *The Electoral Cycle and Patterns of American Politics*, 9 British Journal of Political Science (1979), 129–56; Paul Allen Beck, *A Socialization Theory of Partisan Realignment*, in Richard G. Niemi et al., *The Politics of Future Citizens* (1974); cf. David R. Mayhew, *Electoral Realignments: A Critique Of An American Genre*, Chapter 2, n. 11, at 18–20 (discussing these accounts).

3. David Brooks, *The Coming G.O.P. Apocalypse*, New York Times, June 3, 2019, https://www.nytimes.com/2019/06/03/opinion/republicans-generation-gap.html [https://perma.cc/Q7UG-LWCY].
4. Pew Research Center, *Trends in Party Affiliation Among Demographic Groups*, March 20, 2018, https://www.people-press.org/2018/03/20/1-trends-in-party-affiliation-among-demographic-groups/ [https://perma.cc/T8LG-HHNU].
5. Cf. Pew Research Center, *The Generation Gap in American Politics*, March 1, 2018, https://www.people-press.org/2018/03/01/the-generation-gap-in-american-politics/ [https://perma.cc/P95R-UVEB] (arguing that younger voters' increased racial and ethnic diversity is one reason for the widening generation gap).
6. On the importance of movement parties to transformational constitutional change, see Bruce Ackerman, *We the People, Volume 3: The Civil Rights Revolution* (2014).
7. See Jonathan Rodden, *Why Cities Lose: The Deep Roots of the Urban-Rural Political Divide* (2019).
8. Julia Azari and Marc J. Hetherington, *Back to the Future? What the Politics of the Late Nineteenth Century Can Tell Us about the 2016 Election*, Annals of the American Academy of Political and Social Science, 667: 92–109 (2016).
9. Gary Miller and Norman Schofield, *The Transformation of the Republican and Democratic Coalitions in the US*, Perspectives on Politics, 6: 433–50 (2008); Gary Miller and Norman Schofield, *Activists and Partisan Realignment in the United States*, American Political Science Review, 97: 245–60 (2003).
10. John Sides, Michael Tesler, and Lynn Vavreck, *Identity Crisis: The 2016 Presidential Campaign and the Battle for the Meaning of America* 214–15 (2018); Julia Azari and Marc J. Hetherington, *Back to the Future? What the Politics of the Late Nineteenth Century Can Tell Us about the 2016 Election*, Annals of the American Academy of Political and Social Science, 667: 92–109 (2016); Miller and Schofield, *The Transformation of the Republican and Democratic Coalitions in the US*; Miller and Schofield, *Activists and Partisan Realignment in the United States*.
11. See *Identity Politics Are Stronger on the Right than the Left*, The Economist, November 1, 2018, https://www.economist.com/united-states/2018/11/01/identity-politics-are-stronger-on-the-right-than-the-left [https://perma.cc/247T-MR7A] (arguing that Republican politics is organized around white and Christian identities).
12. See Ira Katznelson, *Fear Itself: The New Deal and the Origins of Our Time* (2013).
13. For one early attempt, see, e.g., Josh Hawley, *Speech at the National Conservative Conference*, July 18, 2019, https://www.hawley.senate.gov/senator-josh-hawleys-speech-national-conservatism-conference [https://perma.cc/EY9Y-S4RW] (arguing for programs protecting working-class families, increased antitrust regulation, greater restrictions on free trade, capital investments in the "heartland," and "an immigration system that rewards and nourishes American labor rather than devaluing it").

Index

Tables are indicated by *t* following the page number

For the benefit of digital users, indexed terms that span two pages (e.g., 52–53) may, on occasion, appear on only one of those pages.

abortion issue, 75–76, 89, 90, 93–94, 98, 124, 199n35, 216n31. See also *Roe v. Wade*
Ackerman, Bruce, 109–10
Adair v. United States (1908), 136
Adams, Henry, 5
Adams, John Quincy, 22
administrative law and administrative agencies, 108, 127, 128, 164
adoption history, use of, 207n46
affiliated presidents, 19, 20*t*, 21
affirmative action programs, 104–5, 124, 143, 148
Age Discrimination in Employment Act, 202–3n36
Alito, Samuel, 108, 120–21, 131, 140–41, 218n74, 223n36, 223n37
Amar, Akhil Reed, 110
American Bar Association, 120
American Constitution Society, 121
American exceptionalism, 10
American Revolution, 9
Americans with Disabilities Act of 1990, 202–3n36
amicus briefs, 121–22, 217n59
Ancient Greeks, 5, 177n8
antitrust laws, 85–86, 138–39, 169, 201n13, 227n13
Appointments Clause, 225n9
apportionment, 207n38, 207n46
appropriations bills, 32–33, 129, 187n6
Aristotle, 47
asymmetric polarization, 31, 73, 119–20, 121, 125, 127, 130–31, 162, 164
authoritarianism, 6, 9
Azari, Julia, 165–66, 167

baby boomers, 162–63
Balkin, Jack M., 12, 20*t*, 79, 80, 110, 125, 133, 178n16, 197n12, 205n6, 218n77
Barnett, Randy, 107–8, 212n91
Baum, Lawrence, 116
  The Company They Keep: How Partisan Divisions Came to the Supreme Court (with Devins), 118
Beard, Charles and Mary, 205–6n14
Berea College v. Kentucky (1908), 136, 221n7
Berger, Raoul, 102, 105–6, 107, 207n42, 210–11n73
Berman, Mitchell, 110
Bernstein, David, 222n25
  Rehabilitating Lochner: Defending Individual Rights against Progressive Reform, 107
Bickel, Alexander, 86, 101–2
  Holmes Lectures (1969), 101–2
  prudentialism and, 109
Biden, Hunter, 58–59
Biden, Joe, 58–59
Big Tech, 169
Bill of Rights, 100–1, 105–6, 112, 129–30, 206n27, 210–11n73
bipartisan agreement, 116, 118, 129
  end of elite consensus and, 121–22, 133*t*, 159
  bipartisan judicial activism, 98
  during New Deal/Civil Rights regime, 31
Black, Hugo, 73, 88–89, 100–1, 102, 110, 208n48
Blackmun, Harry, 72, 73, 120–21, 197n6
Bohr, Niels, 160
Bork, Robert, 102, 103, 105–6, 107, 131, 207n42
Brady Act, 202–3n36
Brazil, 8, 10
Brennan, William, 72, 90, 202n30
Brest, Paul, 102
Brexit, 8
Breyer, Stephen, 96, 199n43

Britain
  democracy in, 8
  fascist movement in, 9
  Thatcher era in, 9–10
Brooks, David, 164
Brown v. Board of Education (1954), 89–90, 97, 100, 101–2, 114, 116, 148, 201n10, 206n26
Brownell, Herbert, 90
Bryan, William Jennings, 27, 28
Buchanan, James, 22, 185n8
Burger, Warren, 207n42
Burger Court, 73, 79, 82, 88–89, 94, 95, 102, 116–17, 207n46
Burns, James McGregor, 224n1
Burton, Harold H., 206n26
Bush, George H. W., 19, 73
Bush, George W., 19, 21, 31–32, 131–32, 182n43
Bush v. Gore (2000), 75, 97, 108, 125–26
Byrnes, James F., 117

Calabresi, Steven G., 225n9
campaign finance
  Citizens United (2010) and, 91, 108–9, 203n42, 218–19n80
  deregulation, 18, 26, 142
  McCain-Feingold legislation, 128–29
  party as database, 18
  Republican vs. Democratic views on, 124
  wealth's disproportionate influence and, 138–39
capitalism, 50–51
Cardozo, Benjamin, 88
Carlson, Tucker, 163
Carolene Products Corp., United States v. (1938), 112–13, 114, 115–16, 123–25
  break down of model, effect on democracy, 123
  Ely's expansion of, 102
  footnote 4 and Supreme Court's protection of democracy, 100, 142
  judicial deference and, 112
  "perverse-*Carolene*" Supreme Court, 143, 222n26
  polarization and, 123–25, 133*t*
  protection of democracy and, 112, 115–16
  reverse-*Carolene Products* effect generated by constitutional rot, 142–47, 222n25
  Scalia on footnote four, 143
Carrington, Paul, 224n3, 225n9
Carter, Jimmy, 12, 20, 22, 73, 88–89, 153
Catholics, 82
census citizenship question, 42, 144–45, 222n30
Chase Court, 94–95
Chevron doctrine, 32, 108, 213n99
Chicago, City of v. McDonald (2010), 91, 107, 212n90
Christian conservatives
  Free Speech and Free Exercise claims of, 104
  harm to, resulting from antidiscrimination laws, 82, 124, 142
  Republican Party and, 27–28, 166, 167–68
  Supreme Court offering protection to, 79, 82, 104–5, 200n7
  Trump and, 20–21, 181n39
Christian evangelicals, 166, 167–68
church–state relations, 89, 200n7
Citizens United v. FEC (2010), 91, 108–9, 203n42, 218–19n80
civil liberties, protection of, 111, 114, 216n31
Civil Rights Acts, 16, 30, 129, 130, 221n4
Civil Rights Cases (1883), 136
civil rights movement, 9, 16, 30–31
civil society, change in, 26–27
Civil War, 3, 9, 15, 34, 36, 39–41, 166, 170, 171–72, 177n1
Clarke, John H., 88, 117, 201–2n22
class actions, 128–29, 138–39, 219n82, 219n83
class conflict, 161, 166, 168–69, 173, 227n13. *See also* middle class; white working-class voters
Cleveland, Grover, 72
climate change, 173
Clinton, Bill
  corporate support for, 166–67
  Democratic Party's identity and, 167
  impeachment, 40, 61
  judicial appointments by, 130–32
  as pre-emptive president, 19–20
Clinton, Hillary, 17, 58–59, 166–67, 172–73
"coalition of the ascendant" (Obama coalition) 18, 28–29, 64, 166–68
Cold War, 17
Comey, James, 38, 41
Commerce Clause doctrine, 211n80
conflict extension, 12, 127, 160, 217n46

Congress, US. *See also* gridlocked Congress; House of Representatives, US; Senate, US
  activity in 1960s and 1970s, 129–30
  corruption, power to investigate, 223n42
  organizational power over Supreme Court, 153, 225n6
  subpoenas issued for Trump's finances, 146–47
  Supreme Court diminishing role of, 213n100
conservatism
  in culture wars, 18
  intense political competition in periods of gridlock and, 140, 218n79
  judicial review and, 81, 90, 91
  movement conservatives, 77, 83, 87–88, 89, 105–6, 110, 115, 117–18, 119, 201n9
  public interest lawyering and, 104, 209–10n62
  in Reagan regime, 13, 104, 119–20, 143
  Rehnquist and Roberts Courts' conservative jurisprudence, 148
  of Republican Party, 16, 81, 83, 119, 129, 171, 183n9, 196–97n5
  social networks of, 120, 148–49
  of Southern Democrats, 31
  of Supreme Court justices, 74, 77, 82, 88–89, 149–50, 201n9
  of Trump, 20–21
Constitution, US
  Article I, section 5, 225n6
  Article I, section 8, clause 9, 225n9
  Article III, section 1, 225n9
  Article III, section 2, 225n9
  Article V, 78–79, 109–10
  durability of, 39–41
  as insurance policy for republic, 48
  judicial role in, 70–71, 78–79
constitutional change, 78–79
  constitutional moments instead of actual amendments, 109–10
constitutional crisis, 7, 38–43
  civil discord as result of, 39
  Civil War as, 39–41
  disagreement over meaning of Constitution, 39, 186n11
  disaster and, 39
  failure of constitution and, 38
  political leaders failing to follow Constitution, 38–39, 42, 186n12
  possibility of constitutional failure and, 42
  purpose of constitutions, 38, 40–41, 186n18
  Trump and, 38, 41–42, 185n2, 186n16
  United States presently not experiencing, 38, 43, 185n3
constitutional hardball, 46, 112, 131–32, 133*t*, 135, 140–41, 151, 188n14
constitutional regimes
  differentiated from presidential models of regimes, 24, 26
  factors constituting change in, 24–25
  next regime, 148–51
constitutional rot, 44–65
  acceleration of, 58–62
  antebellum period, 34, 135–36 (*see also* Slave Power)
  bad news and good news about, 62–65
  causes of, 49, 50, 70
  constitutional hardball generated by, 140–41, 151
  cycle of, 6–7, 12, 62
  defined, 45
  demagogues produced by, 53–54
  dominant party as driver of, 137
  economic inequality and, 49, 50, 52–53, 70, 137–38, 164
  effects of, 135, 151
  federal judiciary as policy vanguard and, 139–40
  federal judiciary's inability to prevent or limit, 137–38, 150, 159
  Finn on, 187n2
  Four Horsemen of, 49–50
  future path out of, 7, 11, 149, 160, 170–74
  judicial failure to protect democracy, 141–42
  judiciary and, 7, 70–71, 135, 137–38
  loss of trust in government and, 46, 49, 50, 133, 134, 135, 140, 151
  media, effect of Trump's attacks on, 57–58
  media's contribution to, 49
  mutual forbearance affected by, 45, 46
  oligarchy and, 45
  originalism and, 4
  periods of, 45 (*see also* Gilded Age [First]; Second Gilded Age; Slave Power)
  polarization and, 7, 49, 50, 70, 135, 151

constitutional rot (*cont.*)
policy disasters and, 49–50
present situation constituting, 7, 12–13, 44
Republican Party hastening, 61–62
reverse-*Carolene Products* effect generated by, 142–47, 222n25
rule of law affected by, 46
as structural consideration, 47–48
Trump's actions and words as part of, 41, 55–58, 59
Trump's impeachment and, 58, 59–60
constitutional theory, 97–111, 204n1
bipartisan judicial activism and, 98, 116
common law theory of constitutional interpretation, 109–10
creation of, 97
future trends and, 110–11
generational change and, 98
historical circumstances shaping, 97
incorporation theory, 210–11n73, 212n85
liberal skepticism about judicial review, 108–10
living constitutionalism, 99–102
long-term secular trend and, 98
lower federal courts and, 98, 205n7
originalism, 102–8, 210n67 (*see also* originalism)
popular constitutionalism, 109
prudentialism, 109
Supreme Court as focus of, 97, 205n7
Supreme Court docket and, 97–98
constitutional time, 6–7, 178n15
judiciary and, 10, 75
transition to new constitutional order, 7, 178n16
Constitution-in-practice, 25–26
consumer rights, 128–29, 138–39, 219n82
contraception, 124
corporations
commercial speech by, 82, 91, 104–5, 203n42
Democratic candidates seeking support from, 166–67
Republican Party favoring, 167–68
corruption, 27–28, 34, 36–37, 58, 60, 138–39
congressional power to investigate, 223n42
in Gilded Age, 62, 63
judicial protection of, 70–71
judicial review to limit, 74
present situation in US politics, 150
court-packing strategy, 131, 150, 151
Cox, Archibald, 41
Cramton, Roger, 224n3, 225n9
criminal procedure, 89, 93–94, 102, 105–6, 207n46
culture wars, 16, 18, 21, 116–17, 149–50, 166, 172–73
Curtis, Michael Kent, 211n74
cycle of regimes, 12–29, 15*t*
constitutional theory in, 97–111 (*see also* constitutional theory)
definition of regime, 179n12
dominant party in, 13
"institutional thickening" of politics during, 108
life cycle of political regime, 14–15, 85–91
living constitutionalism and, 99–102
location in political time, 19–22
New Deal (*see* New Deal/Civil Rights regime)
next regime, 148–51, 159
originalism and, 102–8
partisan regime and, 13–14
political coalitions and, 14
political science and, 179n11
political time, concept of, 178n15
Reagan regime (*see* Reagan regime)
rise and fall of political regimes, 6–7
Trump's place in, 27–29
waning of political time, 22–27
waning of presidential time and, 25
cyclical history, 3–7
Ancient Greeks on, 5, 177n8
Chinese view of, 5, 177n8
despair as reaction in, 6
hope for future in, 6, 65
institutional arrangements, effect of, 6
multiple cycles in play at same time, 5
regime cycles, 12–29 (*see also* cycle of regimes)
three cycles in American politics, 6–7
Trump's place in, 6

Dahl, Robert A., 115, 117, 121, 178–79n9
death penalty cases, 116–17, 124, 217n60, 218n74
Defense of Marriage Act, 205n8
demagogues, 16–17, 27, 53–54, 62–63

democracy
  Carolene Products model, breakdown of, 123
  Carolene Products and democracy protection, 112, 115–16
  conflict over meaning of, 123–24, 125, 141–42, 217–18n64
  Dworkin's "constitutional conception" of, 114
  failure leading to constitutional rot, 45, 188n14
  failure of Supreme Court to protect, 135–36, 143–44, 149
  global decay of, 8, 9
  judicial failure to protect, 10, 123, 159, 160
  judicial protection of, 70–71, 74, 159
  judicial review as safeguard for, 146
  United States becoming less democratic, 44
democratic constitutionalism, 109
Democratic Party, 15*t*, 72*t*, *See also* political parties
  1896 election, effect on, 15–16, 36, 165–66, 172, 180n14
  2016 election outcome and, 165–66
  2020 election outcome and, 7
  asymmetric polarization and, 119, 127, 162, 163
  class conflict in, 161
  conflict extension, 12 (*see also* conflict extension)
  corporate support for candidates of, 166–67
  dominance in New Deal/Civil Rights regime, 13
  dominance predicted after demise of Reagan regime, 64, 159, 161, 170
  egalitarianism of, 168–69
  emerging coalition of 18, 28–29, 64, 166–68
  elites and, 118, 123–24
  immigrants and urban workers forming coalitions in, 36, 166, 167–68
  Jacksonian regime and Slave Power, 15
  judicial appointments and, 132–33
  judicial reform and, 149–50
  judicial review and, 81, 93, 94, 95–96, 110
  limits of a cosmopolitan party, 168–70
  Millennial voters in, 164
  minority rights, protection of, 124
  New Deal/Civil Rights regime and, 86, 90, 92, 129
  Nixon Democrats, 166
  Northern Democrats, 30, 89–90, 91, 166
  polarization and, 12, 30, 125, 137–38 (*see also* polarization)
  Reagan Democrats, 162–63, 166
  Reagan regime and, 90, 92, 131–32
  reconfiguration of, 165–68, 172, 173
  signature issues for, 169
  social movement in new coalition, 164–65
  Southern Democrats, 31, 89–90, 91, 166, 170
  Supreme Court appointments by, 83, 129, 130–31, 140–41
  voting reform and, 150
Democratic Party elites, 124
Democratic-Republican Party, 15*t*, 72*t*
departmentalism, 87–88
Department of Commerce v. New York (2020), 144, 145
depolarization, 7. *See also* polarization
  changing audience for judges and, 118–21, 133*t*
  future of, 11, 161–62, 168–69, 171
  Great Depression and, 16
  judiciary in depolarized world, 113–18, 133*t*, 154
  "long state of courts and parties," 113–14
deregulation, 13, 16, 17
  elites seeking, 52
  Republican Party's economic policies and, 27–28
despair, 3, 6, 46, 48
Devins, Neal (with Baum): *The Company They Keep: How Partisan Divisions Came to the Supreme Court*, 118
disjunctive presidents, 20, 20*t*, 21, 22, 162
District of Columbia v. Heller (2008), 91, 107, 108–9, 212n90
Douglas, William O., 73, 88–89, 101, 153–54
Dred Scott v. Sandford (1857), 136, 146, 221n2
Dworkin, Ronald, 102, 114, 204n50

economic inequality, 12–13, 34–35
  in 1896 election, 166
  constitutional rot and, 49, 50, 52–53, 70, 137–38, 164

economic inequality (*cont.*)
elites, leveraging power to maintain status, 51, 52
federal income tax and, 36
future possibilities after demise of Reagan regime, 161–62, 164, 168
in Gilded Age, 62, 63
immigrants and, 34–36
pension plans and, 52–53
Supreme Court's tendency to increase, 150
surge in twenty-first century, 37
Eisenhower, Dwight D., 19–20, 72, 90, 202n29, 202n30
Electoral College
reform of, 33, 184n22
Republican presidents' reliance on to win, 8, 18–19, 28–29, 159
Eleventh Amendment, 202–3n36
elites. 118, 119, 133*t*, 145
change in views held by, 116
conflict over meaning of democracy and, 124
consensus no longer possible due to polarization, 119–20, 121–22, 133*t*, 136, 159
conservatives accusing liberals of being elitists, 119–20
conservative media denouncing, 163
disciplining of outliers, 123, 126, 133*t*, 216n26
judicial review enforcing values of, 70, 76, 115–16
judiciary belonging to, 117, 120, 131
leveraging power to maintain status, 51, 52
on minority protection, 124
disagreements among, 118
new regime criticizing as out of touch with the public, 87, 103
nurturing of conservative elites, 119
as peer group or "audience" for federal judiciary, 116, 118
in polarized world, 118
Ely, John Hart, 102, 107, 115
Democracy and Distrust, 114
Emoluments Clauses, 60
Epstein, Richard, 106, 211n82
Equal Protection Clause, 79, 100, 101, 125, 129–30
Era of Good Feelings, 15, 170, 171
Establishment Clause, 104
European Union
democratic threats in, 8, 9
economic consequences of globalization in, 8–9
Evangelicals, 82
executive power, 32, 46, 127
executive privilege, 41, 58, 146–47, 223n42

Fair Labor Standards Act, 30, 202–3n36
fake news, 49
family-friendly economic policies, 168, 169
fascism, 9
Federal Arbitration Act of 1925, 128–29, 219n82
federal income tax, 36, 85–86, 136, 201n12, 221n3
federalism, 47–48, 81, 89, 91, 97, 104, 107, 108, 113, 137–38, 210–11n73, 212n85
Federalist, (The Federalist Papers), 207n46
Federalist Party, 15, 15*t*, 52, 72*t*, 170
Federalist regime, 15*t*, 72*t*
Federalist Society, 20–21, 107, 119–21, 130–31, 181n39, 212n91
federal lower courts. *See* judiciary
federal question jurisdiction, 86
filibusters, 31, 32, 127, 131–32
Finn, John, 187n2
First Amendment, 18, 79, 91, 100, 102, 104, 124, 126, 137–38, 214n115
First Reconstruction, 62–63
Fiss, Owen, 102
Fix the Court campaign, 224n3
Ford, Gerald, 72, 73, 88–89
formalism, 110, 114
Fortas, Abe, 73, 88–89
Founders. *See also* Framers
influence of Polybius on, 5
and living constitutionalism, 4–5
Fourteenth Amendment, 86, 101, 106, 107, 170, 207–8n47, 210–11n73, 211n74. *See also* Equal Protection Clause
Fox News, 31, 57, 60, 61, 119, 163
Framers. *See also* originalism
flexible vision of, 103
trying to protect against constitutional rot, 47, 48
values of, 87–88, 204n48
France, unrest in 1960s in, 9
Frankfurter, Felix, 78, 100, 101–2, 110–11, 205n12, 209n60, 213n103

Franklin, Benjamin, 47
Free Exercise Clause, 104
Free Speech Clause, 104, 124
free trade, 227n13
  Trump opposition to, 21, 27
French Revolution, 9
Friedman, Barry, 97, 108, 200n2, 200n3, 200n4, 205n6
Fuller, Melville, 72
Furman v. Georgia (1972), 116–17

Garland, Merrick, 95, 122, 132–33, 150, 221n17
gay rights, 18, 90, 93–94, 111, 124, 167
Gen Xers, 162–63
gerrymandering, 18–19, 28–29, 124, 125–26, 137–38, 142, 143–44
Gilded Age (First), 15–16, 30, 36, 63–64, 146, 148, 172
  characterization of, 62–63
  economic inequality in, 138
  end of, 171
  immigration in, 62–63
  oligarchy and, 53
  as period of constitutional rot, 34, 45, 62, 135–36
  polarization during, 36, 62–63
  populism in, 62–63
  Republicans in, 137
  Supreme Court role in, 85–86
  white supremacy in, 62–63
  yellow journalism in, 63
Gilded Age (Second). *See* Second Gilded Age
Giles v. Harris (1903), 62–63, 136
Gingrich, Newt, 31, 61, 183n8
Ginsburg, Ruth Bader, 96
global financial crisis (2008), 8–9, 49, 50
globalization
  differences in United States from other countries in response to, 10
  economic consequences of, 8–9, 50–51, 52
  social safety net and, 173
  white working class's view of, 18
Goldberg, Arthur, 117
Good Behaviour Clause, 225n9
Gorsuch, Neil, 25–26, 110, 120–21, 122, 131, 132, 140–41, 145, 221n19
Graber, Mark, 94–95, 113, 122, 123, 171–72
Graglia, Lino, 105–6
Grant, Ulysses S., 131
Great Britain, 8, 9
Great Depression, 9, 16, 36, 88, 172, 173
Great Society, 9–10
gridlocked Congress, 32, 44, 76, 127–28, 131, 134, 139–40, 218n77
Griffin, Stephen, 49
Griswold v. Connecticut (1965), 101, 102, 103, 106, 116, 208n52, 208n54, 211n82
Gun Free School Zones Act, 202–3n36

Hannity, Sean, 163
Harding, Warren, 153
Harlan, John Marshall, II, 73, 197n6
Harper v. Virginia Board of Elections (1966), 101
Harris, United States v. (1883), 136
Hart, Henry, 114
Hartford Convention, 170
Hartz, Louis, 10
Hearst newspapers, 63
Heritage Foundation, 119, 120, 121
Hetherington, Marc, 165–66, 167
high politics, 80, 125–26, 133*t*
Hitler, Adolf, 9
Hofeller, Thomas, 144, 145
Holmes Lectures (1969), 101–2
Hoover, Herbert, 20, 22, 88
hope for future, 6, 10, 11, 37, 65, 149, 150–51, 160, 173
hot button issues, to be decided by majority rule, 105, 106, 107
House of Representatives, US, 17, 28, 32, 41, 58, 60, 165
Hughes, Charles Evans, 88, 117
Hughes Court, 88
Hungary, 8, 10
Hunter v. Erickson (1969), 222n25

I Ching, 177n8
identity politics, 163, 166, 167, 168, 173, 227n11. *See also* white identity politics
immigration
  anti-immigrant populism, 8, 27
  conservative policies and, 227n13
  Democratic Party and, 166, 167–68, 222n30
  effects on the politics of redistribution, 34–36
  during Gilded Age, 34, 62–63, 172

immigration (*cont.*)
Republicans' anti-immigrant populism, 167–68
white working class's view of, 18
World War I and, 36
impeachment
of Clinton, 40
congressional use of, 41–42
of Trump, 7, 58, 146
incumbent presidents, likelihood of reelection, 8
Indian Gaming Regulatory Act, 202–3n36
influence peddling, 62, 63. *See also* corruption
Ingraham, Laura, 163
Institute for Justice, 210n68
Iraq War
as policy disaster, 17, 49
Trump's criticism of, 21
Izquierdo, Richard Alexander, 178n15

Jackson, Andrew, 15, 19, 23, 24, 25–26
Jacksonian Democrats, 94–95, 137, 204n52
Jacksonian regime, 15, 15*t*, 72*t*
Janus v. AFSCME (2018), 126, 137–38
Jefferson, Thomas, 15, 19
Jeffersonian Party, 15*t*, 72*t*, 75
Jeffersonian regime, 15, 15*t*, 72*t*
Jeffersonian Republicans, 52, 170, 171
Jehovah's Witnesses, 100
Jim Crow, 62–63, 116, 136, 166, 221n4, 221n5, 221n6, 221n7, 221n8
Johnson, Andrew, 131
Johnson, Lyndon Baines, 19, 23, 73, 88–89
judicial activism, 81–82, 83, 92, 129, 204n46
bipartisan, 98, 129
conservative intellectuals on, 105
defined, 210n69
judicial engagement distinguished from, 105
liberal Democrats and conservative courts in the new regime, 149
originalism and, 105
judicial deference
Carolene Products and, 112
Chevron doctrine and, 32, 108, 213n99
conservative opposition to, 108, 209n60
future scenario for, 110
originalism and, 105
judicial engagement, 81, 82–83, 95*t*, 105, 111, 210n68
judicial minimalism, 109
judicial passivism, 105, 210n71
judicial reasoning
living constitutionalism and, 99
new regimes and, 87
public opinion on, 84
judicial restraint
cycle of regimes and, 95*t*, 211–12n83
defined, 210n71
Frankfurter and, 102, 213n103
future scenario for, 110–11, 149, 214n115
generational shifts in views on, 83, 93–94
legal realism and, 205n13
living constitutionalism and, 99, 100
new regimes and, 69–70, 83–84, 87
originalism and, 105, 106, 208n51
political change of views on, 81, 82–83
pragmatism and, 205n13
prudentialism and, 109
public opinion on, 84
Supreme Court docket and, 81–82
judicial review
in antebellum era, 201n15
Carolene Products and, 112, 143
causes of change in parties' positions on, 91–95
conservatism and, 81, 90, 91
cycle of regimes and, 83, 84–85, 95*t*
democracy safeguarded by, 146
Dworkin on, 114
future scenario for, 110–11
generational shifts in views on, 93–94
high politics and, 80
inability to remedy polarization and current problems, 10–11, 150–51
legitimation of laws and, 76, 130
liberal rights jurisprudence and, 102, 114
liberal skepticism about, 108–10
in life-cycle of a political regime, 85–91
living constitutionalism and, 100
low politics and, 80, 125–26
new regimes and, 69–70, 83–84, 87, 90, 95–96
normative justification of, 216n26
originalism and, 107
party system and, 77–80
polarization, effect of (*see* polarization)
political coalitions and, 75–76
political supports for, 74–77, 81, 115–16, 123, 133*t*, 136–37, 197n8
precedent, and conservative originalism 204n48

precedent in new regime, 93
precedent, need to preserve, 109–10
reasons why politicians prefer, 75–76, 92, 129, 197n15
rise and fall of regimes and, 81–96
separation of powers and, 75
values of national political elites enforced by, 70, 76
judicial time, 71–74, 149
judiciary. *See also* Supreme Court, US
"audience" for, 116, 118–21, 133*t*, 137–38
Carolene Products on role of, 115–16
constitutional hardball and, 131–32, 133*t*, 151
constitutional rot and, 7, 70–71, 135, 137–38, 139–40
in depolarized world, 113–18, 131, 133*t*
gridlock increasing importance of, 127–28, 131
how cycles of constitutional time affect, 10, 75, 159
importance for dominant party to stock courts, 94, 131, 132–33, 137
independent, 47–48
judicial time and, 71–74, 149
as lagging indicator of American politics, 7, 10, 72–73, 116–17, 159
loss of trust in, 140–41
minority and women appointed to, 130–31
new regimes and, 69–70, 86
in next regime, 148–51
partisan entrenchment in, 77–80, 82–83, 125, 128, 129, 141, 159, 160
polarization and, 70, 136–37, 159 (*see also* polarization)
as policy vanguard, 127–30, 139–40
pool from which chosen, 117, 119, 136, 216n36
power and role of, 71, 81, 91, 113, 198n24
Reagan regime and judicial revolution, 26
Roberts on role of, 76, 114–15
Roosevelt and New Deal appointments to, 73
stakes of judicial appointments in polarized era, 130–34, 133*t*
Supreme Court reforms, 148–56, 224n3
as umpires, 76, 114–15, 215n22
Judiciary Act of 1925, 154, 201n8, 226n11, 226n13
justice
avoiding constitutional crisis distinguished from, 40–41
economic justice, 168–69
living constitutionalism and, 4–5
Justice Department, US, 41, 115, 144
Constitution in the Year 2000 project, 209n59
justiciability, 137–38

Kagan, Elena, 74
Kavanaugh, Brett, 25–26, 74, 110, 120–21, 122, 131, 132–33, 140–41, 145, 150, 221n19
Keck, Thomas, 90, 98, 104–5, 213n103
Kelly, Alfred, 103
Kennedy, Anthony, 74, 90, 91, 92, 117–18, 122, 132, 217n60
Kennedy, John F., 19
Kennedy v. Louisiana (2008), 218n74
Kramer, Larry, 109
Ku Klux Klan Act, 221n5

labor unions
decline of, 51, 167–68, 172
Democratic Party and, 166, 167–68, 172
individual arbitration provisions, 219n82
in New Deal/Civil Rights regime, 13
in next regime, 164
public-sector unions, challenges to in Roberts Court, 82, 126, 128–29, 203n42, 219n84
in Reagan regime, 13, 16, 166
weakened by court decisions, 138–39, 221n10
laissez-faire economics, 99
Lawrence v. Texas (2003), 90, 108–9
Legal Process School, 114, 215n14
legal realism, 114, 205n13, 215n11
Leo, Leonard, 120
Levinson, Sanford, 79, 80, 93, 111, 125, 133, 197n12
Lewis, Jeff, 178n1
liberalism, 13. *See also* New Deal/Civil Rights regime
intense political competition in periods of gridlock and, 218n79
judicial review and, 81
judiciary choices representing, 121
protection of civil rights and civil liberties and, 111, 114, 216n31
skepticism about judicial review, 108–10
of Supreme Court justices, 74

libertarian intellectuals, 106, 211–12n83
libertarian rights claims, 104, 207–8n47, 214n115
liberty of contract, 113
Limbaugh, Rush, 163
Lincoln, Abraham, 19, 23, 24, 25–26, 185n8
Lindgren, James, 225n9
living constitutionalism, 4–5, 99–102, 177n6
  critique by originalists, 103
Lochner v. New York (1905), 85–86, 102, 103, 106, 107–8, 205–6n14, 206n15, 208n52, 208n54, 211n82, 211–12n83
Lochner Court, 101, 107, 212n85
Lochner era, 92, 99, 208n56
loss of trust in government, 46, 49–50, 133, 134, 135, 140, 151
Low-Level Radioactive Waste Policy Act, 202–3n36
low politics, 80, 125–26, 133*t*

Machiavelli, 5
Madison, James, 47
majority rule, 84
  living constitutionalism and, 99
  originalism and, 108
Make America Great Again, 20–21, 54, 181n38
Marbury v. Madison (1803), 75
Marshall, Thurgood, 90
McCain-Feingold Act, 128–29, 218–19n80
McCarty, Nolan, 35
McCloskey, Robert, 115, 140–41
McConnell, Mitch, 59–60, 94, 95–96, 132–33, 153
McKinley, William, 15–16, 27, 28
McMahon, Kevin, 77, 140–41, 221n19
McReynolds, James Clark, 72, 88, 201–2n22
media
  conservative media and talk radio, 57, 60, 61–62, 119, 162, 163, 172
  contribution to constitutional rot, 49
  contribution to polarization, 118
  Trump's attacks on, 57–58
Medicaid, 168
Medicare, 18, 21, 51, 169–70
Meese, Edwin, 104, 105–6, 208n56, 209n58, 209n59
middle class, 51
Millennials, 28, 164
Miller, Gary, 165–66, 167
Minersville School District v. Gobitis (1940), 100
minorities
  Carolene Products and, 112
  Democratic Party and, 167–68, 172, 222n30
  judicial appointments of, 130–31
  lack of rights for, 45
  polarization making it difficult to agree on who constitutes, 123, 124
  political process doctrine of *Hunter v. Erickson* and, 222n25
  voter identification laws and, 124
modernization, judicial, 126
Mueller, Robert, 38, 41, 59, 186n17
Mussolini, Benito, 9

National Labor Relations Act, 219n82
National Recovery Act (1933), 88, 201n21
National Republican Party, 15*t*, 72*t*
neoliberalism, 9–10, 13, 16, 28, 161–62, 169, 170, 172–73
New Deal, 9, 63, 78, 88, 94, 97, 100–1, 103, 106, 109–10, 112, 117, 164, 169, 170, 171–72. *See also* Roosevelt, Franklin Delano
New Deal/Civil Rights regime, 15*t*, 92, 93–94, 100, 104, 109–10, 114, 148
  affiliated presidents and, 19
  characterization of, 13
  class issues in, 161
  compromise politics of, 31
  conservatives objecting to liberal court decisions of, 102, 103, 129
  decline of polarization in, 30
  Democratic Party's dominance, 13, 166
  end of, 12, 16 (*see also* Reagan regime)
  liberal agenda and, 129
  pre-emptive presidents and, 19–20
  racial issues, disagreements over, 89–90, 161
  social movements and, 24
  Southern vs. Northern Democrats in, 89–90, 91
  start of, 16, 86, 179n12
  Supreme Court appointments during, 71–74, 72*t*
  Supreme Court during Roosevelt's New Deal and, 72
New Deal settlement, 89–90, 106
New Right, 16, 116–17

Nixon, Richard M.
divided government, yet functional, under, 129–30
firing Cox creating political crisis, 41
as pre-emptive president, 19–20
Supreme Court appointments by, 72, 73, 78, 95, 104, 199n35
Watergate scandal, 40, 42, 145, 186–87n19, 187n21
Nixon, United States v. (1974), 145–46, 147
Nixon Democrats, 166
Northwest Territory, 52

Obama, Barack
administrative agencies used to advance policy goals, 108, 213n99
coalition of the ascendant and, 64
corporate support for, 166–67
Democratic Party's identity and, 167
executive power, use of, 32
failure to inaugurate new regime, 17
judicial appointments by, 130–31
Obama coalition, 18, 28–29, 64, 166–68
political coalition of, 28–29
as pre-emptive president, 19–20, 21
Republican obstructionist policies against, 18, 132
Republicans stopping Supreme Court appointment by, 95, 122, 132, 153
Trump's falsehoods about, 61
Obamacare, 32, 107, 168, 220n92
Obergefell v. Hodges (2015), 95–96, 107–8, 211n79
obstructionist policies
of parties, 18, 31–33, 183n12, 183n16
of Trump, 41, 58
O'Connor, Sandra Day, 90, 92, 108, 120–21
off-the-wall to on-the-wall claims, 80
oligarchy, 45, 50, 52, 53, 138–39
O'Reilly, Bill, 163
organized labor. *See* labor unions
originalism, 4, 177n5
conservative Court of 1990s and, 104
cycle of regimes and, 102–8, 210n67
early version of, 103, 208n55
Kennedy's rejection of, 217n60
liberal attack on, 110, 212n90
liberal version of, 110, 208n48
majoritarianism and rejection of liberal rights claims in, 106
manipulation of, 213–14n111
oldest group of conservative originalists, 105–6, 107
Reagan's commitment to, 104
Warren Court and, 103, 105–6, 107, 110, 208n48
younger generation of conservative originalists, 106, 107
Originalism: The Lesser Evil (Scalia), 106

panic of 1893, 27
Parents Involved in Community Schools v. Seattle School District No. 1 (2007), 91
parties. *See* Democratic Party; political parties; Republican Party
partisan entrenchment, 77–80, 82–83, 125, 128, 129, 141, 159, 160
partisan regime, 13–14
party as database, 26
party coalitions. *See* political coalitions
Patent and Plant Variety Protection Remedy Clarification Act, 202–3n36
Peckham, Rufus, 72
Pence, Mike, 64
pension plans, 52–53
People's Party, 62–63
Persilly, Nate, 218n68
Pew survey (2018), 164
Planned Parenthood of Southeastern Pennsylvania v. Casey (1992), 90
Plessy v. Ferguson (1896), 62–63, 116, 136, 207–8n47
Poland, 8, 10
polarization, 3. *See also* Democratic Party; Republican Party
asymmetric, 31, 73, 119–20, 121, 125, 127, 130–31, 162, 164
Bush (G. W.) and, 31–32
Carolene Products model and, 123–25, 133*t*
causes of, 34, 183n7
changing audience for judges and, 118–21, 133*t*
collapse of distinction between high and low politics, 125–26, 133*t*
constitutional rot and, 7, 49, 50, 70, 135, 151
cycles of, 6–7, 30–37, 112–34, 133*t*, 178n1
decline in future of, 170
disagreements among educated elites and, 118
disciplining of outliers, 123, 126, 133*t*, 216n26

polarization (*cont.*)
disjunction and, 162–64
elite consensus no longer possible, 119, 121–22, 159
envisioning how dysfunctional polarization may recede, 160
federal judiciary as policy vanguard, 127–30, 139–40
during Gilded Age, 36, 62–63
judicial appointments, importance in polarized era, 130–34, 137
judicial failure to offer constitutional renewal in time of, 10, 137–38
judiciary and, 70, 113–18, 127–30, 133*t*, 136–37
long cycle of, 30–31
during New Deal, 30
party activists driving, 217n46
permanence of, 33–37
present situation constituting peak of, 7, 12, 16–17, 140–41
ranked-choice voting as a potential remedy for, 33
Reagan regime and, 12, 26, 31–33, 64
spoils of government and, 113, 115–16, 123, 125, 133*t*
stakes of judicial appointments in polarized era, 130–34, 133*t*
Trump and, 64
political coalitions, 14
cross-party alliances forming, 36, 37, 161–62, 173
incoherence likely to reduce polarization, 36, 163, 173
judicial protection of, 127
judicial review and, 75–76
loss of members, 162–63
need to reproduce itself in next generation, 164
new constitutional regimes and, 25
of Obama and Democratic Party, 28–29
post-Civil War changes in, 36
Trump's Republican coalition compared to 1896 election, 27
Police, protests against in spring 2020, 164
political crises, 40, 41, 43
political economy of republican government, 50–53
political mobilization and reform, 7, 10, 164
cycles of, 36–37
difficulty of political reconstruction in face of larger and more complex state, 23, 24
future possibilities, 160, 164
in Progressive Era, 63
Supreme Court reforms, 148–56, 224n3
political parties. *See also specific parties*
after Civil War, 33
base strategy of, 31–32
conflict extension, 12 (*see also* conflict extension)
conflict over meaning of democracy, 123–24
dominant party in constitutional regime, 24, 128–29
dominant party setting political baseline, 13, 128
future possibilities in new regime, 161
generational shifts and, 164, 226–27n2
ideological coherence within, 89–90, 115–16
intense political competition in periods of gridlock and, 128, 140
judicial review and, 77–80, 84, 85, 115–16
during New Deal/Civil Rights regime, 31
obstructionist policies of, 18, 31–32
party as database, 26
polarization and, 12, 90 (*see also* polarization)
reconfiguration of, 165–68
Supreme Court appointments by, 71–74, 72*t*, 77, 83, 88, 130–31, 140–41, 153, 201n9 (*see also specific presidents and political parties*)
political supports for judicial review, 74–77, 81, 115–16, 123, 133*t*, 136–37, 197n8
political time
divergence from judicial time, 72–73, 149
waning of, 22–27, 165
Pollock v. Farmers' Loan & Trust Co. (1895), 136
Polsky, Andrew, 13–14
Polybius, 5, 47
Poole, Keith, 35
popular constitutionalism, 109
populism
anti-Big Tech, 169
anti-immigrant, 8
in both political parties, 37, 169–70, 173
in Gilded Age, 62–63
Republican Party's populist nativism, 16–17, 161
Post, Robert, 109, 226n13

Powell, Lewis F., 197n6
pre-emptive presidents, 19–20, 20*t*, 21, 23, 76
presidential immunity, 146–47
presidential leadership. *See also* executive power
  continuous lying and, 57
  presidential regimes differentiated from constitutional regimes, 24, 26
  gridlocked Congress and, 32
  Skowronek's theory of (*see* Skowronek, Stephen)
  transformative, 26–27, 165, 182n50
  waning of political time and, 25
privatization, 13
Progressive Era (First)
  depolarization in, 171–72
  Gilded Age corruption leading to, 36, 63
  start of, 171
  turbulence of, 11
Progressive Era (Second). *See* Second Progressive Era
propaganda, 49, 60
proportional representation, 33
prudentialism, 109
public good
  relationship to constitutional rot, 44
  republic's commitment to pursue and promote, 44, 45, 58
  trading devotion to public good for pursuit of personal aggrandizement, 45, 47
  Trump failing to consider, 58
public opinion
  generational shifts in views about judicial review and, 83, 85, 93–94, 162–63, 164, 226–27n2
Pulitzer newspapers, 63

Racism, 62–63, 116, 124, 136, 164, 166
Racial issues
  in 1896 election, 166
  affirmative action, 124, 142
  and elites 124, 142
  in political coalitions, 18, 77, 161, 162, 164, 166, 172
  in Gilded Age, 62–63
  Jim Crow, 62–63, 116, 166, 221n4, 221n5, 221n6, 221n7, 221n8
  in New Deal/Civil Rights regime, 89–90, 161, 166
  political parties and identity issues, 167
  in Progressive Era 173
  in Reagan regime, 13, 18, 166
  Republicans' use of, 166, 168
  Roosevelt's judicial appointments and, 77
  Supreme Court shift of sympathies on, 79, 82, 124
  white working class and, 18
ranked-choice voting systems, 33, 184n22
rational basis test, 113
Reagan, Ronald
  1980 election, 16
  compared to FDR, 23, 25–26
  Justice Department's Constitution in the Year 2000 project and, 209n59
  neoliberalism and, 9–10
  Justice Department's role in advocating originalism, 104, 209n59
  as reconstructive president, 19, 87–88
  relationship to Supreme Court, 88–89
  Trump comparing himself to, 20–21
Reagan Democrats, 162–63, 166
Reagan regime, 15*t*, 72*t*, 93–94, 96, 99, 121, 125, 131–32, 149, 161, 162, 163, 167–68
  asymmetric polarization in, 119–20
  backed by social movement, 24,
  bureaucracy, conservative view of, 32
  campaign finance deregulation and, 18
  characterization of, 13
  congressional gridlock late in regime, 129–30
  conservatism of, 13, 104, 119–20, 143
  constitutional doctrine changes and, 24–25
  Constitution-in-practice and, 25–26
  crumbling and demise of, 17, 18, 64, 159
  culture wars and, 18
  economic inequality intensified in, 12–13
  judicial activism and, 92
  judicial revolution and, 26
  liberal criticism of, 109
  nearing end of, possible scenario for, 110
  organized labor weakened during, 166
  party coalitions in, 173
  polarization and, 12, 26, 31–33, 90, 113–14
  Reagan Democrats in, 162–63, 166
  Republican Party's dominance in, 13, 128–29, 137
  Republican Party's polarization during, 73, 137
  start of, 12, 13, 16, 86
  Supreme Court appointments during, 72*t*
  Trump and, 8, 30

Reconstruction, 164, 170, 171–72
Reconstruction Amendments, 91
Reconstruction Republicans, 131, 132–33, 170
reconstructive politics, waning effectiveness of, 22–27
reconstructive presidents, 19, 20–21, 20*t*, 25, 26–27, 87–88, 201n20
regimes. *See* cycle of regimes
regime theory, distinguished from realigning elections theory 13–14
Rehabilitating Lochner: Defending Individual Rights against Progressive Reform (Bernstein), 107
Rehnquist, William, 77, 116–17, 154–55, 208n53
Rehnquist Court, 81, 82, 90, 91, 94, 97, 106, 107, 108, 148, 207n46, 212n85
Reich, Charles, 100–1
Religious Freedom Restoration Act (RFRA), 200n7, 202–3n36
religious right. *See* Christian conservatives
republic and republicanism
  decaying through constitutional rot, 45
  defined, 44
  Framers' view of, 52
  insurance for, 47–49
  judicial protection of, 70–71
  political economy of, 50–53
  subject to decay, 44, 47, 141
Republican Party, 15*t*, 72*t*, *See also* political parties
  1896 election, reconfiguration of, 15–16, 36, 165–66, 172, 180n14
  2016 election outcome and, 165–66
  2020 state elections and, 159
  asymmetric polarization and, 162
  baby boomers and, 162–63
  campaign finance and, 18, 124
  climate-change denialism and, 173
  conflict extension, 12 (*see also* conflict extension)
  conservatism of, 16, 81, 83, 119, 129, 171, 183n9, 196–97n5
  creation of, 15, 52
  deregulation and economic policies of, 27–28
  dominance from 1860 to 1932, 13–14
  dominance in Reagan regime, 13, 128–29, 150, 159
  exit of dissenters from, 163, 166–67
  Gen Xers and, 162–63
  history of first Republican regime, 15–16
  judicial review and, 81, 89–90, 92, 93, 94–95, 96
  liberal Republicans become increasingly rare, 31
  McKinley and, 27
  Millennial voters in, 164
  Obamacare repeal efforts of, 32
  obstructionist policies of, 18, 31–32, 183n12, 183n16
  polarization and, 12, 30, 31, 32, 73, 113, 118, 122, 123–24, 125, 127, 128, 129, 130–32, 137, 159, 162, 166, 167, 183n12, 183n15, 196–97n5
  political entrenchment of, 160
  populism in, 16–17, 27, 161
  party evolution following 1896 election, 166
  reconfiguration of, 165–68, 169–70, 171, 172, 173
  religious right and, 27–28
  social issues, failure to move to center on, 169
  Supreme Court appointments by, 72, 73–74, 77, 78, 83, 88, 94, 140–41, 148, 149–50, 201n9
  taking up progressive critique of judicial review, 102
  Trump and, 17, 44, 61, 64, 144, 162, 167, 171
  vulnerability of, 17, 159
  white working-class voters and, 18, 21, 27–28, 161, 163, 164, 166, 167–68, 169
  winning Electoral College but losing national popular vote, 18–19, 159
Republican Party elites, 124
Republican regime, 15–16, 15*t*, 20, 24, 27, 72, 137
Roberts, John
  confirmation hearing (2005), 114–15, 131–32
  in *Department of Commerce v. New York*, 145
  on judicial role, 76, 114–15
  as median (swing) Justice, 117–18, 122, 140–41, 220n92
  in *Obergefell v. Hodges*, 107–8
  as part of conservative majority on Supreme Court, 131

in Reagan Justice Department, 115
in *Rucho*, 143–44
in *Shelby County*, 143–44
siding with liberal justices, 144, 145
Roberts, Owen, 88
Roberts Court
as "anti-*Carolene*" Supreme Court, 143, 222n26
commercial speech, choice of cases involving, 82, 91, 104–5, 203n42
conservatism of, 90, 91, 95, 148
consumer rights limited by, 128–29
judicial creativity of, 94
judicial review and, 81
McCain-Feingold legislation hobbled by, 128–29
originalism and, 106
public-union challenges, choice of cases involving, 82, 128–29
religious claims, choice of cases involving, 82
Voting Rights Act weakened by, 128–29
Roe v. Wade (1973), 75–76, 78, 89, 90, 93–94, 95–96, 97, 102, 106, 107, 108–9, 111, 116, 211n82, 212n90
Romer v. Evans (1996), 90
Roosevelt, Franklin Delano. *See also* New Deal
1932 election, 16
Carolene Products and, 112
compared to Jackson and Lincoln, 23
court packing plan of, 131
Democratic Party constituency and, 166
history repeating judicial era of, 95, 149
judicial appointments of liberals by, 77
originalist arguments of, 103
overwhelming majority held by, 23
as reconstructive president, 19, 87–88
and Supreme Court, 73, 88–89, 94, 99–100, 103, 206n16
Supreme Court appointments by, 73, 78, 96, 117
Roosevelt, Theodore, 135–36, 205–6n14
Rosenthal, Howard, 35
Ross, Wilbur, 144–45
Rove, Karl, 31–32
Rucho v. Common Cause (2019), 126, 137–38, 143–44
rule of law, 46
rural voters, 27–29
Russia
2016 US election interference by, 59
social media's manipulation by, 8–9

Sachs, Albert, 114
same-sex marriage, 98, 111, 124
Sanders, Bernie, 172–73
Scalia, Antonin
on *Carolene Products* in *Schuette v. BAMN*, 143
Chevron doctrine, defense of, 108
as conservative icon, 128
in *Obergefell v. Hodges*, 211n79
"has left the building," 111
Originalism: The Lesser Evil, 106
as part of older group of conservative originalists, 105–6, 107
replacement on Supreme Court, 95–96, 122, 132, 153
Supreme Court appointment of, 77
Schechter Poultry Corp. v. United States (1935), 88, 201n21
Schlesinger, Arthur, Sr., 5
Schlesinger, Arthur, Jr.: *The Cycles of American History*, 5
Schofield, Norman, 165–66, 167
school desegregation, 91, 207n38, See also *Brown v. Board of Education*
school prayer, 207n38, 207n46
Schuette v. BAMN (2014), 143
Second Amendment, 91, 107, 203n37
Second Gilded Age
and constitutional rot, 31
economic inequality in, 138
leading to Second Progressive Era, 63–64, 171
parallels to First Gilded Age, 62, 173
Second Progressive Era, 7, 11, 63–64, 171, 173
Second Reconstruction, 128–29
Segall, Eric, 110
Senate, US
2020 election outcomes and, 28
filibusters, 31, 32, 127, 131–32
malapportionment of, 165
Judiciary Committee, 132
Supreme Court appointments, approval by, 77–78, 132, 140–41, 152, 225n5
Trump impeachment and acquittal, 59–60
separation of powers, 47–48, 75

September 11, 2001 terrorist attacks, 21, 31–32
sexuality, battles over, 18, 124, 216n31. *See also* gay rights; same-sex marriage
Shapiro, Martin, 198n20
Shelby County v. Holder (2013), 91, 126, 137–38, 143–44, 205n8, 219n81, 222n25
Siegan, Bernard, 106, 211n82
Siegel, Reva, 109
Silverstein, Gordon, 198n20
Sixteenth Amendment, 36
Skowronek, Stephen, 13, 19–22, 20*t*, 23, 24, 25, 108, 165, 178n15, 178–79n9, 180n14, 180n26
Slave Power, 15, 30, 45, 52, 135–36, 137
social insurance programs, 13, 52
social movements, 26–27, 94, 130, 164–65. *See also* Republican Party, movement conservatives
Social Security, 18, 21, 30, 51, 169–70
Souter, David, 73, 120–21, 153, 197n6
Southern politics, 30–31
Soviet Union
  demise of, 17
  propaganda, use of, 49
spoils of government, 113, 115–16, 123, 125, 133*t*
state liability and immunity, 91, 104–5, 202–3n36
Steel Seizure Case (1952), 145–46, 187n21
Stephanopoulos, Nicholas, 143, 222n26
Stevens, John Paul, 72, 73, 74, 153, 197n6
Stewart, Potter, 88–89, 197n6, 202n24
Strauss, David, 109–10, 126
Sugar Trust Case (1895), 136
Sunstein, Cass, 109, 110, 204n50
Supreme Court, US. *See also specific courts by name of chief justice and also specific names of individual justices*
  amicus briefs, 121–22, 148–49, 217n59
  audience for, 120–21, 137–38
  confirmation votes in Senate, 131–32
  and conservatism, 74, 77, 82, 88–89, 149–50, 201n9
  as conservative bastion in next regime, 149–50
  constitutional theory focusing on, 97
  Constitution-in-practice and, 25–26, 178–79n9
  court-packing strategy, 131, 150, 151
  cycle of regimes and, 83, 95*t*
  as Dahl's majoritarian institution, 115, 121
  divergence of Justices' views from appointing party, 78
  docket chosen by, 79, 81–82, 92, 97–98, 148–49, 199n40, 226n11, 226n13, 226n14
  docket reforms, 154–55
  as Dworkin's "forum of principle," 114
  evolving power of, 75
  federal income tax and, 36
  Graber on "constitutional yo-yo" effect, 122
  how cycles of constitutional time affect, 10
  ideological compatibility of nominees with president, 78–79
  inherently political nature of, 214n115
  internalization of professional norms above politics, 143
  Jim Crow and, 62–63
  judicial creativity and ambition, acceleration in middle of regime of, 94
  as lagging indicator of American politics, 7, 10, 72–73, 116–17, 149, 159
  lifetime tenure of justices, effect of, 72–73, 149, 159
  likelihood of a president having opportunity to make appointment to, 153, 216n33
  litigants' identity, as factor in choice of cases to be heard, 82, 226n15
  McCloskey's view of, 115, 140–41
  moderate Republicans on, 72, 197n6
  new regimes and, 69, 86, 128
  number of justices on, 131
  party opportunities for appointments to, 71–74, 72*t*, 153
  polarization in Reagan regime, 149, 154–55
  pool from which nominees chosen, 117, 119, 153–54, 216n36
  reflecting times in which justices live, 146
  reforms, 148–56, 224n3
  regular and predictable appointments suggested for, 152
  Republican appointments to, 72, 73–74, 77, 83, 88, 140–41, 201n9
  Senate approval of appointments to, 77–78, 132, 140–41, 152, 225n5
  Slave Power and, 52
  sunrise provisions for reforms, 155–56

swing votes on, 79, 90, 92, 117–18
term limits suggested for, 152–54
unanimous opinions, 121–22
The Supreme Court and the Idea of Progress (Bickel), 101–2
Sutherland, George, 88
Sweet, Alec Stone, 198n20
swing votes (median Justices), 79, 90, 92, 117–18

Taft, William Howard, 226n11, 226n13
Taft Lecture (1989), 106
Taney, Roger, 52
Taney Court, 131, 148, 204n52
taxes. *See also* federal income tax
2017 tax bill, 37, 53
in New Deal/Civil Rights regime, 13
in Reagan regime, 13, 16, 17
and upward redistribution, 52–53
Tea Party, 162, 163, 167
technology change, effect of, 26, 172
anti-Big Tech, 169
Teles, Steve, 104, 209n59
Thatcher, Margaret, 9–10
third party, possible emergence of, 64
Thomas, Clarence, 24–25, 77, 83, 90, 106, 111, 128, 131, 140–41, 145, 153–54, 223n36, 223n37
toleration, loss of, 45, 46
Trademark Remedy Clarification Act, 202–3n36
transitional period, unpleasantness of, 7, 12, 178n16
Tribe, Laurence, 102
Truman, Harry S., 19, 145
Trump, Donald
2016 election and, 58–59, 140–41, 172–73
2020 election and, 7, 8, 28–29, 58, 64, 95–96, 159
as affiliated president, 21
anti-immigration stance of, 27
"birther" lies about Obama, 61
census litigation and, 42, 144–45, 222n30
congressional investigations of, 58
conservatism of, 20–21
conservative base of, 163
conservative media organizations supporting, 162, 163
constitutional crisis and, 38, 41–42, 185n2, 186n16
continuous lying by, 57–58
corruption of, 58–59, 60
in cyclical view of Constitution, 6
despair about future of democracy and, 3
as disjunctive president, 21, 22, 182n47, 182n48
Emoluments Clauses ignored by, 60
Federalist Society and, 120
foreign policy, manipulating for personal political gain, 58, 59
immigration and, 37
impeachment, 7, 58, 146
lower federal court appointments by, 95
media attacks by, 57
not pre-emptive president, 21
not reconstructive president, 20–21, 182n47
obstructionist policies of, 41
as populist demagogue, 16–17, 21, 55–58, 64, 162
position in life cycle of Reagan regime, 19–22
Republican Party and, 17, 44, 60, 61, 64, 162, 167, 171
Supreme Court nominees chosen by, 95, 120, 122, 132
as symptom of decadence of Reagan regime, 30
tax returns, refusal to divulge, 146–47
travel ban upheld, 137–38
Ukraine scandal and, 58–59
white working-class voters and, 21, 27
Trump v. Deutsche Bank (cert. granted), 146
Trump v. Hawaii (2018), 137–38, 144
Trump v. Mazars (cert. granted), 146
Trump v. Vance (cert. granted), 146
trust. *See* loss of trust in government
Turkey, 8, 10
Tushnet, Mark, 109
and constitutional hardball, 188n14
Twain, Mark, 5, 177n14

Ukraine, 58–59, 60, 61
United States v. See name of opposing party
US Department of ______. *See name of specific department*

Van Devanter, Willis, 88
Vietnam War, 16, 49
Violence Against Women Act, 202–3n36

voting. *See also* gerrymandering
black disenfranchisement, 136
Carolene Products and, 112
electoral reform suggestions, 33, 150, 184n22
immigrants becoming voters, 35–36
poll tax and, 101
ranked-choice voting systems, 33, 184n22
realigning elections, 13–14
respect for electoral integrity, 46
restrictions on, 28–29, 150, 218n68
Trump allegations of voter fraud, 61
universal white male suffrage, 45
voter identification laws, 124, 125–26, 142
Voting Rights Act of 1965, 30–31, 89–90, 91, 98, 124, 125–26, 128–29, 130, 137–38, 142, 143–44, 183n7, 205n8, 218n68, 219n81

waning
of political time, 22–27, 165
of presidential time, 25
War on Terror, 17
Warren, Earl, 72, 73, 79, 88–89, 90, 100, 105
Warren Court
adoption history and, 207n46
Black's role on, 208n48
choice of claims heard by, 79
congressional enactments requiring legitimation by, 130, 219n85
conservatives and, 89, 92
The Federalist and, 207n46
generational change of views on, 201n10
identity of litigants in cases heard by, 82
judicial activism of, 212n85
judicial creativity of, 94
liberal constitutional thinkers' view of, 97, 101–2
liberal (or moderate) coalition on, 72, 90
originalism and, 103, 105–6, 107, 110, 208n48
rights revolution of, 114, 130
state monitoring and, 219n86
Watergate scandal, 40, 42, 145, 186–87n19, 187n21
Wechsler, Herbert, 101–2, 114, 215n14
West Virginia State Board of Education v. Barnette (1943), 100
Whigs, 15, 15*t*, 64, 72*t*
White, Byron, 78
White, Edward, 72
white identity politics, 27–28, 163. *See also* white working-class voters
white males as targets of antidiscrimination laws and affirmative action, 124, 142
white supremacy, 62–63, 166
white working-class voters
Democratic Party and, 167–68
family-friendly economic policies and, 168, 169
Republican Party appealing to, 18, 21, 27–28, 166, 167–68, 169
Whittington, Keith, 87–88, 103, 210n67
Wilkinson, J. Harvie, III, 107, 212n85, 212n91
Cosmic Constitutional Theory: Why Americans Are Losing Their Inalienable Right to Self Governance, 107
Wilson, Woodrow, 72, 88, 201–2n22
Windsor, United States v. (2013), 205n8
women
Democratic Party and, 167–68, 172
judicial appointments of, 130–31
lack of rights for, 45
World War I, 9

yellow journalism, 63